Getting Started in

Entrepreneurship

The Getting Started In Series

Getting Started in

Entrepreneurship

Jack M. Kaplan

John Wiley & Sons, Inc.

New York • Chichester • Weinheim • Brisbane • Singapore • Toronto

This book is printed on acid-free paper. ∞

Copyright © 2001 by Jack M. Kaplan. All rights reserved.

Published by John Wiley & Sons, Inc.

Published simultaneously in Canada.

This publication is designed to provide accurate and authoritative information in regard to the subject matter covered. It is sold with the understanding that the publisher is not engaged in rendering legal, accounting, or other professional services. If legal advice or other expert assistance is required, the services of a competent professional person should be sought.

Designations used by companies to distinguish their products are often claimed as trademarks. In all instances where the author or publisher is aware of a claim, the product names appear in initial capital letters. Readers, however, should contact the appropriate companies for more complete information regarding trademarks and registration.

ISBN 0-471-29456-X

Printed in the United States of America.
10 9 8 7 6 5 4 3 2 1

Acknowledgments

I relied on the contributions of many people in the preparation of this book. A tremendous amount of assistance was given by colleagues and practicing entrepreneurs.

I owe a special thanks to Lori Puritz, Executive Assistant of Datamark Technologies, in preparing and editing the manuscript, and to Laurence Charney, Area Director of Sales, MNYA, of Ernst & Young, LLP, who provided me with the resources and research in preparing the IPO chapter on going public. My gratitude is also due to Eric Hirsh, who authored the intellectual properties chapter. I would like to thank my wife, Dr. Eileen Kaplan, for her patience, as well as my daughter, Karen, and my sons, Paul and Andrew, who made a number of thoughtful editorial suggestions.

Credit is also due to Airié Dekidjiev, Senior Editor at John Wiley & Sons, for her assistance. Additionally, the executive and management team at Datamark Technologies and a number of reviewers provided invaluable feedback on the early draft and final version. Their insight helped me to mold the book and organize my efforts.

My thanks to the following who participated:

Ann Chamberlain, Richards & O'Neil, LLP

Fanny Chin, Inner Works Enterprises

Jessica Forbes, Columbia University Ph.D. Candidate

Margaret Green, Creative Enterprises

Steve Hanson, BR Guest

Larry Meistrich, Shooting Gallery

Robert Meyers, Fairfield Resources International

Kevin O'Connor, DoubleClick

Mati Weiderpass, Watch World International

Ray Wetterstrom, Plural

Contents

Chapter 6

Chapter 7

Chapter 8

Chapter 9

Discovering Value in Intellectual Property: The Competitive Edge   218

Chapter 10

Building the Resources and Setting Up the Company   248

Introduction

Entrepreneurship is a vocation for which there is no true apprenticeship. Working in a corporation, or even a small business, does not prepare you for the challenges, long hours, social sacrifices, and financial commitment that will be needed for a career running your own company. If you have found that your calling is to become an *entrepreneur*, how can you comprehend the rewards and pitfalls of this professional choice, compile the necessary resources to begin, as well as locate the information and skills to support every step of the process? From starting a business and getting funding to growing and perhaps even selling your company, this book has been written as your best resource. The path to quick and easy ways to creating and starting your business, how to raise capital, building relationships, and launching an Internet business—these topics break the steps of the process into easily digestible components that replace the mystery with an effective plan. For beginners, aspiring entrepreneurs, and those already in the process of running their own businesses, this book will be your guide, mentor, and most reliable ally in the ever-competitive and even hostile business environment of today.

entrepreneur
derived from the French *entreprendre*, "to undertake." Someone who is willing and eager to create a new venture in order to present a concept to the marketplace.

The entrepreneur must know how to compete and thrive in a dynamic, uncertain, and risky environment. New opportunities and threats appear at short notice and usually require a rapid response. Updated practices and information are essential—yesterday's strategies will leave you and your company behind the global and technological trends of tomorrow. This book will answer your demands by providing you with the best tools to be current. It will also equip you to seek out, analyze, and critically implement the ever-increasing and crucial supply of entrepreneurial information by utilizing resources such as the Internet and the cutting-edge new business solutions.

CHALLENGING THE ROLE OF ENTREPRENEURS

Business-minded individuals and companies are changing their economic vision to respond to and gain from the entrepreneurial approaches of today. Why this shift? In your bookstore, take a look at the shelf material surrounding this volume; more and more business educators, writers, and self-starting thinkers are writing for the ever-growing field of entrepreneurial counsel and managing. Why, then, should you buy this particular book?

This book will provide you with background needed to be a successful entrepreneur, to manage resources effectively, and to be knowledgeable about consumers of entrepreneurial behavior. The text emphasizes how you can more effectively start and manage a growing company, and it highlights important issues in current entrepreneurial practices. There are five specific ways this book represents a new and valuable addition of business writing.

1. *Experience.* I have had over 15 years of experience with start-up companies and currently manage and co-own Datamark Technologies, Inc., a loyalty and stored value processing company. In addition, I have taught entrepreneurship management both to traditional day MBA students and to more experienced managers and professional employees in weekend and evening programs. My work as a teacher has gained me a number of able young business protégés who have stepped up to the challenges of entrepreneurship. So I not only am in touch with the most recent academic research findings and the best new company practices, but am constantly advising other businesspeople on the concerns and trials facing beginning entrepreneurs today. I can impart this experience, knowledge, and counsel directly to you through this book.

2. *Management Information.* This approach will give you more than the impetus to begin your start-up—it will emphasize the crucial importance of entrepreneurial management that is critical to the staying power and success of your business. Competitive advantage for your venture is the basis of every piece of information in this text, especially through an emphasis on the strategy function.

3. *From Idea to Opportunity.* This is not merely a concept-oriented book. It will aid you in making your vision a reality. Such vital topics as negotiating your technologically oriented global market as well as anticipating and creating business opportunities will be addressed in order to broaden your business perspective.

4. *Current Topics.* The key issues of the business climate are not an afterthought or an appendix in this text. I will introduce topical factors such as Internet start-up choices, legal issues for the entrepreneur, and intellectual property issues early in the game as well as integrate these topics throughout so that your understanding of them will be in top form.

5. *Internet Emphasis.* You've already noticed how this text has stressed the importance of the Internet to your new business. This is not a topic taken lightly or presented shallowly. This book devotes a complete, up-to-date chapter in creating a business from a technology idea, preparing a plan to ensure that practices are accepted and implemented effectively, and launching an Internet business in today's environment.

FEATURES DESIGNED TO AID LEARNING

As a future or developing entrepreneur, your time is extremely valuable. This text is organized by providing important information in the following areas to maximize productivity:

- ✔ *Learning objectives* at the beginning of each chapter map and anticipate your progress, allowing you to review the introduction as well as home in on the most desirable topics for your business needs.
- ✔ *Real business problems* and challenges will help you conceptualize the knowledge to practice the disciplines you will be integrating into your company.
- ✔ *Key terms* are explained in the Glossary at the end of the book, so that you can keep your information topical and introduce current terms into your important business dealings.

✔ *Profiles* feature companies from the retail, Internet, and technology sectors of the economy, providing perspective to the particular issues and questions raised in that section.

✔ *Networking* sources and web sites at the end of most chapters aid in finding topics and companies crucial to the network building necessary in developing both your vision and your growing business.

Are you ready to take on the invigorating challenges of the entrepreneurial profession? You can take the first step by turning to Chapter 1.

Developing Ideas and Business Opportunities

Objectives

1. Identify the various sources to generate potential business ideas.
2. Exploit the existing need to turn an idea into an opportunity.
3. Prepare an opportunity analysis.
4. Prepare a cash flow forecast for your business.

INTRODUCTION

For an entrepreneur, a business idea is a concept that will give you the material to envision and start your own business. You may already have ideas and just need ways to screen their potential. Or, you know you have what it takes to be an entrepreneur, but you need inspiration to generate possible paths for your skills to take. The business idea, opportunity/analysis, and preparing a cash flow forecast for the product or service will form the subject matter of this chapter. To begin, start off by reading this profile about an entrepreneur who was faced with this issue and targeted her idea to create a profitable business opportunity.

DO YOU HAVE A BUSINESS IDEA?

Maybe you have some starting concepts but question how original they are. You may be surprised to hear that not all

Profile: Fanny Chin of Inner Works Enterprises— Building an Idea

Businesspeople are not the only ones keeping work and personal calendars in their overscheduled and demanding environment. The amount of organization required for raising children inspired one entrepreneur to pitch calendars to a new market niche, packaging them as educational tools and modes of personal expression for children and adolescents.

Fanny Chin emphasized the visual and creative potential in calendar building. She quickly seized on already popular elements such as markers and stickers for the product packet. Then she built her appeal base not only by targeting the desires of kids, her proposed users, but by directing the product at the concerns of parents, her proposed buyers. Fanny's product invention, Creative Calendar®, proved to be a benefit for harried parents who were relieved to have their kids keeping their own schedules. The product delivered on three distinct selling points: a chance to feed the creative impulses of busy kids, an opportunity to provide young customers with organization tools needed for most adult occupations, and the means to create a memento of childhood for years to come.

Fanny came up with this concept as a student in her MBA class in new product development. Yet it was not her class or even her own marketing skills that jumpstarted her product—it was her idea and angle above all that led to this business opportunity.

To recap:

✔ Idea: keeping a calendar.

✔ Angle: a coloring calendar for kids.

✔ Need: overextended parents and busy kids looking for mutual solutions.

✔ Opportunity: marketing a product package through emphasis on accessories and direct appeal to an unexploited need.

entrepreneurs come up with unique ideas. (See Figure 1.1.) You can be innovative without that initial generative impulse. Here are four ways to build upon already existing material and still provide a profit-driven concept:

1. Develop ideas as an extension of an existing product (a keyboard that accepts a smart card for security or e-commerce).

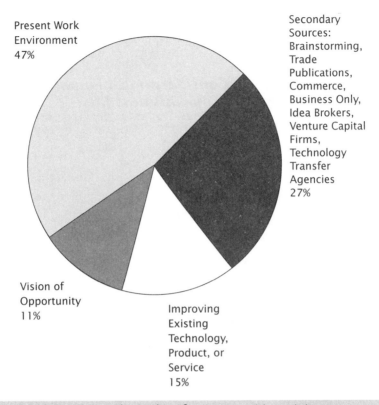

Present Work Environment 47%

Secondary Sources: Brainstorming, Trade Publications, Commerce, Business Only, Idea Brokers, Venture Capital Firms, Technology Transfer Agencies 27%

Vision of Opportunity 11%

Improving Existing Technology, Product, or Service 15%

FIGURE 1.1 Where ideas for opportunities originate.

2. Create an improved service (faster delivery or an Internet e-commerce hotel concierge service).

3. Market a product at a lower price (think Amazon.com).

4. Add value to an existing product or service (linking branded products, such as IBM PCs just for the Internet).

IDEA ASSESSMENT

Let's say you do have an idea for a new business. What opportunities are there for putting your idea into practice? Is this something that has been overdone? Or has it been executed poorly in the past? Or has no one else ever thought of it? In short, is your idea a potential dead end, a productive angle on an opportunity, or an entirely unexplored chance to create a business?

Capital Considerations: Financing and Revising Your Business Idea

Next, consider briefly the financial elements that would help you to start up this new idea:

✔ How much more capital/investment money is needed? Where will you go for this kind of financial support?

✔ How long will you be able to handle the initial losses using your own resources?

✔ What other resources can contribute to extend your involvement so that you can turn your initial losses into profits?

✔ How long might it take to develop the business so that it will make a profit?

✔ What kind of profit margin do you think might eventually result from your product or service?

✔ How will you market the realistic but optimistic loss or profit narrative to investors so that they will want to get involved with your business?

Remember, whether you generate an idea yourself or are connected with someone else who wants to develop an idea in a shared context, the questions you answer should still follow these suggestions.

Where to Look for Information

Once you have developed your idea, you can move on to assessing the information that will help you in convincing others, including loan officers, potential investors, and those in your personal life, of its validity. This will mean direct and thorough research on the potential of this idea. You will rely on hard facts and statistics to turn this opportunity into a potential venture. See Figure 1.2 for some common sources of information on potential markets that might help your development and presentation.

FIGURE 1.2 Where to find information.

Experts in field	✔ Contact well-known entrepreneurs to get advice.
Internet searches	✔ Visit web sites of companies with new products or technologies.
Library research	✔ Use college libraries to access references and specialized bibliographies.
Questionnaire surveys	✔ Use mail, phone, Internet, or professional interviews. Write and prepare questions to give you the right data.
Existing research	✔ Use investment banking firms, advisory services, or consulting firms to gather data and ask to receive findings.
Trade associations	✔ Visit trade shows, and read trade publications.
Market research firms	✔ Hire a firm to prepare a report or market survey for the proposed idea.

Evaluation Process

There is no question that you will need plenty of encouragement and support while developing a business idea. But in order to turn this idea into a concrete business, you'll need to face some hard facts and take a heavy dose of reality. However, keep in mind that armed with this information you can legitimately decide if you will be able to proceed and work to sustain your venture bolstered by your awareness of the challenges facing your business.

Approximately two million businesses are started each year. Anywhere from 50,000 to 100,000 file for bankruptcy within 10 years. This bankruptcy rate does not seem exceptionally high, but business failure extends beyond bankruptcy. Now consider that 85 percent of businesses actually end within five years. They are not all bankrupt, yet their owners have decided to close shop—for a host of reasons. Many do not have the needed investment to carry them through the start-up process (six months to a year between opportunity analysis and opening the doors for business). Others die out because they topple on a shaky basis of poor business planning at the initial stages. Still others disappear due to a lack of business resources and management expertise and simple dearth of experience.

Profile: Larry Meistrich, Chairman and CEO of Shooting Gallery

In 1990, Larry Meistrich had an idea. He wanted to offer filmmaking with artistic freedom to produce creative vision. He was tired of the way things were done in the movie production business and frustrated with the way big studios operated. Larry wanted to improve the situation for the artists. His goal was to provide a platform to display their creative energy and a place where new talent and ideas could merge to become a unique and exciting experience. Larry's idea was to effectively create a film commune— a place for filmmakers to run the machine that produces the films. The result is a high-quality product for less money. His idea emerged as Shooting Gallery, which soon became the East Coast leader in independent film and a distinguished provider of production services as well as a fully integrated studio and multimedia company.

Today, the company is an integrated solutions provider that develops original programming and offers a full spectrum of services and facilities for the multimedia marketplace. Shooting Gallery is now poised to become a global leader in the communications arena, including film, television, commercial video, music, broadband, and Internet.

Shooting Gallery has produced roughly 100 films, commercials, and music videos. Credits include such critically acclaimed projects as Kenneth Lonergan's *You Can Count on Me* (Grand Jury Prize and Waldo Salt Screenwriting Award at 2000 Sundance Film Festival), Billy Bob Thornton's *Sling Blade* (1996 Academy Award—Best Adapted Screenplay), and Nick Gomez's *Laws of Gravity*.

Larry Meistrich demonstrates a unique ability to seek out ideas and bring to the screen the exceptional work of innovative filmmakers.

You may experience anxiety when you think that of those initial two million ventures starting each year, only one in 10 will reach its 10th birthday. But don't allow an uncontextualized statistic to end your viable and potentially profitable business idea. Many start-up owners conceive of their ventures as sidelines to their "real" professions. They never make the emotional and practical investment needed to ensure continued success. Note that 1.3 million of these businesses never legally register as corporations or partnerships because owners don't intend them to grow.

If you are committed, the odds will rise considerably

in your favor. We can estimate that as an owner you can have a one-in-four chance of keeping a new business going for eight years if it is full-time and incorporated; and if you then change owners, the business can survive another eight years, at that same rate of one in four. Now that we've contextualized this, you can see how those initial figures could seem misleading. The actual eight-year survival rate for incorporated start-ups is about 25 percent.

Yet remember an important piece of information—you might not want your business to last that long. Ask yourself what different outcomes could spell success for you. Do you want to tie up your assets for a significant period of time if you are confident of the turnaround, or does the thrill for you lie in the rush of the start-up period? Does success to you mean long-term survival or does it mean developing your company during a window of opportunity, then selling it at a high gain?

However long you ultimately want to stick with your business, the fact is that you will need to develop it in a logical and stable manner to reap any kind of reward. Now that we've looked at the statistics and you've done your own research related to the specific needs of your venture, let's formulate a plan and a schedule. This will help you to conduct the most thorough inquiry yet into the potential of your idea/opportunity—otherwise known as the opportunity analysis. (See Figure 1.3.)

OPPORTUNITY ANALYSIS: FIVE PHASES TO SUCCESS

The opportunity analysis consists of five distinct phases:

✔ Phase 1: Seize the opportunity.

✔ Phase 2: Investigate the need through market research.

✔ Phase 3: Develop the plan.

✔ Phase 4: Determine the resources needed.

✔ Phase 5: Manage the distinguishing features of the business.

These phases sometimes overlap, but should follow in logical order.

Does the opportunity:

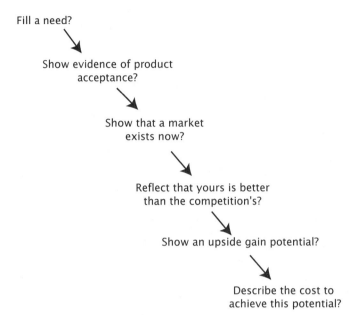

Fill a need?

Show evidence of product acceptance?

Show that a market exists now?

Reflect that yours is better than the competition's?

Show an upside gain potential?

Describe the cost to achieve this potential?

FIGURE 1.3   Evaluating the opportunity.

Phase 1: Seize the Opportunity

To evaluate the opportunity, read the following questions keeping in mind both your personal and your professional experience.

- ✔ What are the clues that indicate this idea and opportunity?
- ✔ What are the conditions that permit the opportunity to occur?
- ✔ How will the future of this new product or service change the idea?
- ✔ How great (in terms of time) is the window of opportunity?

A window of opportunity is a time horizon during which an opportunity exists before something else happens to eliminate it. A unique opportunity, once shown to produce wealth, will attract competitors, and if the business is easy to enter, the industry will become saturated. You have to get in quickly and be able to get out before revenues become dispersed in an overdeveloped market.

To give yourself greater room to maneuver on the threshold of a start-up idea, consider creating your own window of opportunity. Successful companies find and exploit markets that others have missed or that new technologies have suddenly created. For example, advertising has obviously been around for some time, but when DoubleClick started, Internet advertising was a brand-new field. Its founder helped to create a wildly successful business by taking advantage of an unforeseen opportunity.

The factors that help the business entrepreneur create opportunity are given in Figure 1.4.

Phase 2: Investigate the Need through Market Research

It's necessary to identify, measure, and document the need for the product or service. This means making a specific financial forecast that will testify to the actual potential and anticipated return for this proposed product or service. This process is not the end—it's only the beginning. We'll explore the topic of marketing more fully in Chapter 2—but for now, we'll consider it as it fits into the opportunity analysis.

Here is your chance to interact with the actual climate surrounding your company, so you will be prepared in the early stages of your *new venture*. Larger companies often outsource research to a marketing company, but this process will identify the steps and questions you will need to custom-design your personal research and conduct it productively.

 new venture a new business providing products/services to a particular market.

Preliminary Questions This is the point when you can solidify the purpose and object of your research. Those who are developing a particular product will want to focus on a certain brand of question that can tell them about product features and distribution. A more service-oriented entrepreneur will consider other inquiries, directed at identifying the sources and beneficiaries of that service. Consider what you want now—you'll be

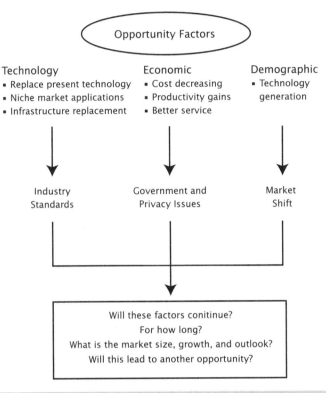

FIGURE 1.4 What factors create opportunity?

saving time and money later on. You will find these areas and questions to be potential material to direct the development of your research.

✔ *Need.* Will this product be serving the customers' real needs? What is the overall market for the business? Are there special niches that can be exploited?

✔ *Angle/Competition.* What is different about your product or service that will cause the customer to choose it over your competition's product or service?

✔ *Proprietary Questions.* Can the product be patented or copyrighted? Is it unique enough to get a significant head start on the competition? Can the process be easily copied? Will the business concept be developed and licensed to others, or developed and sold?

✔ *Cost and Manufacture.* How much will the customer be willing to spend for the product? How much will materials and labor time cost? How much capital will be needed in the future? Now?

✔ *Advertisement and Packaging.* What type of advertising and promotional plans will be used to market the product? Will you bank on traditional methods of promoting related products or services?

✔ *Sales.* What distribution and sales methods will be used? Will you rely on independent sales representatives, company sales force, direct mail, door-to-door sales, supermarkets, service stations, or company-owned stores?

✔ *Transport.* How will the product be transported—company-owned trucks, common carriers, postal service, or airfreight?

✔ *Employees.* Can the company attract employees with the necessary skills to operate the business venture? Who are the workers? Are they dependable and competent?

Start with Data Collection Now that you've established key questions about your potential business, you need to find the answers. Data collection can come from a variety of sources. The more sources you consult, the more valid your results will be considered to be. Yet don't go overboard—you can become overwhelmed with all of the available data out there. So keep in mind that you want your questions to be as specific as possible, your sources to be as relevant as possible, and your data collection only as extensive as you will need for the initial investment and planning to run smoothly.

Design and Execute a Study to Get the Answers You will be taking your data findings from secondary resources to support your preliminary research. In short, you've looked at other sources with the appropriate questions and expectations. Now it's time to create your own personal source by asking businesses and experts direct key questions.

You will need to choose a small number of relevant companies that will represent the total group. First, find out who is out there; next, find out who you can speak with that will give you an idea of what the varieties of companies might say, so you don't waste time and money. Remember, you are doing this to start a business, not to become a research expert. Now you will ask your representative companies and experts your study questions, based on the most unbiased model you can find. You don't want questionable data, so you have to avoid the pitfalls. Make sure that all the participants are asked the same questions in the same manner. Don't skimp on the details here— make the results really reflect the true account by sticking to an exact and objective method of questioning. You will have to train survey recorders and telephone interviewers, and perhaps monitor them, to ensure these results.

Analyze the Data At this stage you have primary data. What is it telling you? How can you interpret it? Again, think of the secondary sources that you examined. How did they interpret their results? Using the most thorough sources as your model, write a final report. This ensures that a record exists for the future and that others in the organization can refer to the study as necessary.

Does all of this sound too extensive—and expensive? Many entrepreneurs must do their market research with limited funds. You can cut costs with these recommendations:

✔ Use search engines, web pages, and online databases.

✔ Use the telephone instead of mail surveys and door-to-door interviewing.

✔ Avoid research in high-cost cities; test more than one product at a time.

✔ Avoid collecting unnecessary data.

One source might be a university. Professors, students, and staff are often involved in projects that enable them to extend their assignments with the entrepreneur's market research survey.

Phase 3: Develop the Plan

Once an opportunity has been identified, decisions must be made regarding performance and staffing. Who is going to do what? How will decisions be made? You need to develop a business plan that will stretch your assets as far as possible, while ensuring flexibility. It should be broad enough to incorporate some unexpected changes in your aim for success and profitability.

Your plan will be the backbone of your business, helping you in times of crisis and motivating you at points of indecision. An extremely valuable outcome of preparing and writing the plan at this stage is identifying flaws and coming up with the means to address them. You will find yourself compelled to examine closely your prospective venture.

If you are discovering irreversible errors and insurmountable flaws, you may discover that you will have to abandon this particular opportunity. Is it discouraging to return to the idea stage? Of course, but consider two things: You've already learned a great deal that will help you the next time around, and you've just saved yourself and your investors a large amount of time and money. Don't be blind to serious misgivings. If you can walk away at this stage and begin again with a strong attitude, those already involved will be suitably impressed.

A business plan maps out the particular components of and future tasks for your business, all in about 30 to 40 pages. Similar to a real map, it should answer some basic questions: How far will the business have to go? What is the exact destination? How will the goal be reached? What is the anticipated arrival time at each of the various stops? A good plan will do the following:

✔ Determine the viability of the business and application in selected markets.

✔ Provide guidance in planning and organizing the activities and goals.

✔ Serve as a vehicle to obtain financing and personnel for the business.

A more detailed version of the business plan is found in Chapter 4, but you can greatly benefit from considering these basic elements now.

Phase 4: Determine the Resources Needed

For any business, asking questions about your own resource capabilities is crucial. It is particularly the case, however, with a start-up venture that uses new technology for its service or as its product. You need to make sure that you have the skills to match—and triumph over—your competition. This sounds like Darwinian survival of the fittest, but consider it in an updated form—survival of the most skilled.

So, what are your capabilities and resources? Let's check, using these questions:

✔ *Do you have business and financial support?* Can the business operate in a cost-effective manner? Who will be on the management team? How can you fill gaps in management and/or financial knowledge?

✔ *Are you prepared for personal contacts and networking?* Who will make contacts at the right companies? How should the network be set up? Are you going to be able to devote time to meeting people by traveling? Phone work? E-mail correspondence? Will you put contact making not only on your priority list but also on your daily calendar?

✔ *Have you considered financing requirements?* Can the business last (especially in this business opportunity, which requires capital to sustain the company over possibly a one- or two-year period)? Will there be investors who might be willing to come on board at a later date?

✔ *Where are your technical skills based?* Do you have the technical skills necessary? Who has the know-how—you or your coworkers? Will you need to figure in additional training to your start-up costs? Is there someone who can translate technical jargon to investors?

Phase 5: Manage the Distinguishing Features of the Business

You've set up the opportunity, written the plan, and assessed your resources. Now you need to run your business, applying your management structure and style to any questions, difficulties, and successes that come your way.

If any advice is pivotal here, it's the key emphasis on the act of investing. You've invested time, money, experience, and energy in setting up. Now you'll need to follow the path blazed by the most successful businesses and invest in people, business procedures, and information technology. How will you do this?

Keep Planning The most successful entrepreneurs know where they fit in the market and where they want to be. Planning should account for and accommodate changes in designing, testing, and marketing to prepare for the business opportunity. How can you follow their lead?

- ✔ Test the business concept.
- ✔ Determine the improvement needed.
- ✔ Anticipate the necessary time frame.
- ✔ Define problems and anticipate barriers.
- ✔ Align strategic partners for the process.
- ✔ Assist in preparing a pricing strategy and anticipate future direction.
- ✔ Be competitive at all times.

Deliver a Total Solution Traditionally, small companies have assumed unchallenged territory and special distribution channels for their products. Today, however, all companies are playing in the same markets and providing the entire range of service for their customers. Investors and customers want to buy a whole product or service.

Cultivate Advanced Resources The layoffs of highly skilled workers from major corporations that you read about every day are actually creating an important opportunity for your company. These trained and effective personnel are looking to apply their business skills and experience to start-ups. The results to your business could include access to small companies and major corporations, capital, and productive market knowledge.

Now let's consider a new technology that is effectively transforming day-to-day services. Consider how a business plan was crucial in making this opportunity a business reality.

CASE STUDY: NEW PAYMENT IDEA, NEW OPPORTUNITY

With the advent of smart cards, consumers will soon be able to load electronic cash on a card and use it to perform any number of the seemingly unending small-value payment transactions, avoiding the need to carry exact change or rely on change machines. They will be used, for example, at such places as laundromats, vending machines, parking meters, bridge and toll road crossings, and fast-food outlets. Service providers will also benefit from reduced operating costs and increased business.

Cost-conscious shoppers can use these cards to receive discounts and/or bonus points by using their cards frequently at their favorite stores. Service providers, too, will benefit by being able to access a customer's shopping preferences and then let the customer know of special offers that might be of particular interest.

Business travelers or vacationers may someday eliminate many of the nuisances and annoyances they have come to expect as part of traveling. These cards can help people avoid long lines for ticketing and seat assignment. They may even be used to unlock rental cars and hotel rooms without first having to check in at rental car agencies or hotel desks.

Smart cards provide consumers with an alternative method to perform financial transactions faster and with increased security. For example, with the aid of card-compatible personal computers and interactive TVs, smart cards will make tasks such as home banking and home shopping much more attractive.

Successful companies find and exploit markets others have missed, or they explore new markets that recent technologies have created. Most businesses believe that they are too big to pursue a poorly defined market. That's why so few large companies have spotted new opportunities.

WHAT'S PROTECTING YOU?

One question that you might encounter in your work conducting research and formulating a business plan is whether this idea/opportunity/product/service needs to be protected by a *patent* or *copyright*. Take the following evaluation screening to get an idea.

Evaluation Screening

1. Is the service, product, or idea unique to get a head start on competition?

2. Does your service or product represent a breakthrough (either high-tech or different from others)?

3. Have you fully explored other less expensive protective measures that may give all the legal protection needed at this point?

4. Has an attorney discussed the options and recommended that a patent be pursued?

5. Are you able to risk up to $2,000 on a patent search and application?

If you answered yes to more than one of these questions, you should seriously consider seeking legal protection for the idea and opportunity. However, if a *nondisclosure agreement* that essentially protects the idea for the first two years will suffice, then seriously con-

patent
federal governmental grant to an inventor giving exclusive rights to an invention or process for 20 years from date of patent application filing. A U.S. patent does not always grant rights in foreign countries.

copyright
an exclusive right granted by the federal government to the processor to publish and sell literary, musical, and other artistic materials. Honored for 50 years after the death of the author.

nondisclosure agreement
legal agreement stipulating that the signer not disclose confidential information about the company and/or product.

sider that the first option. What about marketing this to a larger company as a customer? Most companies have their own internal research and development organization dedicated to monitoring and meeting the needs of their product or service line. The best method for submitting an idea is to contact the company and ask for their disclosure conditions to review an idea.

Some companies, however, will sign your nondisclosure form, while others will not. Most will have their own protection forms to sign, which essentially state that, while they may agree to look at or discuss an idea, their research departments may have already thought of the idea long before. Let an attorney have the last word. Get a second (or even a third) legal opinion before committing to any legal expenditure.

PREPARING A CASH FLOW FORECAST

Why Should You Prepare a Cash Flow Forecast?

As stated earlier, one of the major problems that start-up companies face is cash flow. On several occasions, profitable companies have failed because of lack of cash. As the manager of your cash, you can anticipate temporary cash shortfalls and have sufficient time to arrange short-term loans if needed.

working capital
the amount of funds available to pay short-term expenses. Seen as a cushion to meet unexpected or out-of-the-ordinary expenses. It is determined by subtracting current liabilities from current assets.

A cash flow forecast shows the amount of cash coming in and cash going out during a certain month. The forecast will also show a bank loan officer (or you) what additional *working capital*, if any, the business may need. Additionally, it provides evidence that there will be sufficient cash on hand to make the interest payments on a revolving *line of credit* or to cover the shortfalls when cash outlays are greater than cash receipts.

Computer spreadsheet programs such as Microsoft Excel or any variety of full-faceted business software can be very useful for cash flow worksheet development. Reliable cash flow projections can bring a sense of order, well-being, and security to your business. The most important tool owners and managers have available to control the financial liquidity of their business is the cash flow worksheet.

How Do You Get Started?

Step One: Consider Your Cash Flow Revenues
Find a realistic basis for estimating your sales each month.

For a start-up, the basis can be the average monthly sales of a similar-sized competitor that is operating in a similar market. Be sure to reduce your figures by a factor of about 50 percent a month during the start-up year. There are also publications available in libraries and bookstores that discuss methods of sales forecasting.

For an existing company, sales revenues from the same month in the previous year make a good basis for forecasting sales for that month in the succeeding year. For example, if the trend in the industry predicts a general growth of 4 percent for the next year, it will be entirely acceptable for you to show each month's projected sales at 4 percent higher than your actual sales the previous year. Include notes to the cash flow to explain any unusual variations from the previous year's numbers.

Step Two: Consider Your Cash Flow Disbursements
Project each of the various expense categories (normally shown in your ledger) beginning with a summary for each month of the cash payments to suppliers as well as your wages, rent, and equipment costs (accounts payable).

Each month shows only the cash you expect to pay out that month to your suppliers. For example, if you plan to pay your supplier invoices in 30 days, the cash payouts for January's purchases will be shown in February. If you can obtain trade credit for longer terms, then cash outlays will appear two or even three months after the stock purchase has been received and invoiced.

An example of a different type of expense is your insurance expenditure. Your commercial insurance premium may be $2,400 annually. Normally, this would be treated as a $200 monthly expense. However, the cash flow will not see it this way. The cash flow wants to know exactly how it will be paid. If it is to be paid in two installments, $1,200 in January and $1,200 in July, then that is

line of credit
short-term financing usually granted by a bank up to a predetermined limit; debtor borrows as needed up to the limit of credit without need to renegotiate the loan.

how it must be entered on the cash flow worksheet. The same principle applies to all cash flow expense items.

Step Three: Reconciliation of the Revenues and Disbursements The reconciliation section of the cash flow worksheet begins by showing the balance carried over from the previous months' operations. To this it will add the net inflows/outflows, or current month's receipts and disbursements. This adjusted balance will be carried forward to the first line of the reconciliation portion of the next month to become the base to which the next month's cash flow activity will be added and/or subtracted.

Making the Best Use of Your Cash Flow

Cash flow plans must be modified constantly as you learn new things about your business and paying customers. Since you will use this cash flow forecast to regularly compare each month's projected figures with each month's actual performance figures, it will be useful to have a second column for the actual performance figures right alongside each of the "planned" columns in the cash flow worksheet. Look for significant discrepancies between the planned and actual figures. (See Figure 1.5.)

For example, if the business's actual figures fail to meet your cash receipt projections for three months in a row, this is a signal that it is time to revise the year's projections. It may be necessary to apply to the bank to increase the upper limit of your revolving line of credit. Approaching the bank to increase an operating loan should be done well in advance of the date when the additional funds will be required. Do not leave cash inflow to chance.

DESIGNING A CASH FLOW WORKSHEET

There are a variety of ways a cash flow forecast could be presented. The best way is to show only revenues from operations and the proceeds from sales.

The format should be a double-width column along the left side of the page for the account headings, then two side-by-side vertical columns for each month of the

FIGURE 1.5 Sample cash flow—planned versus actual.

Item	April Planned	April Actual	May Planned	May Actual
Cash Revenues/Cash In	$22,000	$18,500	$24,000	$22,500
Cash Disbursements/Cash Out				
Wages	$10,000	$11,500	$11,000	$12,000
Commissions	$2,000	$1,500	$2,000	$2,000
Rent	$3,500	$3,500	$3,500	$3,500
Equipment payment/computers	$12,000	$12,000	$12,000	$12,000
Total cash out	$27,500	$28,500	$28,500	$29,500
Reconciliation of Cash Flow				
Opening cash balance	$5,000	$5,000	($500)	($5,000)
Add: Total cash revenues in	$22,000	$18,500	$24,000	$22,500
Deduct: Total cash disbursements out	$27,500	$28,500	$28,500	$29,500
Closing Cash Balance (Carry forward to next month)	($500)	($5,000)	($5,000)	($12,000)

year, beginning from the month you plan to open (e.g., the first dual column might be labeled "April Planned" and "April Actual").

From there, the cash flow worksheet breaks into three distinctive sections. The first section (at the top left portion of the worksheet, starting below and to the left of the month names) is headed "Cash Revenues" (or "Cash In"). The second section, just below it, is headed "Cash Disbursements" (or "Cash Out"). The final section, below that, is headed "Reconciliation of Cash Flow."

SUMMARY

Once a business idea is determined to be worthy of further consideration, you must assess its potential. Often, after you select an approach to the market and do the necessary research, you will need to revise your concept, adding refinement and sophistication to your original spark of an idea.

Generally, there is a great deal of useful information

that is readily available. Often our market research objectives must be modified to use available information. In some cases, you may choose to survey the market to acquire data geared specifically to your needs. In every case, you must apply some judgment to the data since you are trying to project your future prospects.

When you complete this step, the planning and developing process starts. All ideas must be screened and evaluated to determine the feasibility of the opportunity. The best ideas are evaluated through the development, test marketing, and managing the resources to successfully launch the business.

From the market research results, you must fine-tune your plan. You should also be able to provide the answers to the following questions: What segment(s) of the market can your product or service serve? What does it have to offer the market? Who are your customers? How will you promote and market the product or service?

Preparing a monthly cash flow forecast highlights the actual cash effect and timing of the company's revenue and expenses. For example, the company may generate revenue in September but not actually receive the cash until October or November. Used properly, this will provide you with the means to keep your business decision making on track and your inventory purchasing under control. It will also serve as an early warning indicator when your expenditures are running out of line or your sales targets are not being met. Your idea should be tested thoroughly by preparing a cash flow forecast.

In the next chapter, we'll take the next step to apply the marketing plan for your business.

ADDITIONAL RESOURCES

Allbusiness.com (www.allbusiness.com): "Solutions for growing business."

Digitalwork.com (www.digitalwork.com): "Your business workshop."

Edge.low.org (www.edge.low.org): "A peer-learning community for growing your company."

Entreworld (www.entreworld.org): "A world of resources for entrepreneurs."

Ideacafe.com (www.ideacafe.com): "A fun approach to serious businesses."

Office.com (www.office.com): "This new way we work."

Onvia.com (www.onvia.com): "The premier emarketplace for small businesses."

Small Business Administration (www.sba.gov): "Helping small businesses to succeed."

Smartonline.com(www.smartonline.com): "Small-business answers from small-business owners."

Workz.com (www.workz.com): "Helping small businesses grow and prosper online."

Analyzing the Market, Customers, and Competition

Objectives

1. Understand the five steps for a successful marketing plan.
2. Know how to prepare a market analysis.
3. Know how to use electronic commerce (e-commerce) marketing.
4. Analyze your market, customers, and competitors.

INTRODUCTION: HOW WILL YOU MARKET YOUR VISION?

By now, you have solidified your idea and have used the recommendations in the first chapter to investigate its worth and work through possible problems. You may even have already sold others on your idea and gained their financial and/or mentoring support. But now you need to understand and use the business strategies that will give you a competitive advantage and get your product to the market at large.

The process that I am referring to is marketing, a term you have heard before and probably know a few things about. But what will you need to know for your business to succeed?

You want your product to sell. In order to help you achieve that, you are going to have to understand your customers, their profile, markets, and pricing as well as be able to plan for your company's future strategies in each of these areas. This chapter will provide you with the information and tools you'll need to do just that. Throughout, I'll be explaining the two important elements to understanding your role in the marketing game—the components of marketing strategy and the keys to understanding and dominating the competition.

A number of techniques and strategies can assist you in effectively analyzing a potential market. By using them, you can gain in-depth knowledge about the specific market and can translate this knowledge into a well-formulated business plan. Effective marketing analysis also can help a new business position itself and make changes that will result in increased sales

Electronic commerce (e-commerce) is now becoming a marketing competitive necessity for many businesses. It will change the way you do business and how you market your services and products. In this chapter we will address these issues and offer guidelines to follow in attracting new marketing opportunities.

The business begins with customers, so unless you obtain and keep customers, you will not sustain the business. By far the best asset for a business is its customers, where market analysis begins.

FIVE STEPS TO FORMULATING A SUCCESSFUL MARKETING PLAN

How can you utilize marketing techniques to your advantage? Let's consider the following areas and how you can answer questions and anticipate concerns from a marketing perspective. Keep in mind that we'll be broadening our understanding of many of these topics later on in this chapter to help you prepare a *marketing plan.*

1. *Getting the Product Out: Sales and Distribution.* Start with how a business will get its products or services to customers. Will the business employ its own sales force for direct marketing or will dealers, distributors, or jobbers be used? Have any of these distribution people been specified or identified? On what basis have they been or

 marketing plan
a written plan for achieving the marketing goals and strategies of the venture, usually on an annual basis. Business plans always contain a marketing plan section.

Profile: Stephen Hanson—Vision and Marketing Plan for BR Guest

For the past 14 years, Stephen Hanson of BR Guest has brought his vision of stylish, popular, and value-oriented restaurants to New Yorkers and diners from all over the world.

His first taste of the restaurant business came in the early 1970s when he worked as a maître d' at the original TGI Friday's while earning a business degree at New York University. Promoted to the position of manager after graduation, he sharpened his business acumen and marketing skills there before embarking on an entrepreneurial path. In 1974, he collaborated with two college friends to open the enormously popular Westchester nightclub, Peachtree's.

While still in the nightclub business, Hanson changed directions and pursued a career as a commodity broker. Several years later he sold his interest in Peachtree's and left commodities as well to help run his family's designer sportswear company, Betty Hanson. After nine years as an executive in the fashion design business, he left to return to his first love, restaurants.

In 1987, Hanson created the first of his burgeoning group of Manhattan restaurants, Coconut Grill. The 150-seat bistro-style restaurant became a fixture on the Upper East Side. On the heels of his success with this first solo venture, Hanson opened his second restaurant, the Mediterranean-inspired Isabella's, on the Upper West Side. Here, his touch masterfully converted a previously jinxed corner into a buzzing destination frequented by celebrities such as Steve Martin, Jerry Seinfeld, and Alec, Billy, and Stephen Baldwin, as well as neighborhood residents and workers of all ages.

In 1994, Hanson opened his third venture, the 220-seat Park Avalon, on Park Avenue South. There, Mediterranean-American cuisine served in a loftlike, trilevel dining room attracted high-profile customers from the worlds of photography, advertising, and entertainment as well as local residents.

Two years later, Hanson ventured west across Union Square to open Blue Water Grill in the marbled-lined former home of the Bank of Metropolis. With its bilevel dining rooms, outdoor café and a 150-seat jazz room, the restaurant was an instant success. Blue Water Grill is now the city's 10th most popular restaurant, according to the *1999 Zagat Survey*. It was also named 1998's "best seafood restaurant" by *Time Out New York* magazine.

Capitalizing on his success with seafood, Hanson opened Ocean Grill on the Upper West Side in 1997. Ocean Grill's elegant 160-seat dining room is reminiscent of a luxury liner. Its lively outdoor café was featured in the hit movie *You've Got Mail* with Tom Hanks and Meg Ryan. In 1998, Hanson followed with the 220-seat Atlantic Grill on the Upper East Side. The Cape Cod–inspired dining room, flanked by a bustling bistro-style section, features both a raw bar and a sushi bar.

His marketing plan was to expand into totally new territory in the year 2000 with his seventh venture, Ruby Foo's Dim Sum and Sushi Palace, on the Upper West Side. This trilevel, 10,000-square-foot and 400-seat restaurant was designed by renowned architect David Rockwell. It was to be a feast for the senses as well as the palate. A 50-foot-high sushi bar and massive curving staircase add drama to the Pan-Asian cuisine, which includes "New York's best dim sum," according to *New York* magazine's Hal Rubenstein. A critical success, awarded two stars by *The New York Times*, the Ruby Foo's concept has expanded into booming Times Square.

Hanson shows no signs of slowing down on either his vision or his market plan.

will they be selected? How will they be compensated? If a business chooses to rely upon its own sales force, what skills and training will that require?

2. *High Quality, Low Cost: Pricing.* You should consider pricing as part of your overall marketing strategy. For example, the manufacturer of designer women's apparel might pursue a high-priced strategy, then discount liberally as a means of generating sales.

You will need to generate a rationale to explain your strategy in this area and anticipate its impact on gross profit. A detailed price list will be helpful, whether you are handling the marketing of the product, getting advice from mentors, or considering outsourcing marketing to a company that specializes in it.

3. *Raising Visibility: Advertising, Public Relations, and Promotion.* In many instances, public relations will play an important role in your attempts to generate sales. Focus on the concept and creative content of the communications campaign, the media you will utilize, and the extent to which each will be employed.

Many start-up or early-stage companies will not have large advertising budgets. For them, public relations can be the answer. Entrepreneurs can contact local media— newspapers, radio, and television—that often write or broadcast stories on new businesses in the community. If response is favorable, this can mean free advertising directed at a large audience.

4. *On the Spot: Site Analysis.* In some instances, particularly if your business is retail-focused, you'll need to take the location into account as you work on your marketing plan. Think about the demographics of your neighborhood, its environment, and the cost of maintaining a facility.

5. *Future Marketing Activities.* Your plan should consider sales strategies aimed at sustaining growth. For example, a company's immediate plans might involve penetrating only the domestic market, while in the future the same company might consider a license for its products in some international markets or perhaps even a joint venture.

PREPARING THE MARKETING ANALYSIS AND PLAN

Marketing analysis is sometimes called a feasibility study or marketing plan. This process will help you develop a plan that leverages your strengths and accounts for your weaknesses in determining the demand for the product or service.

Marketing analysis is also the process of determining a plan that provides you with a sense and an indication of demand. The analysis addresses the key questions: Is there a market to build a viable business? Who are your competitors? Will you be the first to launch? Is governmental regulation an issue? What new products are in the pipeline? How much financial support will you need in order to start up? This analysis also describes the research for collecting and analyzing marketing information on the demographics and on consumers' needs as well as buying habits on which to base decisions.

Identifying Customers

The first step is identifying the most likely customer for the business. Who will buy the product? Often the decision maker and the buyer are the same person, particularly with consumer-product goods. You should also develop a profile of the potential customer or the target audience you are serving. This profile is usually based on the following factors:

✔ *Market Profile.* A market profile helps a company identify its current market and service needs. How profitable are existing company services? Which of these services offer the most potential? Which (if any) are inappropriate? Which will customers cease to need in the future?

✔ *Current and Best Customers.* If you are already in business, identify the company's current clients to determine where to allocate resources. However, if you are a start-up company, prepare a preliminary list of potential customers. This will help you define the best customers to segment this market niche more directly.

✔ *Potential Customers.* By identifying potential customers, either geographically or with an industry-wide analysis of its marketing area, a company increases its ability to target this group, thus turning potential customers into current customers.

✔ *Outside Factors.* This analysis focuses on changing trends in demographics, economics, technology, cultural attitudes, and governmental policy. These factors may have a substantial impact on customer needs and, consequently, expected services.

Niche or Target Markets

A niche market is a small segment of a large market ignored by other companies. For many firms, niche markets are too small to be attractive to large competitors; yet your firm can do quite well with them. The plan is to select a niche market in which your business can grow and gain a competitive advantage.

Target marketing is the strategy used by most successful businesses today. Usually, a company ignores segments that are too small because the product will not generate sufficient growth to compete effectively.

The market segments are selected and targeted. Marketing tactics are developed for each target market; this is called strategy market segmentation. Target your markets and develop a marketing program for penetrating each segment. Your business plan as described in Chapter 4 will help you identify the markets and selection. Each of your target markets should be treated almost as a separate marketing program.

One-to-One Marketing

One-to-one marketing requires learning the profile or details about individual customers to identify which are most valuable to the company. By tailoring or customizing your product or service to the customer, you will enhance your company's value to each one.

One-to-one marketing is fast becoming a competitive imperative. As companies learn more about their customers, they will use this knowledge to create and sell products and services to loyal customers. The key steps to be a one-to-one marketer are:

✔ *Identify your customers, or get them to identify themselves.* Consider all options for collecting names: sales transactions, contests, sponsored events, frequent-buyer programs, 800 numbers, credit-card records, simple survey cards, and quick one-question polls when customers call.

✔ *Link customers' identities to their transactions.* Credit-card records are especially useful, but not necessary. Often the best way to build individual customer transaction records is to approach business differently. Consider membership clubs to make it possible to link information about purchases with people.

✔ *Calculate individual customer lifetime value.* Knowing what a customer is likely to spend over time will help you decide which customers are most desirable (because their business is more profitable) and how much to invest in keeping them. In this light, unusual and seemingly expensive offers can make powerful economic sense.

✔ *Practice just-in-time marketing.* Know the purchasing cycle for the product or service and measure it in months or years. Identify when a customer is planning to buy the next product, and enter the customer's shopping process. Time your marketing material to meet that person's needs rather than your quarterly sales goal. Send handwritten postcards or marketing materials, or use a new catalog for selling.

✔ *Ratchet up your customer-satisfaction program.* Even your customer-survey questions can be tailored to a customer's wish list and buying preferences. Customize your responses to meet customer demand.

✔ *Treat complaints as opportunities for additional business.* Call back complaining customers; don't make them chase you down. By responding quickly, you can turn a complainer into an advocate for your product.

✔ *Enhance your product with information.* Build in some form of information that will keep customers coming back. For example, a tofu maker could provide special recipes to those who respond to back-of-the-package coupons.

Database Marketing

Database marketing lets you analyze sales trends and profile prospects to target your best customers. Until recently, start-up and small companies did not use database marketing. It was expensive to build the systems, and considerable time was needed to set up the database and data. However, due to falling costs of hardware and software, this technique is becoming popular for most businesses. By installing a database marketing system, you could systematically analyze sales trends to make smarter purchasing decisions. Such a system can combine a database full of information about the customers' buying habits to give the buyer answers to key marketing questions such as:

✔ Which products and colors sold best?

✔ Which vendors were most profitable?

✔ What time of year was best for selling a particular item?

With this knowledge, buyers can rearrange their sales approaches and meet sales projections.

FIVE STEPS TO SUCCESSFUL DATABASE MARKETING

1. *Pinpoint your objectives.* Are you looking to increase your customer base? To double sales of a product line? To encourage repeat business? Make sure you understand your goals before you automate. Companies that are drawn to the technology without knowing what they want to get out of it will be very disappointed.

2. *Choose the software that best fits your goals.* If, for instance, you need a system that's tied tightly to sales-rep activity in the field, use or outsource a management program with database capability that defines customers by market segment, revenue, and geographical location.

3. *Determine who should be in the database.* First, figure out what types of customers have the most potential. Then construct the database, using everything from salespeople's contacts to lists bought from outside suppliers.

4. *Develop a plan.* Only after your objectives are laid out and your database is constructed will it be time to devise a marketing program. Generally the program will fall into one of three categories: direct marketing, rewards for repeat purchases, or relationship-building promotions for longtime customers that generate profits.

5. *Measure results.* Generate periodic status reports in which you determine items such as cost per contact and cost per sale. If you want to be really careful, don't launch your program full tilt. Start with a small prototype. If you like what you see, expand to include the entire database.

DEFINE THE MARKET POSITION

Positioning means understanding how your customers perceive your product or service in direct relation to how they perceive your competitor's product or service.

How do you want the market to think of your product? To a large extent, by your promotional activities, you can position your product or service. Try to develop a company personality. Make your company mean something to its potential customers.

Consumers will group your business with others based on their perceptions of similarities. There are various factors that influence your position in the customer's mind. Geographic location, presentation of a site, annual sales, number of employees, and the period of time in business are merely a few of the elements that can link you to other businesses and determine how you will distinguish yourself from your competition.

Prepare the Industry and Market Segment Analysis

An industry and market segment analysis starts with research data on the size, growth, and segments of the industry. Review secondary sources at the library. Trade magazines, publications, or published articles may be useful in determining how attractive the industry is. Information on size of market, rate of growth, availability of suppliers, or new technology should be documented before the marketing plan is determined.

Define the Market Segment

The market segment defines the market by product feature, lifestyle of target consumers, and season. To become the leader, you must capture the biggest portion of sales in its market segment. It is also the process of identifying a specific set of characteristics that differentiate one group of consumers from the rest. For example, although many people drink coffee, the market for coffee can be segmented based on taste and price. Some individuals prefer high-quality coffee made with special coffee beans because of its

> ### *Market Postioning Guide*
>
> 1. What industry are you competing in? Can you identify cycles of success or failure that affect competitors or tighten the market?
>
> 2. Your business should offer a competitive position in this industry. How attractive is it compared to alternative positions?
>
> 3. How strong is your competitive advantage? What resources will be required to maintain it?
>
> 4. Can your competitors easily imitate your plan to their own advantage?

taste; many others cannot tell the difference between high-quality and average-quality coffee. The price is higher for high-quality coffee such as Starbucks, so the market niche is smaller for these offerings than it is for lower-priced competitors. This process of segmenting the market can be critical for new businesses with very limited resources.

Also measure yourself against existing and potential competition. How can you position your business to win? Use the market positioning guide (see box) to formulate a plan for understanding the market that you and your competitors are in.

KNOW YOUR COMPETITION AND PREPARE A COMPETITIVE ANALYSIS

You should also provide a detailed assessment of the competitive environment by creating profiles of your competitors. It is helpful to know the key players in each firm with which your company will be competing—their personalities and positions in the companies.

Also review how they compete for business in terms of product, service, location, and promotion. Do the competitors meet price competition? In many situations, various competitors compete with different methods. Some go after the price-sensitive segment of the market while others seek the business of those who want service, quality, and so forth.

It is particularly important to identify which businesses will provide the most significant competition and what they will likely do. Analyze the situation by using the following questions. (See Figures 2.1 and 2.2.)

Product or Service

✔ How is the competitive product or service defined?

✔ How is it similar to or different from your own?

✔ Does the competition cater to a mass or target market?

✔ What features of the product are superior?

✔ What strengths or weaknesses of the competition can you exploit?

Price

✔ What is the competitor's pricing strategy?

✔ Is the competitor's price higher or lower?

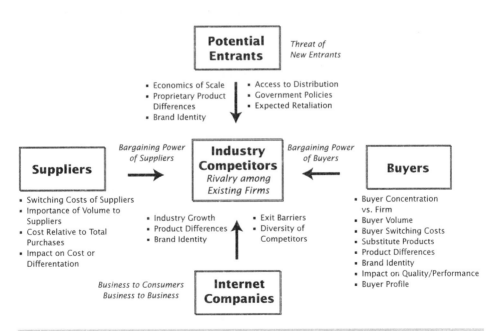

FIGURE 2.1 Evaluating the competition—marketing analysis.

FIGURE 2.2   Evaluating the competition.

| Factor | Attractiveness | |
	High	Low
Competition among existing firms	Competition is minimal but will become intense.	The industry is declining and mature.
Bargaining power of buyers	Buyer volume is high, and buyers are willing to negotiate.	Buyers face few switching costs.
Bargaining power of suppliers	Many substitutes and sources are available.	Supplies are limited; products are differentiated.
Internet companies	No competition is defined on the Internet.	Many companies are entering this market.
Potential threats	There are complex barriers, and costs are high to enter market.	There are few simple entry barriers to enter the business.

✔ What is the competitor's gross margin for similar products?

✔ Does the competitor offer terms, discounts, or promotions?

Industry Competitors

✔ Define where the competition is located in terms of new, Internet, or potential threats of existing companies.

✔ What are the strengths and weaknesses of each?

✔ How will e-commerce companies affect your business?

✔ How can your suppliers or buyers affect your competition?

Selling/Promotion

✔ How does the competitor advertise? Analyze the web site.

✔ How much does the competitor spend on advertising, web site development, and promotions?

✔ What marketing vision or plan is the competitor selling?

Management

✔ How strong is the competitor's management team?

✔ What is the team's background or experience?

✔ How does the company recruit new key employees?

✔ How does the company compensate employees?

Financial

✔ Is the competitor profitable?

✔ What volume are sales and market shares?

✔ Does the company spend money for research and development (R&D), Internet and web site development, and so on?

✔ Is the competitor properly capitalized? How strong is its cash flow?

PREPARE THE PRICING AND SALES STRATEGIES

Once the marketing analysis and competition review are established, you can begin to develop the pricing and sales plan. Pricing is one of the most difficult decisions to make for your product or service. A number of factors can guide you to price your product or service, including the degree of competitors, seasonal or cyclical changes in demand, distribution costs, customer services, and markups.

Pricing procedures differ depending on the nature of the business—retail, manufacturing, or service. The general methods discussed next might be applied to any type of business. They also demonstrate the basic steps in adopting a pricing system and how that system should relate to the desired pricing goals. With this general method in mind, you can formulate the most appropriate pricing strategy.

Pricing is key to the process of controlling costs and showing a profit. It is a very effective marketing tool that you must learn and master. It also conveys an image and affects demand, helping you target the market segment you are interested in.

Pricing Methods

There are three methods you should consider in pricing your product or service.

Value When considering the price to charge for your product or service, you must realize that price should not be based simply on cost, plus a modest profit. Instead, price should be based on the value of your product or service to the customer. If the customer does not think this price is acceptable, then you should consider not only a price change, but also a new image for the product or service. Demonstrating value is part of pricing a new strategy.

Rationale Explain why your prices are different from those of your competitors. For instance, does your business perform a service faster or more efficiently? Lower prices can be justified that way. Or, is your product created with greater care and better materials? A higher cost can communicate this.

Positioning One way of positioning is to charge a high price when competition is at a minimal level. Another option is to match competition by pricing slightly under competition to expand your market share. A third approach is to substantially underprice the market so as to exclude competitors altogether.

MARKET PENETRATION— SELLING THE PRODUCT

Market penetration determines specific methods you can use to sell products and services to customers. You always need to review the methods employed for the sales and distribution in relation to the customer. Some of the selling options include the following.

Direct Sales Force

Direct sale forces are salespeople who work directly for you and are paid either straight salary, salary plus bonus, or straight commission. The advantage of a direct sales force is you can control them as full-time employees. You have more control in training them to sell, price, and service the product. The disadvantage is the added expense in maintaining a full-time sales force. You will pay salary, travel, office support, and benefits for each salesperson.

Sales Agents

A sales agent works as a subcontractor to sell products or services. Agents are paid by commission, which is calculated as a specified percentage of the price. They receive their commissions after the company collects from the customers. The sales agent pays for expenses such as product samples, travel, office, telephone, and supplies that are incurred in selling the product or service.

Usually a specified territory is given to a sales agent where he or she can sell the product or service. In addition, a performance contract is used and signed by the sales agent, which outlines a minimum number of sales to be made annually.

The advantages of using sales agents are that you do not incur sales cost until the product is sold, and you can quickly build a large sales force and have the product or services sold nationwide in a relatively short period of time.

There are disadvantages to using sales agents as well. They usually sell other products or services as part of a complete line handled by the sales agent. They tend to push the easier-to-sell products or services and those for which they have already established a large customer following. You will have little control over the sales agents, since they are subcontractors and do not work directly for the company. Therefore, they can be extremely hard to manage in regard to pricing, follow-up, and service.

Trade Shows

Sales are achievable while exhibiting at a trade show. Many trade shows are available, but finding the right one can be difficult. Consider which trade shows you should attend to meet target customers.

The advantages include identifying many sales prospects because they come directly to your business. It is an excellent chance to meet people in the industry whom you could otherwise never have an opportunity to meet. You can also demonstrate your product and answer any questions from prospects about your product or service. In addition, you can establish a successful business relationship by inviting them to a follow-up breakfast, lunch, or dinner meeting.

You should develop screening questions to identify solid sales leads. This is an excellent method to meet the key players in the industry and learn what is happening. The contacts you make can ultimately provide significantly increased business that will better establish and increase your market share.

Marketing and Electronic Commerce Opportunities

Electronic commerce (e-commerce) is becoming a marketing and competitive necessity for start-up and growing companies. It will change the way many companies market their products and do business. It may even render purchase orders and invoices obsolete. Therefore, it is worth your while to shop for, invest in, or lease electronic commerce technologies. For you, it will mean competing more readily for domestic and global sales and delivering new products for the electronic commerce marketplace.

How Electronic Commerce Works

Electronic commerce is more than simply exchanging electronic mail messages or creating your company's informational site, or home page, on the Internet's World Wide Web. It also enables you to buy and sell electronically as well as reduce or eliminate paperwork and its associated costs and delays. Additionally, it can automate and streamline your buying and selling activities, including marketing, ordering, shipping, invoicing, and making payments. Previously, most electronic commerce transactions traveled over private telecommunications networks operated by individual companies. While this may continue to a limited degree, the Internet will become the electronic commerce of choice for most companies.

Electronic Commerce Guidelines

You should define your business needs first and then worry about the electronic commerce technology. Ask yourself, "How can I use the Internet and today's communications capabilities to increase sales? How can I use them to decrease the costs of operating my business? How are my competitors doing this?" Then research the products and services already available in the market to get the job done. If you cannot find any, consider teaming up with technology experts to create your solution. You should also equip your company for Internet electronic mail (e-mail). This will enable you to correspond electronically with business partners and offer to send and receive transactions online, in the form of text documents.

Finally, be sure that any services you consider provide safety measures, such as authentication (to confirm the identity of users and computers involved in the process); encryption (to protect the confidentiality of each transaction and message); and firewalls (to block private computer systems from outside hackers).

Advances in Wireless Communications

Many businesses already rely on cellular phones, pagers, and other wireless devices to outmaneuver the competition. As manufacturers and service providers make advances in digital technology with crisper sound and less static, wireless communication will expand its features to business for marketing opportunities. This includes electronic mail, Internet access, and smart phones to allow companies to market and use electronic commerce to advance the business.

Home Page Opportunities

You should consider creating a home page to market and provide information about your products or services on the Internet. A home page can also serve as a natural jumping-off point for electronic buying and selling. However, creating a home page may not be the right choice for every company. Too many web sites have no business reason; they exist simply to exist. Good sites are driven by a business objective that needs to be solved, and the Internet is the best way to solve it. Therefore, understand the risks of making payment transactions on the Internet.

Secure Payment Over the Internet

Because of the public nature of the Internet, consumers have been reluctant to use it for transmitting payments. Before it can be part of business as usual, electronic commerce must provide the same levels of privacy, integrity, and trust inherent in existing business practices. Fortunately, these problems can be overcome through the use of digital certificates.

Digital certificates are electronic credentials that bring greater security and integrity to Internet commerce. Using advanced encryption techniques, digital certificates give messages a unique electronic signature that identifies the sending party, ensures that the message was not altered or copied en route, and verifies that the message was sent and received. A rigorous certificate management system provides a strong assurance that people are who they claim to be. In this way, electronic commerce can have the same levels of security and integrity as brick-and-mortar businesses.

Businesses of all sizes can use digital certificates to bring security and identification to a wide range of network-based transactions, including e-mail, credit card transactions, software distribution, electronic data interchange (EDI), and intranet identification. It is expected that these newly secure applications will usher in an era of enhanced collaboration and productivity as companies increasingly turn to the Internet to conduct business.

Automating Transactions for the Business

Electronic data interchange technology enables companies to exchange and process business transactions, including purchase orders and invoices, electronically with their suppliers and corporate customers. In recent years, e-commerce providers have developed PC-based EDI systems that run over their private networks and reduce some of the costs and complexity of EDI for smaller companies.

Most companies currently engaged in electronic

commerce use computer software and modems to dial into telecommunications networks. Via network-based electronic mail, EDI, and/or databases, they transact business and share information with their suppliers. It is expected that as the technology becomes less expensive, earlier-stage and growing companies will implement EDI to support commercial transactions.

An Intranet or Your Own Private Internet

An ever-increasing number of larger companies are creating intranets, or restricted networks based on Internet technology, which provide employees with fast, easy access to their colleagues and to internal databases and systems.

Many midsize and smaller companies also will consider creating intranets over the next five years, primarily because such "private Internets" not only streamline internal information sharing but also can serve as a foundation for electronic commerce capabilities. Two companies now battling each other as leading intranet providers are Microsoft and America Online (AOL).

If you have a small company with all of your employees in one room, you probably don't need an intranet. But as soon as you have multiple floors or want to connect different locations, an intranet becomes helpful.

Media Advertising

If your business is small, you can use regional or local newspapers to reach your targeted customer. This can be a good medium for reaching a larger geographical area and to test the acceptability of your products and services. However, the cost of space and producing a professional ad can be high. This requires a larger advertising budget and more time than other market-penetration methods. You must choose media advertising for market penetration carefully because of price constraints and the need for quick results and rapid sales.

If you have determined that television advertising could be an effective way to reach your customers, try to purchase small blocks of local television time at a reduced rate. This will depend on the supply and demand for television advertising time in the local area.

Media-buying services usually charge 5 percent of the total bill and provide expertise in buying various types of media. Advertising agencies charge in a variety of ways, such as a fee, a per-project charge, or a commission based on the media rate.

Flyers and Handbills

Flyers consist of handouts that give the customer a reason to purchase a product or service. They often contain a discount coupon to attract potential customers.

Many start-up businesses, such as pizza deliverers, car washes, and housecleaning services, use this market-penetration method to establish and grow a repeat-customer base. With all the new software programs and quick copiers, this can be a cost-effective way to reach a small market area. You can also track how many customers are attracted by counting the coupons used.

The disadvantage of using flyers is evident when trying to cover a large geographical area. In this case, you would be better off using print media and running an ad that contains a coupon.

To distribute flyers, give them out at the business as bag stuffers or enclose them as business-mail inserts in someone else's mailings. They can also be given out in shopping centers, distributed at trade shows, or placed on counter displays.

Keep track of which distribution methods bring in the most sales by asking customers where they heard about the offer. Ask satisfied customers to pass on flyers to their friends and neighbors.

Direct Mail

Direct mail is sending sales literature to potential customers by mail. Direct-mail marketing provides a medium to reach a large number of customers quickly. It is selective because it allows owners to measure the response easily.

The disadvantage of using mail is that the cost is up-front. The mailing piece, mailing lists, and postage are paid for without any guarantee that sales will be generated. The effectiveness of a direct mailer is only as good as the actual mailing list, followed by the right offer and sale.

Telemarketing

Telemarketing is the use of telephone communications to sell merchandise directly to consumers. It is one of the fastest-growing direct market channels available and has become a direct-marketing tool. In many cases, firms have switched to fully automated telemarketing systems. Telemarketing systems now can use automatic-dialing and recorded-message players (ADRMPs) to dial numbers and play advertising messages that are voice activated and even that record orders from customers or forward the call to an operator.

Implementation and Plan of the Marketing Process

For a start-up business, the management team must coordinate and implement the marketing process. If the team lacks expertise in market planning, assistance is available from sources such as the Small Business Administration (SBA), Small Business Development Centers, universities, and marketing consultants.

Tracking the Progress of Marketing

Follow-up of the plan involves tracking specific results of the marketing effort. Sales data by product, territory, and sales representatives are a few of the specific results that should be followed. Any weak areas will provide you the opportunity to redirect or modify the existing marketing efforts to allow the business to achieve its goals and objectives. The marketing plan will also be useful in preparing the business plan. Details of how to develop the business plan are discussed in Chapter 4.

We will now apply what we learned in this chapter to a sample marketing plan for a technology company. The following illustrates a marketing plan and reviews as well as analyzes the products, pricing, strengths, and weaknesses of a company.

SAMPLE MARKETING PLAN— DATAMARK TECHNOLOGIES, INC.

Datamark uses its expertise in smart cards and magnetic stripe technology to develop applications and solutions to meet the rapidly growing demand for marketing frequency programs. Existing and previous loyalty programs have normally been too expensive, complicated, and paper-intensive, thus leading to lack of customer participation. As competition increases in retailing and other industries, companies are searching for new ways to understand customers and retain them. Datamark offers an inexpensive, easy-to-implement PC solution for these companies.

Datamark's strategy is focused on the frequency program's benefit to the customer. The company enables its clients to identify:

✔ Their most profitable customers.

✔ What these customers purchase (how often, how much).

✔ What customers' buying preferences are.

Clients use these solutions to better understand their customers and purchase habits in order to introduce new services that create added value for their customers. The Datamark marketing database drives all aspects of the marketing mix: advertising, promotion, pricing, and site selection; and it can be customized to meet the individual client's needs.

The objective is to establish an ongoing relationship with the client that will enhance the company's return on investment. Industry surveys have found that 80 percent of revenues are generated by 20 percent of customers. Datamark can help companies identify those 20 percent of their customers.

Review of the Product Analysis

The products should be compared to products offered by competitors in terms of quality and features. Unique attributes that are important to customers should be identified and highlighted. The products should also be considered from the physical standpoint, for size and appearance can be important attributes. As an example, smart cards can hold 1 to 10 pages of information regarding a customer.

Other important marketing characteristics for smart cards are:

✔ *User-Friendliness.* Will customers feel comfortable using the product?

✔ *Reliability.* Will the card work? Will the user feel 100 percent confident about the card's reliability? What backup system is in place?

✔ *Cost-Effectiveness.* How does delivery cost compare to the customer's perceived value of the service?

✔ *Compelling Use.* The initial application must be universal and valuable to compel a critical mass of people to accept it. Does the product fit the bill?

Figure 2.3 summarizes the marketing opportunities for smart cards. Figure 2.4 shows the advantages of smart cards as they relate to the cardholder, merchant, and issuers.

Guidelines for Product Development

You may feel that product development may be the least of your concerns when starting a smart card business. To ensure success, you will need to focus on this issue. One-product companies are unlikely to survive. Any product has a limited life, although some products have longer windows of opportunity than others. If you are planning product development, you must be able to establish or extend a line of products and use innovation to improve and reintroduce ideas.

Guidelines for Pricing Influenced by Cost and Competition

You can price products according to their costs or by the market. Ultimately, competition exerts a strong influence on pricing. Product differentiation can moderate or minimize the influence of competition, but it can never

---

FIGURE 2.3   Smart card marketing opportunities.

- Product

  Compelling use: Application must attract critical mass of users.

  Versatility: Multiple uses → more value.

  Cost-effectiveness: Is service's perceived value worth the delivery cost?

- Price

  Start-up: New high-tech products command price premium.

  Transition to maturity: Will price cover costs? Eliminate unprofitable services.

  Maturity: Will competitive price-cutting begin?

- Selling

  Direct sales force versus distributors for selling smart cards. The sale is complex, and a direct sales force provides better service and control.

- Promotion

  Smart card's promotional issues: The industry must create a need for new technology and replace existing magnetic stripe cards.

FIGURE 2.4   Advantages of smart cards.

Participant	Advantage	Description
Cardholder	Convenience	No need for correct change.
		Safer than carrying cash.
Merchant	Reduced cost	Reduced cash handling.
		Reduced vandalism/theft.
Issuer	Additional revenue	Float/interest.
		Unused balances.
		Additional fee income.
		Expanded cardholder base.
Acquirer	Additional revenue	Additional merchant service charges.
		Expanded merchant base.

---

completely insulate the company. Pricing for smart cards should take into consideration features compared to competitive products and the value perceived by the customer. In general, customers seem to be willing to pay more if they perceive superior quality for how smart cards will add convenience to their quality of life.

Guidelines for Selling Technical Products

Sales carried out by an internal sales force are preferred rather than using agents or brokers to sell smart card services. This plan is preferred because:

- ✔ The company can handle the administration of a sales force.
- ✔ Sales territories are concentrated and can be easily measured.
- ✔ The company wants to retain primary control of distribution and the selling process.

Other issues Datamark has considered: whether to use specialists and generalists as salespersons; the assignment of territories; the number of accounts to be assigned to an individual salesperson; and determination of compensation, including salary and commission.

To promote smart cards, a complex product, Datamark has used a more sophisticated promotion approach—a combination of trade shows, press kits, web sites, demonstrations, and other promotions.

Summary of the Company's Strengths and Weaknesses

The model in Figure 2.5 measures Datamark's strengths and weaknesses as they relate to the factors of management financing, product sales, and marketing. The company prepared the factors that affect the business and how attractive each is in terms of high or low priorities.

SUMMARY

Writing the marketing plan is the first step in the marketing process. The marketing plan is one of the most important parts of a business because it communicates most directly the nature of the intended business and the manner in which that business will be able to succeed. Specifically, the purpose of the marketing process is to explain how a prospective business intends to manipulate and react to market conditions in order to generate sales.

FIGURE 2.5 Measuring your strengths and weaknesses.

	Attractiveness	
Factor	High	Low
Management team	Team has proven skills and abilities.	People with right skills are not available.
Financing	You have comfortable cushion or can raise capital if needed.	You have a narrow time horizon to make money.
Product development	Complete product line.	One product of limited life.
Sales force	Strong contacts; specialist skills.	Limited contacts; generalist skills.
Marketing	Deep and tightly focused.	Untargeted.
Operations	Strategic alliances help improve execution.	Learning is done in a vacuum.

Source: Datamark Technologies, Inc.

You must prepare a marketing plan that is both interesting and thought-provoking. The plan cannot simply explain a concept; it must sell a prospective business as an attractive investment opportunity, a good credit risk, or a valued vendor of a product or service.

The degree of detail and support that should be provided may depend on the market share one requires in order to ensure success. If the market potential is commonly understood to be large and only a very small market share is projected, little support information may be needed. Conversely, this detailed information becomes more critical as relevant market share increases.

The marketing plan must establish realistic goals and objectives. The goals must address the market share, penetration, sales, and pricing strategies. Pricing strategies must consider such factors as market competition, customer demand, life cycle of products, and economic conditions.

The marketing strategy describes how the business will implement its marketing plan in order to achieve desired sales performance. This involves focusing attention on each salient marketing tool a company has at its disposal. Elements such as distribution, pricing strategy, advertising, promotion, site analysis, and related budgets all may merit discussion, depending on their importance in relation to the company's overall market strategy. While meticulous detail is probably unnecessary, it is important that you gain a general understanding of how the business intends actively to market its product or service.

Once the marketing analysis and competition review are established, you can begin to develop the pricing and sales plan. Pricing is one of the most difficult decisions to make for your product or service. A number of factors can guide you to price your product or service, including the degree of competition, seasonal or cyclical changes in demand, distribution costs, customer services, and markups.

It is important for the new business to take a total marketing approach to the customer and attempt to design a marketing plan that ultimately can provide a high level of customer satisfaction. Database marketing lets you analyze sales trends and profile prospects to target your best customers. Until recently, start-up and small companies did not use database marketing due to the money and time needed. However, due to falling costs of hardware and software, this technique is becoming popular for most businesses.

Marketing research need not be extensive, sophisticated, or expensive, but must determine what customer satisfaction means for the target market. It should also provide other critical information about the target market used to develop marketing strategies. In some cases you can survey the market to obtain information geared specifically to your needs. However, you must use your judgment since you are protecting future marketing plans.

Electronic commerce is becoming a marketing competitive necessity. Consider using home pages to market your products and economic capabilities for customers to buy on the web site. However, your site must provide the same levels of privacy and trust so consumers will not be reluctant to use it for payment transactions.

With a marketing plan in place, we will use Chapter 4 to prepare a detailed business plan and test the feasibility of the business. This will include the nine components and steps toward a completion of a business plan.

ADDITIONAL RESOURCES— DATABASE SEARCHES

Lexis/Nexis
Reed Elsevier
P.O. Box 933
Dayton, OH 45401
(800) 227-4908
www.lexis-nexis.com

Prodigy.com
445 Hamilton Avenue
White Plains, NY 10601
(800) 776-3449
www.prodigy.com

Westlaw
West Publishing Company
620 Opperman Drive
P.O. Box 64526
St. Paul, MN 55164-0526
(800) 328-0109
www.westpub.com

Internet Providers

The number of Internet providers grows daily. Check with your favorite software store and with people you know who have Internet access.

Starting Home-Based Businesses, Opening Franchises, and Buying Existing Businesses

Objectives

1. Identify the different types of businesses.
2. Understand the advantages and disadvantages of each business type.
3. Choose what type of business is most appropriate for your situation and needs.

INTRODUCTION: CHOOSING THE RIGHT BUSINESS

What type of business should you start? There are in essence five kinds of businesses; the first, start-up ventures, was explored in previous chapters. The second, Internet companies, will be discussed in detail in Chapter 8. In this chapter, we will examine:

✔ Home-based businesses.
✔ Franchises.
✔ Buying existing businesses.

There are several paths for you to follow when starting and growing a business. You must consider many different factors when deciding which kind of organization to pursue. In our discussion, we will highlight the positive and negative attributes of each type of business and, more importantly, outline the steps you should follow in your decision-making process.

This chapter is designed to help you start thinking and acting in a manner that improves your chances for success. It will guide you through starting your business and identify the hidden traps of failure as well as the ingredients for success.

One of the first tasks is choosing the kind of business you want to run. In this chapter, we will discuss each type of business along with the advantages and disadvantages of starting it.

HOME-BASED BUSINESSES

There are many advantages to start and manage a home-based business. However, you must address the following questions:

Should I Run a Home-Based Business?

Not all businesses lend themselves to being home-based. Those that do soon outgrow a home office. One important consideration to keep in mind is whether your home can accommodate the business at a later stage after it has grown.

For instance, if selling is a major part of your business, a home office may be very appropriate. One example would be a wood floor resurfacing company that attracts business through advertising and simply uses the home as a base of operation to handle sales calls. If the technological needs of your business are simple (requiring just a computer, fax, copier, and printer, for instance), a home-based venture makes sense.

What Issues Should Be Considered?

Discipline Obviously, anyone starting a home business must be highly motivated. But that is only one key consideration. When working at home with your family

Profile: Richard M. Schulze—CEO and Chairman of Best Buy Co., Inc.

Richard Schulze, founder of Best Buy Co., Inc., knows how to replay success—again and again. Ernst & Young's 1999 Entrepreneur of the Year, Schulze started at zero and built the nation's largest retailer of consumer electronics, personal computers, entertainment software, and appliances. But he almost lost everything—twice.

Having given up college to work for his father's electronics distribution company, Schulze immersed himself in the business. He soon realized that his father, who has since passed away, was not interested in his ideas for improving operations. After five years, Schulze quit and started his own retail audio store.

Every business has its share of ups and downs, but few have had shifts as dramatic as those experienced by Best Buy. Starting as The Sound of Music, Schulze's fledgling stereo component retail chain grew to nine stores. Then, in 1981, disaster struck. A tornado hit St. Paul, Minnesota, destroying his largest and most profitable store. The storeroom was spared, however, so Schulze decided to gather his 65 employees from all of his other stores and hold a "Tornado Sale" in the parking lot. He only expected to liquidate the stock, but customers waited in a two-mile-long line to get into the lot. To be sure that no one went away empty-handed, Schulze brought in inventory from stores untouched by the twister.

Realizing he had hit upon a winning concept, Schulze bet the farm on his new retail strategy. "I asked customers what they truly wanted when shopping for technology products," says Schulze. Their response was simple: "a hassle-free shopping experience, broad selection of name-brand products readily available on shelves, informed sales assistance, service when needed, and a quick and easy checkout process." With this information in hand and using his family's assets, Schulze built his first superstore, repositioned the company, added many new product categories, and renamed it Best Buy.

Then, in the winter of 1996, disaster struck again. In anticipation of a busy Christmas season, Schulze made the decision to borrow heavily in order to add a whopping $300 million in additional inventory, most of it computers. Meanwhile, news spread about the launch of Intel's new mul-

(Continued)

Richard M. Schulze Profile Continued

timedia Pentium chip. The timing could not have been worse for Best Buy, which found itself buried under a mountain of obsolete PCs. Earnings in 1997 were a mere $1.75 million, and Best Buy's stock, which had traded as high as $22 a share in 1994, fell to around $5 a share.

Over a 14-month period, Schulze presided over one of the most dramatic—and fastest—recoveries in modern retailing. He made changes to everything from marketing to management to inventory controls. He abandoned the chain's famous "No, No, No" pricing strategy: no money down, no monthly payments, and no interest. This had translated to no profit, say analysts. The merchandise mix shifted away from low-margin items like VCRs and computers and toward more profitable goods such as software, home appliances, and office furniture.

Earnings for fiscal year 1998 rose to $94.5 million, a 5,500 percent increase over 1997, "our darkest hour," according to Schulze. The home-grown management team that had run the company for years gave way to 40 new vice presidents, mostly brought in from the outside. The medicine was bitter, he says, but "it had to be done."

present, you may become easily distracted. It is important that the work be done in a professional environment. To accomplish this, you will need to set up a separate office to create a dedicated space and establish parameters with your family so they respect your work schedule.

Consider the following questions:

- ✔ Is there enough space for a business?
- ✔ Will the space fit the business that is being considered?
- ✔ Will your family not interfere in the operation of the business and the business not cause problems in your family?
- ✔ How will schedules be handled, and how will privacy be maintained?

Regulations Home-based entrepreneurs also need to be aware of the laws and regulations governing businesses in general and those governing what types of businesses may operate from a home. Zoning regulations may prohibit certain businesses from being home-based.

Some states prohibit home businesses from dealing with poisons, explosives, medical products, and other items. Be sure to consult an attorney and both the U.S. Department of Labor as well as your state's department of labor.

Some advantages of starting a home-based business:

✔ *Convenience.* You can roll out of bed and work in your pajamas, if you choose. There is no dress code or commute.

✔ *Control.* You have more control and flexibility operating a home business than working for an outside company. You can have lunch when you want, do errands in the middle of the day, and work any hours you choose.

✔ *Lower Costs.* It's cheaper to set up a business at home rather than lease or build an office space. In addition, you can take advantage of tax write-offs for home offices, though you should be very careful what you deduct. The Internal Revenue Service looks very closely at home office write-offs.

There are some significant disadvantages you should also consider.

✔ *24/7.* When you work from home, you are never far from work. Clients and customers know they can reach you 24 hours a day, seven days a week. It can be difficult to take a vacation from work, and if you do take time off, it can mean there is no revenue coming in.

✔ *Restrictions on Growth.* Your business may expand faster than you expect, and you may outgrow your home office space.

✔ *Difficulty Attracting Employees and Appearing Professional.* It may be difficult to attract employees who are willing to work out of your home. In addition, customers or clients may perceive you as less professional because you operate in a home environment.

✔ *Distractions.* You have to be disciplined and not be distracted by family members or chores that need to be done around the house.

Profile: Lauren Rosato of Lexpress International

Another company's misfortune sowed the seeds of opportunity for Lexpress International, a home-based multilingual translation business with more than 300 clients and $250,000 in billings a year.

Hired as a financial officer to assist in the attempted turnaround of New York–based Lexitech International Documentation Network, Lauren Rosato soon became a jack-of-all-trades to keep Lexitech afloat. When Lexitech finally went out of business in 1990, Rosato took the client list and her experience and launched Lexpress International. Operating out of her apartment in Greenwich, Connecticut, Rosato started with $5,000—a mix of savings and family loans. She spent $2,000 on marketing and brochures and the rest on a computer, a modem, and a fax machine that doubled as a copier. "I didn't have any overhead or inventory. It was all about who I knew and building contacts," Rosato says.

Initially, she obtained work from Lexitech clients. But that didn't last long. Translation is very project-based. A major company might need you for a translation assignment only once every year or two. So Rosato set about networking to build up her client base. She focused on doing text translations in southwestern Connecticut, where there weren't many other multilingual translation businesses. She used direct mailings, and networked through international trade associations and graduate school contacts to gain access to company contacts. Her timing was good. She caught a wave of companies locating in Fairfield County, less than an hour from New York City, as well as a trend toward corporate globalization.

Customers range from individual businesspeople who need business cards in several languages to multinational corporations that need major translation projects, such as a manual in 40 languages. Clients include Tiffany & Co., Mercedes-Benz Leasing, and American International Underwriters. Rosato has also developed a niche business doing linguistic evaluations of new product and service names globally.

Though nine-year-old Lexpress became profitable by year four, Rosato purposely keeps the business small and often turns business away. She has one full-time employee and is looking to hire another part-time. Married with two young children and working from her home in Norwalk, Connecticut, Rosato says, "I have controlled the growth of my business for quality of life."

✔ *Isolation.* Home-based businesses are often one-person companies. Be sure you can handle working in an isolated environment without the social interaction that an office offers.

FRANCHISES

If you are considering buying a franchise, you should address the following questions:

What Is Franchising?

The standard definition is "an arrangement by the manufacturer or sole distributor of a trademarked product or service that provides exclusive rights of local distribution to independent retailers in return for their payment of royalties."

The person offering the franchise is the franchiser, while the individual who purchases it is known as the franchisee. The franchise agreement usually gives the franchisee the exclusive right to conduct business in a specified area. In return, the franchisee agrees to pay the franchiser a fee and usually a percentage of gross sales as well.

Should I Consider Buying a Franchise?

A franchise can be a very attractive way to operate your own business because of these advantages:

✔ *A Proven Product.* Unlike starting a new company from scratch, you will be selling a product or service that the public already knows. This familiarity often means you will have many presold customers and you will not have to spend resources to establish the credibility of the company.

✔ *Established Business Plan.* If you start your own business, you will have to experiment to find the right administrative and business procedures. This involves a lot of trial and error. However, in a franchising situation, you may be able to receive training and management assistance in both day-to-day operations and administrative tasks like record keeping. In fact, some franchisers require franchisees to enter into a training program to educate the new owner in all aspects of operating the franchise. McDonald's, for example, requires all franchisees to take classes in accounting, personnel management, marketing, and production. Additionally, some franchisers offer toll-free numbers so that franchisees can ask questions about any aspect of the business.

✔ *Financing Assistance.* A franchise can be started with less capital and front-end support than would be necessary for launching a company from scratch. Many franchisers will provide financial assistance to qualified franchisees. Additionally, the franchisee can pool money with other franchisees to share in advertising and insurance costs. This pooled money can be used for advertising on a national scale, which would be difficult to do starting a company on your own.

✔ *Knowledge of Market and Capital Requirements.* As we have discussed in previous chapters, an essential ingredient in starting a new business is a thorough understanding of your market, including market conditions, competitive factors, and sales and profit potential. Additionally, you must know your capital requirements such as costs for real estate, construction, and equipment. Typically, a franchiser will provide at least some of this information to the franchisee. The franchiser may have a profile of the potential target customer and provide strategies for use after the operation has begun.

✔ *Operations and Quality Control.* Entrepreneurs often run into problems of quality control with their suppliers when starting a venture. The franchiser will typically identify suppliers who meet their quality standards. Sometimes the franchiser actually provides the supplies. This standardization minimizes the risk to the franchisee.

Along with those advantages come some distinct disadvantages. Franchising may not be the route for you because of the following:

✔ *Restrictions in Decision Making.* Unlike starting your own venture, as a franchisee you will not be your own boss. Typically, a franchiser will have preapproval on such key decisions as the location of the business. Franchisers also commonly enforce design and appearance standards. Complying with these standards may be expensive and limit your creative freedom.

✔ *High Start-Up Expenses.* Your initial franchise fee is frequently nonrefundable and is often a sizable amount. Sometimes it can be as much as several hundred thousand dollars. Royalties and group advertising fees also eat into your revenue. And remember that the franchiser takes a portion of your earnings, but doesn't share in your losses.

✔ *Selection and Price Restrictions.* You may be restricted in establishing selling prices, introducing new products and services, and adjusting the supply cycles to meet current demands. Moreover, the franchiser may set your hours, limit your market territory, dictate dress codes, design advertising campaigns, or demand adherence to certain bookkeeping methods.

Types of Franchising

There are essentially three types of franchises available, which are displayed in the next box:

1. Dealerships.
2. Brands.
3. Services.

Should I Invest in a Franchise?

First, you must reflect on your own strengths and weaknesses to determine if you have the personality necessary for a successful franchise. Second, you must investigate thoroughly the franchise to determine its legitimacy.

Franchise Type	Arrangement	Examples of Actual Companies
Dealerships	Typically in automotive industry; manufacturers use franchisees to distribute their product lines.	John Holz Honda; Tom's Ford Motor Cars
Brands	Internationally known brands for items such as food or hotels use franchisees to expand.	McDonald's; Subway; Midas; Jiffy Lube; Comfort Inn
Services	Personnel agencies, income tax preparation companies, realtors, and other service companies offer established names and use franchisees to expand.	Kinder Care; Living and Learning; Computer Tots

Investigating the Franchise

Assessing the reputation, financial stability, and arrangements of potential franchisers is crucial.

- ✔ *Is the franchise reliable and stable?* If not, the investment cost will be lower, but the risk will be much higher. However, unproven franchisers can offer more long-term profitable rewards.

- ✔ *How financially stable is the franchise?* You must ascertain the long-term financial condition of the franchiser. You should examine the success rate of each of the franchisees in the organization. Also, find out how the franchiser's profits are generated. Some of this information can be obtained from profit-and-loss statements. You may also consider contacting some of the franchisees directly to determine their successes and identify problems that occurred.

Conducting a Self-Examination

1. Are you a self-starter? What projects have you undertaken during the past 10 years? Were they successful? Why or why not?

2. Do you have the ability to provide leadership to those who will work for you? How have you managed people in the past?

3. Are you willing to take risks to some extent? Can you afford a large non-refundable deposit that could run hundreds of thousands of dollars?

4. Can you make solid business decisions? What kind of training or education have you had to help in key areas such as accounting, record keeping, finance, personnel management, and marketing? Do you think you might need additional training in some of these areas before embarking on such a venture?

5. Are you willing to go along with decisions even when you do not agree with them? There may be many times when your creative freedom will be restricted. Can you accept that?

Consider each of these points. Draw on your past experience and your personal patterns to answer them rather than on how you perceive yourself or would like others to perceive you.

If you can honestly answer yes to many of these questions, then you may have the personality and experience necessary to operate a franchise.

✔ *What is the profit potential for the new franchise?*
You should ask the potential franchiser for financial projections to calculate future earnings. You must also determine the profit potential for the geographic market in which you would like to operate. You can obtain information about market conditions from local economic periodicals in your library as well as from a plethora of web sites of franchise associations and from government statistics.

The following checklist summarizes some concerns when evaluating a potential franchiser, but is by no means a complete list.

✔ What is the franchiser's reputation?
✔ What are the opinions of current franchisees?

✔ Is the franchiser now involved with any litigation or has it been in the past?

✔ What kind of training and start-up assistance is available?

✔ What kind of continued assistance is available?

✔ What is the management structure of the organization?

✔ Are the location and territory protected?

✔ What are the operating practices of the franchise?

✔ What are the franchise's start-up and continuing expenses?

✔ How can the purchase be financed?

✔ What are the terms of renewal and termination?

BUYING AN EXISTING BUSINESS

Up to this point, we have discussed start-up ventures, home-based businesses, and franchises. There is another alternative: to purchase an established company. Buying an existing business is another lower-risk way to enter a new venture.

Should I Buy an Existing Business?

To some extent, buying a business is less risky, because its operating history provides meaningful data on its chances of success. However, it is important that a detailed analysis is performed.

One important factor is the seller's reasons for offering the business for sale. Often these are personal and career reasons, such as a readiness to retire and the absence of a successor, or another opportunity perceived as a better fit. If the business reason for selling is personnel problems or that the business cannot stand up to competition, you must decide that what is missing is a quality of management that you can provide, or that major changes are required to turn the business around.

A detailed review of the business must be performed before a binding offer is made. Is the company's history and network of business relationships clear? Are its finan-

---

Profile: Mark Logan of VISX Inc.

Mark Logan's arrival at VISX Inc. is the story of a man who bought an existing company and brought it back to life. Logan acquired a company mired in financial shortages, bad business agreements, conspiracy, and a hostile board of directors, and turned it around in less than two years.

Today, VISX's laser vision-correction equipment is used in more than 60 countries around the world. It is the only laser manufacturer with approval to treat low, moderate, and high myopia, astigmatism, and hyperopia.

The lasers are sold to clinics rather than to individual doctors, allowing multiple doctors to use the equipment for many procedures, thus increasing the revenue from each unit. VISX's license agreements entitle a per-procedure fee.

The company's goals for the future involve the development of a new platform for surgical lasers scheduled to be launched by 2002. At the same time, the company is constantly improving its present systems, updating software and hardware, and retrofitting.

---

cial statements represented? What do they say about the business? Are there any unstated dangers or risks? Are there any hidden liabilities? Often, a review of the financials by your banker and accountant can be valuable.

How good an organization is it? How is the business perceived by its customers and suppliers? What will be the effect of an ownership change on the customer base, supplier relations, and so on? How much customer loyalty is to the business and how much to the current owner? Does the company have a niche? If so, is it the one in which you want to operate? Is there a competitive advantage to the operation that is sustainable? Are its assets useful to you? Will key personnel remain with the business?

Testing the Viability of the Business by Asking the Right Questions

There are many important evaluation-related questions that should be asked to screen an existing business:

1. What is the overall market for the business? What are the market segments that your business will be in? Are there special niches that can be exploited?

2. Is it a new product or service proprietary? Can it be patented or copyrighted? Is it unique enough to get a significant head start on the competition? Can the process be easily copied?

3. Has the product been taken to trade shows? If so, what reactions did it receive? Were any sales made? Has it been taken to distributors? Have they placed any orders?

4. What distribution and sales methods will be used—Internet web sites, independent sales representatives, or company sales force?

5. Can the company get, or has it already lined up, the necessary skills to operate the business? Who are the workers? Are they dependable and competent?

6. How much capital will be needed now? How much more in the future?

One single test rarely determines the ultimate success or failure for a business. In most situations, a combination of ingredients influences the outcome. Therefore, it is important that these variables be identified and investigated before the business is put into practice. The results of a test viability approach enable you to judge the business's potential.

Avoid the Common Mistakes

From manufacturing, sales, or distribution, there are a series of common mistakes that you should be aware of and avoid at all costs. They are listed as primary or secondary for your review in buying a business.

Primary Mistakes

✔ Trying to make the business appeal to everyone.

✔ Starting out with too little cash.

✔ Failing to detect bad credit risks early.

✔ Setting the wrong price.

✔ Making grossly inaccurate sales projections.

✔ Failing to match management experience to industry experience.

✔ Not understanding the competition.

✔ Not having a niche strategy.

✔ Not having competitive advantage.

Secondary Mistakes

✔ Mistaking a hobby for a business you plan to buy.

✔ Bleeding the business for quick cash.

✔ Not using enough managerial sense to plan and anticipate.

✔ Acting on blind faith.

✔ Not calculating potential sponsors or customers.

✔ Having unrealistic time horizons to make the business profitable.

Key Ingredients for Buying an Existing Business

When you buy a business, make sure you have the skills and capital to generate a successful operation. The key financial tools to consider in analyzing the business are the profitability of the business, the ability of the business to generate cash, and the overall health of the business, as indicated by ratio and percentage analyses. You should review all of the financial statements carefully and understand the significance of the values projected.

If the projected financial statements indicate that success is feasible, then the business can become a tool for securing loans and for soliciting investors to finance growth. The projected financial statements, if they are based on reasonable assumptions and good research, will indicate the amount of money you will need to establish the business and maintain it until the business becomes self-supporting. The projections should also indicate when the borrowed debt can be repaid and how much return investors can expect.

THE FINANCIAL PLAN

One of the first steps to make your business secure is to establish a financial plan to measure financial performance.

There are several perspectives in measuring financial performance. The first perspective is to view performance in terms of sales volume percentage of increased sales or new business. Many Internet companies measure success in terms of increased sales volume. However, if the expectation that additional sales mean higher profits, which may not be the case, certainly increasingly sales is a part of the financial plan. However, to stop at that point is shortsighted.

The second perspective is to measure profits. This is the difference between revenues and expenses as reported in the income statements. Sales must be profitable. A firm can determine the profitability of products and customers. It can also provide incentives to its sales force to encourage more profitable sales.

The third method is to measure cash generated. Just because a company has an income statement that shows that it is profitable does not necessarily mean it is generating cash. If your company uses accrual accounting, you recognize a sale when as an example, a customer takes title to the product, even though the cash may not be exchanged for some time. Accrual accounting does not recognize that cash was required to purchase materials, labor, and other resources in advance of the sale and the recognition of the cost of goods. Frequently businesses, though profitable, may be running out of cash, since a sale occurs and the cash from the sale is collected at a later date. It is important, especially for undercapitalized companies, to project cash flow and note any periods where it will have inadequate cash or secure outside financing so that the company is not forced into bankruptcy.

These financial methods give you some idea of the nature of financial goals that may be set for your company. Obviously, how high they are set depends on the nature of the business, the opportunities available, and management's objectives.

PREPARE AN ANNUAL BUDGET

The annual budget presents a month-by-month projection of revenues and expenses over a one-year period. The budget is the foundation for projecting the other financial statements. It presents a more detailed accounting of expenses than does the income statement. In a budget, expense details are usually grouped by department or functional area, such as general and administrative. The details of a standard budget are broken down into the following major categories:

✔ *Sales.* The detail should include all or some of the following: sales by product line and sales by customer, geographical region, and goals for each sales representative.

✔ *Cost of Goods Sold.* The detail should include both material and shipping costs as well as any allocated overhead if the company is a manufacturer. If sales are identified by product line, the cost of goods sold for each product line should be calculated in order to determine gross profit by product line.

✔ *Gross Profit.* The detail should include, where possible, the gross profit by whatever categories the sales are broken out into (e.g., product line, geographical region, etc.).

✔ *Operating Expenses.* The detail should classify expenses by research and development, selling and marketing, and general administrative. Within these categories the detail should reflect the budgeted expenses by category, such as salary, benefits, rent, telephone, and so on. Some expenses should be broken down even in detail, such as salary by employee and allocation of rent expenses.

✔ *Operating Profit/Debit.* If product lines can identify operating expenses, an operating profit/debit for each product line should be calculated.

✔ *Other Income and Expense.* This category usually includes interest expense, which should be detailed by each type of debt (e.g., lease, bank loan, etc.).

✔ *Income before Taxes.* This amount is calculated by taking operating profit and factoring in other income and expenses. It denotes the income that will be subject to corporate income tax.

✔ *Income Taxes.* This is the management's estimate of what taxes will be owed on its earnings. Detail should reflect amounts owed for federal and state taxes.

✔ *Net Income.* This is the amount available for dividends or reinvestment in the company.

✔ *EBIT.* This is the earnings (net income) before interest expense, interest income, and income taxes. It measures the profitability of the company's current operations as if it had no debt or investments.

✔ *EBITDA.* This is the earnings before interest expense, interest income, income taxes, depreciation, and amortization. It measures the profitability of a company's operations without the impact of its debt, investments, and long-term assets.

PROJECTED CASH ACTIVITY

The projected cash activity presents a month-by-month projection of receipts and disbursements over a one-year period. The budget is the foundation for projecting the activity. The sales from the annual budget are used to project receipts, and the expenses are used to project disbursements. The details of the projected cash activity are broken down into the following major categories:

✔ *Receipts from Sales.* The detail from sales, the payment terms the company extends its customers, and the company's collection history are used to project receipts from sales.

✔ *Other Receipts.* Other receipts includes bank loans, equity investments, tax refunds, or any other inflows of cash not related to the operations of the company.

✔ *Disbursements from Expenses.* The detail from expenses and the payment terms granted your company should be used to project disbursements from expenses.

✔ *Other Disbursements.* This includes capital equipment acquisitions and payment of debt, including capitalized leases or bank debt and dividends.

FINANCIAL STATEMENTS

The financial statements are the method by which the company communicates its financial condition (balance sheet) and financial performance for a given period (income statement and statement of cash flow). Financial statements should reflect the operation of the business in the same way that management view its business. When these statements are used to forecast what the business would look like given certain events, they are referred to as pro forma statements.

There are three basic financial documents that are used by most businesses:

1. The balance sheet (also called the statement of financial position).
2. An income statement or profit-and-loss statement (P&L).
3. The statement of cash flows (also called source and use of funds).

Balance Sheet

The balance sheet provides a picture of the financial position of the business at a particular point in time, generally at the end of a financial period (such as a month, quarter, or year). It is essentially a snapshot of a company's resulting financial position, encompassing everything the company owns (assets) or owes (liabilities), as well as the investments into the company by its owners and the accumulated earnings or losses of the company (equity).
The balance sheet equation is:

Assets = Liabilities + Shareholder equity

Assets and liabilities are current if they can be converted into cash within one year. Otherwise they are considered long-term. Inventory is considered current because it sells within one year.

The balance sheet on the following page shows that shareholders' equity or the net worth of the company is $923,080, calculated by subtracting the total liabilities of $752,726 from the total assets of $1,675,806.

The Balance Sheet

Assets		Liabilities and Equity	
Current Assets		*Current Liabilities*	
Cash	$127,395	Accounts Payable	$311,418
Accounts receivable	541,798	Current portion of debt	128,777
Inventory	422,517	Accrued expenses	108,777
Prepaid expenses	87,614	Accrued taxes	29,700
Total current assets	$1,179,324	Total current liabilities	$578,672
Property, Plant, and Equipment		*Long-Term Debt*	
Land	123,719	Notes payable—bank	121,999
Buildings	248,502	Mortgage payable	52,055
Equipment	367,198	Total long-term debt	174,054
Less: Accumulated depreciation	(389,414)	Total liabilities	752,726
Total property	350,005		
Other Assets		*Shareholders' Equity*	
Investments	79,661	Paid-in capital	698,700
Patents	48,625	Retained earnings	224,380
Organization expense	18,191	Total equity	923,080
Total other assets	146,477		
Total Assets	$1,675,806	Total Liabilities and Equity	$1,675,806

When analyzing a company's balance sheet, managers and investors alike must view it in terms of its type of business. For example, one would expect to see that fixed assets accounted for a greater percentage of total assets in a manufacturer, as opposed to a distributor or professional services company. Additionally, the balance sheet should be analyzed with respect to the volume of the company's business. For example, receivables should be compared to sales to determine how quickly the company collects its cash, or current liabilities compared to expenses to see if it is paying its short-term obligations in a timely fashion.

Although the company does not have a great deal of cash, the fact that its current assets are well in excess of its current liabilities indicates it is able to meet its current obligations. The fact that its total debt of $303,831 is less than its fixed assets means it is likely that the debt was used to finance equipment purchases rather than operations. Its positive retained earnings indicate overall profitability.

Ratios can also be used to analyze a balance sheet. The following are some of the most commonly used ones.

Current Ratio This is the total current asset divided by the total current liabilities. Current assets and liabilities are those items expected to either generate cash or require the disbursement of cash within the next year. The current ratio indicates the ability of the company to meet its obligations for the next year.

Although a satisfactory value for a current ratio varies from industry to industry, a general rule of thumb is that a current ratio of 2:1 or greater is fairly healthy. Thinking in terms of dollars, a 2:1 ratio means that you have $2 of current assets from which to pay every $1 of current bills. A smaller current ratio may mean that you have successfully negotiated to pay the suppliers later than the usual 30 days, which essentially gives the company an interest-free source of cash.

Let's say the current assets are $15,000 and current liabilities are $10,000; this yields a current ratio of 1.5:1. In this scenario, the entrepreneur could improve the current ratio to 2:1 by paying $5,000 of the current liabilities with the current assets, reducing both by $5,000. If the suppliers were willing to wait for payment without charging you interest, this would probably be a bad idea (unless a financing agreement requires you to maintain a current ratio of 2:1).

Quick Ratio Also called *acid-test ratio*, this is very similar to the current ratio but includes only those current assets that can be most readily used to pay bills today—cash and accounts receivable. The quick ratio excludes inventory, which must first be sold and the cash collected before it can be used to pay liabilities. It also excludes current assets

 acid-test ratio method of judging firm's ability to meet current debt quickly. The formula: Total cash + receivables / current liabilities. One common standard ratio is one to one (1:1).

such as prepared expenses, which are never converted to cash (they are simply assets paid for in advance). As a result, the quick ratio is a good indication of how well you are able to meet the current liabilities in a crunch situation. In general, the entrepreneur should try to maintain a quick ratio of 1:1, which means you have $1 worth of cash and accounts receivable for every $1 of total current liabilities.

Debt Ratios Debt management ratios can help the entrepreneur evaluate the business's liabilities. Debt is associated with risk; so, the greater the debt, the higher the return rate will be. If the liabilities are large compared to the equity or the assets, potential lenders and investors may feel you are already too indebted and the business is not a good investment risk.

Debt-to-Worth Ratio Also called debt to owners' equity, this ratio compares the total liabilities of the business to the total owners' equity or net worth (the value of the total assets minus the total liabilities from the balance sheet). This ratio gives insight as to whether the company's previous funding has been through equity (sales of stock) or debt.

Total Debt to Total Assets This is total liability divided by total assets (from the balance sheet). Unlike the current ratio, it compares all the assets and all liabilities. In other words, it shows the ratio of what you owe to what you own.

This discussion of ratios is not meant to be all-inclusive. Each industry and business will have a set of ratios that are especially helpful to it. The point to remember is that ratios are nothing more than a comparison of two numbers. So, if you find a ratio that is helpful to you in the financial management of the firm, by all means, use it.

Income Statement

The statement of operations—also known as income statement, profit-and-loss statement, or a P&L statement—summarizes the revenue and expenses on a monthly basis for one year or an annual basis for several years. It divides expenses into broad categories, such as cost of goods sold and operating expenses. The cost of goods sold would represent the resources that went into the production of the

Income Statement

Revenues	$4,126,311
Less: Cost of goods sold	($2,051,625)
Gross margin	$2,074,686
Less: Operating expenses	
Research and development	($211,721)
Sales and marketing	($678,520)
General and administrative	($301,109)
Profit before taxes	$1,191,350
Less: Taxes	($369,729)
Income (or loss)	$ 821,621

products ultimately recognized as sales. These costs would include materials, labor, and manufacturing expenses. Two more terms for costs of goods sold are:

1. *Inventory costs*—costs that are assigned to inventory before being sold.
2. *Production costs*—costs that are identified with the product.

Operating expenses are costs that are not identified with the product. The major categories include research and development, sales and marketing, general and administrative, and financial expenses.

The statement shows how the business made a profit by displaying how much money it took in through sales and how much money it costs to run the business. The equation used to determine net profit or loss is:

Net profit (or loss) = Gross sales – Total expense

You should be aware that operating income is not the same as net profit. It is determined by subtracting costs from sales and does not include taxes or interest charges. Operating income is the amount the business earns after expenses but before taxes. It is sometimes called EBIT (earnings before interest or taxes).

When analyzing the income statement, you need to view it in terms of the type of business and how long the company has been involved in its current operations. Many companies change their type of business over time through acquisitions, divestures, or diversification. Ratios can also be used to analyze the statement of operations. Some of the more commonly used ones are as follows:

Return on Owner's Equity (ROE) This ratio compares the net profit of the business to the equity (net worth) of the business. It is calculated as net income after taxes (from the income statement) divided by total owner's equity (from the balance sheet).

$$\text{Return on equity} = \frac{\text{Net income}}{\text{Shareholders' equity}}$$

To relate return on equity to the debt-to-worth ratio, remember that given a fixed total asset figure, the greater the debt, the lower the net worth. Therefore, given two companies of identical asset size and profitability, the company with the higher debt-to-worth ratio will also have a higher return on equity ratio. When potential lenders and investors consider the risk of investing in the business, they will look at the return on equity ratio.

Level of Reliability of ROE Return on equity is not a totally reliable measure of financial performance for the following reasons:

✔ Returns are examined without the rush factors of the business.

✔ The assessment is measured in an annual time frame, and long-term decisions may not be reflected.

✔ Book value is used for shareholders' equity rather than market.

Therefore, return on equity should be examined in relationship to the business and environment rather than just mechanically.

Return on Total Assets This measures how efficient the business is using the assets in negotiating net income. This is calculated as the net income after taxes (from the income statement) divided by the total assets (from the balance sheet). Assets are used to generate profits. Therefore, the return on total assets is a measure of how effectively you are employing the assets of the business.

Gross Profit Margin, Operating Profit Margin, Net Profit Margin Gross profit margin (or percent) is the ratio of gross profit (gross sales minus the cost of goods sold) divided by gross sales, expressed as a percentage. The operating profit and net profit margins are the operating income divided by gross sales and net income divided by gross sales, expressed as percentages. All three percentages should usually be included on the income statements. To analyze the profitability, compare these percentages to the industry's averages or those of the immediate competitors (if you can obtain this information). Of course, you will always want to compare the current year's profitability percentages to the percentages from the company's previous years in order to determine how well you are progressing.

Taxes You will also be required to withhold federal and state taxes from employees. Each month or quarter (depending on the size of the payroll), deposits or payments will need to be made for funds withheld from wages. Generally, federal taxes, state taxes, Social Security, and Medicare are withheld from employees' salaries and are deposited later. If payments are late, there will be high interest and penalties assessed. In addition to withholding taxes, you may be required to pay a number of taxes, such as state and federal unemployment taxes, a matching FICA and Medicare tax, and other business taxes. These taxes will need to be part of the plan since they will affect cash flow and profits.

The federal and state governments also require you to file end-of-year returns of the business, regardless of whether you earned a profit or not. A tax accountant should advise you in handling these expenses. The accountant can also assist you in planning or budgeting appropriate funds to meet any of these expenses.

Statement of Cash Flows

The statement of cash flows summarizes where cash comes from and how it is used over a period of time. It begins with net income from the income statement then shows adjustments for items that do not involve cash (such as payable and depreciation); other nonoperational sources and applications of cash are listed next (such as fixed asset purchases and financing proceeds and payments). Then the increase or decrease in net cash balance is calculated. The statement shows the movement of funds through a business over time. The format used in the box shows how the sources of funds are accumulated. This includes changes in operations, new sources of capital such as debt and equity, the sale of fixed assets, and all the uses of funds. The bottom line is the net change in working capital.

When analyzing a company's cash flows, you need to determine if the numbers are showing in the positive or negative. Examine the relationship between cash available through operations and cash from investment. You can also examine if growth in receivables is due to increased sales or poor collection results. Is an increase in debt matched with fixed assets, or is the debt being used to fund operations? The statement of cash flows is usually overlooked by investors, but can frequently disclose information about how a company manages its cash.

Footnotes to the Financial Statements

Financial statements are usually accompanied with footnotes. Like the statement of cash flows, these are often overlooked but contain valuable information. Certain footnotes are especially important.

General Description of Business The first footnote usually includes a general description of the company's business and a recent history, usually detailing any events that have a material impact on the company's current financial statements, such as an acquisition, increased competition, and so on.

Statement of Cash Flows

Year Ended December 31, 1998

Cash Flows from Operating Activities

Net income (loss)	($262,381)
Adjustments to reconcile net income (loss to net)	
Cash provided by (used in) operating activities	
Depreciation	99,182
Issuance of common stock in lieu of compensation	0
Bad debts	14,875
Deferred taxes	(241,800)
	(390,124)

Changes in Operating Assets and Liabilities

Accounts receivable	(12,387)
Loan receivable, employee	0
Prepaid expenses and other current assets	(32,213)
Accounts payable and accrued expenses	56,845
Income taxes payable	(4,892)
Net Cash Provided by (Used in) Operating Activities	(382,771)

Cash Flows from Investing Activities

Purchases of certificates of deposit	(250,000)
Purchases of property and equipment	(59,158)
Net Cash Used in Investing Activities	(309,158)

Cash Flows from Financing Activities

Repayment of loan	(14,644)
Issuance of common stock	6,423
Issuance of preferred stock	2,500,000
Acquisition of treasury stock	(363,398)
Net Cash Provided by (Used in) Financing Activities	2,128,381
Net Increase (Decrease) in Cash	1,436,452
Cash, beginning of period	48,021
Cash, End of Year	$1,484,473

Supplemental Disclosures of Cash Flow Information

Cash paid during the period for:	
Interest	$380
Income taxes	$0

Acquisitions and Divestures/Discontinued Operations If the company has acquired or sold either the assets or stock of a company, the details of the transactions will be included in this footnote. Additionally, if a company discontinued a material segment of its business, the details of the discontinuance will be included.

Intangible Assets This footnote details any intangible assets the company has on the balance sheet, such as goodwill, capitalized patents, or capitalized research and development. The viewer should make note of how much the company capitalized during the year and how quickly it is being amortized.

Debt The debt footnote will classify the debt on the balance sheet by loan instrument and by bank. It will also include the current interest rates and may disclose how much financing is available in the future as well as the pay off schedule of the company's present debt.

Legal Proceedings This footnote must disclose any material legal proceedings either by or against the company. This should always be reviewed to determine if any legal proceedings could significantly affect the financial viability of the company.

Subsequent Events This footnote details any unusual and material events that have taken place after the date of the financial statement, but before the issuance of the financial statement.

BREAK-EVEN TECHNIQUE

The break-even technique is a decision-making model that helps you determine whether a certain volume of output will result in a profit or loss. The point at which breaking even occurs is the volume of output at which total revenues equal total costs. The technique can be further used to answer the question, "What is the profit associated with a given level of output?" To use this technique, you need only three types of information: fixed costs of operation, variable costs of production, and price per unit.

Fixed costs are expenses that do not change in the short run, no matter what the level of production and sales. Variable costs vary with the volume produced. They are usually expressed in terms of per-unit variable costs. Total costs are the sum of fixed and variable costs. Price is the total amount received from the sale of one unit of the product. Multiplying the price by the number of units sold yields the amount, which are revenues. Profit is what remains when the total costs are subtracted from the total revenues. The break-even point is the level of output or sales at which total profit is zero—in other words, where total revenues equal costs.

Break-Even Formula

A quick way to calculate the break-even point is to use a formula. According to this formula, the price per unit (P) multiplied by the number of units sold (X) is equal to the fixed costs (F) plus the variable costs (V) multiplied by the number of units produced. That is,

$$P(X) = F + V(X)$$

In our example, the fixed costs (F) are \$40,000; the variable costs per unit (V) are \$15; and the price per unit (P) is \$20. We find the break-even point (X) by plugging these values into the equation:

$$
\begin{aligned}
20(X) &= 40{,}000 + 15(X) \\
20X - 15X &= 40{,}000 \\
5X &= 40{,}000 \\
X &= 8{,}000 \text{ units}
\end{aligned}
$$

Pros and Cons of Buying an Existing Business

Purchasing a business has its pros and cons. The primary advantages are:

✔ *Established Business.* The acquired firm has an established image and track record. You can tap into the business's strategies and continue them, assuming that the business is profitable at the time of purchase. There is already an established customer base. Also, you will know immediately about that particular market. While a franchiser can give you information about the franchise's markets in general, when purchasing an existing business you will get details about your particular market by examining the company's records.

✔ *Lower Costs.* The total cost of acquiring a business could be lower than trying to buy a franchise or starting from scratch. Although you will have to pay for goodwill, which refers to the company's intangible assets such as the company's brand name or customer relationships, you save construction costs by buying the company's established facilities.

✔ *Fewer Personnel Changes.* You do not have to hire new employees like you would for a start-up or franchise. Current employees also have established relationships with customers and suppliers.

✔ *More Creative Freedom.* You will not be restricted in choices about decor, dress codes, bookkeeping, product selections, or personnel policies.

There are important disadvantages for you to consider as well.

✔ *Seller's Motivation.* Why is the business for sale? Often it is for personal or career reasons, such as a readiness to retire or another opportunity. However, some businesses are sold because they are having problems. You must review key documents such as profit-and-loss and cash flow statements. Furthermore, you should arrange to interview important constituents involved in the business. The key question is: "Are there problems and if so can they be fixed?" For example, if the location is poor, that cannot be easily solved. However, if the problem lies in poor management, that situation can be solved by bringing in new managers.

✔ *Key Employee Losses.* Often, when a business changes owners, key employees also leave. You should therefore speak to current employees to ascertain their intentions. Incentives can play an important role in persuading key employees to stay.

✔ *Overvaluation.* At times, the actual purchase price can be inflated because of the established image, customer base, and suppliers. This will drastically lower the return on investment for the new owner.

How Do I Locate Acquisition Candidates?

You should consult professional business brokers that act on the seller's behalf. However, since these individuals are paid on commission, they are working for the seller and may try to sell a company that is less than perfect. Be sure to consult lawyers and acquisition specialists. Also, accountants, attorneys, and bankers may know of good acquisition candidates. Finally, do not overlook the classified sections of trade magazines.

SUMMARY

Home-based businesses are one of the fastest growing markets in the United States. The American Association of Home Based Businesses estimates that 24 million people are operating from home. These include marketing or sales professionals and contracting, service, and professional or technical people. They all require self-discipline, organization detail, and flexibility to succeed.

Franchising can be a very attractive way to operate your business. There are three types of franchises available: dealerships, brands, and services. Consider your investment, conduct a self-examination, and investigate the franchise before you make a final decision.

There are several ways to find a business for sale. Trade associations, business groups, and brokers are good sources for information on properties, locations, and markets. Always first determine why the business is for sale. Does it have new competition, customer base, product obsolescence, or cash flow problems? Study the business, research the market, and know the trends and the business community to maximize your chances of greater success.

In the financial area, you must be concerned with managing cash, assets, and profits. Cash flow must be monitored on a regular basis and evaluated when flows vary greatly.

This chapter provided a brief discussion of three basic financial statements:

1. *Balance Sheet.* Assets = liabilities + owner's equity (capital). The balance sheet provides an estimate of the company's value on a particular date.

2. *Income Statement.* Compares the revenue against its expenses to determine its net profit (or loss).

3. *Statement of Cash Flows.* Shows the change in working capital over a period of time by listing the source and the uses of funds.

Keep in mind that financial statements should be used as tools in the evaluation process since they rely on historical data.

This section involves areas such as financial and marketing analysis that may require expertise that either you or the team is unable to contribute. In those instances where you do not have this expertise, it is recommended that outside advisers be hired. Trying to save money by performing these tasks alone could end up costing you more than the fees.

Ratio analysis is a tool designed to help you interpret the financial statements. Ratios can describe the company's ability to meet its current obligations and show how effectively it uses its resources and profitability. To benefit from ratio analysis, you should compare the company's ratios to those of other companies in the same line of business. Many agencies and organizations regularly publish such statistics.

ADDITIONAL RESOURCES— FRANCHISE REFERENCES

American Franchisee Association (AFA)
53 West Jackson Boulevard, Suite 205
Chicago, IL 60604
(800) 334-4232

*Entrepreneur's Guide to Franchise Business
    Opportunities*
Rieva Lesonsky, Editor
Entrepreneur Media, Inc.
2392 Morse Avenue
Irvine, CA 92714
(714) 261-2325
(800) 421-2300

The Complete Franchise Book
Dennis L. Foster
Prima Publishing
P.O. Box 1260
Rocklin, CA 95677-1266
(800) 632-8676

The Franchise Consulting Group
1888 Century Park East, Suite 1900
Los Angeles, CA 90067
(310) 552-2901

Franchise Opportunities Handbook
Superintendent of Documents
U.S. Government Printing Office
710 North Capital Street, NW
Washington, DC 20402
(202) 512-1800

Chapter

4

Preparing a Winning Business Plan

Objectives

1. Understand the value of writing a business plan.
2. Learn the eight detailed components of a business plan.
3. Determine your target audience.
4. Know the five steps toward the completion of the business plan.

INTRODUCTION

When a CEO-founder of a new computer software firm in Washington, D.C., recently visited a banker to request a $50,000 line of credit to enter into the software world, the business plan was close by. When the president of a plastic card manufacturer wanted to establish a set of five-year goals based on the company's current financial projections, a business plan was also available. Also when the management team of a company on the east coast of Florida sought outside investors to finance their expansion into a financial service for Internet e-commerce, they made sure that their business plan was first-rate. All entrepreneurs recognize the value of the business plan for securing capital and growing their businesses.

The business plan can take many forms—from a glossy, professionally produced document to a handwritten manuscript in a three-ring binder that serves as

Profile: Christy Jones of pcOrder—A Winning Business Plan

Christy Jones started her first company, Trilogy Software, at 19. At 26, she sold her equity interest and founded pcOrder. Today, at 29, she runs a company with almost $22 million in sales that is revolutionizing the way the computer industry sells hardware.

"The grand vision is to have every single computer bought using pcOrder technology," says Jones. That technology is a practical outgrowth of artificial intelligence, the field that Jones was studying as a Stanford undergraduate when she cofounded Trilogy, the leading provider of enterprise solutions for sales and marketing. The software "recognizes" which of thousands of parts will work best in a given computer. PcOrder's pricing uses Trilogy's core technology.

Making the rounds with her business plan pitch, she met Ross Cooley, the former senior vice president and general manager of Compaq's North American business and operations. "Lightbulbs went off," says Cooley. "I realized that if you just changed things a little bit, there could be this tremendous potential for PC makers to level the playing field and compete against the direct guys."

Cooley talked Jones into changing the business plan. Jones convinced Cooley to join the company as chairman and CEO. The combination offered a powerful mix of experience, contacts, intellectual firepower, and fresh ideas to launch the business.

Christy had the foundation of a great business plan. Her new plan combined Internet software applications, product content, and partner connections that allowed manufacturers, distributors, and resellers to configure, price, and sell products over the Web. Her revisions of the plan included the real-time product information that streams from pcOrder's database of over 600,000 products. "This could make pcOrder the A. C. Nielsen of the computer industry," says Cooley.

Following the announcement of a $30 million deal with Ingram Micro, the world's largest computer distributor, Jones used the buzz from that deal to turn the company's IPO into one of 1999's blockbusters, to the tune of $46.2 million. While it is unlikely that every computer will one day be bought using pcOrder technology, Jones seems ready to capture a sizable slice of the business-to-business e-commerce market, which is projected to grow from $8 billion in 1997 to $327 billion in 2002, according to Forrester Research.

Profile: Margaret Green of Creative Enterprises—Using a Business Plan

Margaret Green's association with active sportswear began in 1995 when she became a designer of Ellesse, SPA, a major manufacturer of tennis and ski apparel in Perugia, Italy. After three years she returned to New York City and worked with Ellesse, USA, designing tennis, golf, and ski apparel. She designed licensed products for the professional sports leagues—NFL, NBA, and NHL.

In 1997, she formed Creative Enterprises, a turnkey business offering marketing programs for targeted consumers for importing high-quality apparel products. The company focused on the active sportswear sector of the apparel industry and provided a menu of services, from concept development to the delivery of products or fulfillment centers. These marketing and design programs brought a competitive advantage to the customer's brand name.

Margaret Green realized that preparing a business plan was essential to a new venture. The plan would serve as a guide and instrument for raising capital. After completing the financial analysis section, it indicated that the business would reach a revenue base of $1,925,000 in three years, with a pretax profit margin of 55.5 percent. Additionally, the cumulative negative cash flow after the first year was expected to be $73,125. Therefore, she estimated an initial investment of $175,000 was needed to fund the business activities and implement the client programs.

As a result of her efforts, a large garment manufacturer in South Korea with 25 years' experience and over $23 billion of product manufacturing pledged development resources. Discussions were also underway to determine the extent of the manufacturer's participation as a strategic investor.

documentation for the goals, objectives, strategies, and tactics of a company. The plan is the preferred mode of communication between entrepreneurs and potential investors. You will find that just completing the steps outlined for developing a business plan forces you to introduce discipline and a logical thought process into all of the planning activities. Additionally, a properly prepared plan will greatly improve your ability to consistently establish and meet goals and objectives for employees, investors, and management.

In this chapter, we will establish the value of a business plan and a step-by-step procedure to follow. We will also discuss why certain information is required, how it should be presented, and its importance.

WHAT IS A BUSINESS PLAN?

A business plan is a written document, between 25 and 40 pages, of where the business is going and how it will grow. It must include all pertinent aspects of the business including current status and projected results.

In most companies, business plans are used at a minimum to:

✔ Set the goals and objectives for the company's performance.

✔ Provide a basis for evaluating and controlling the company's performance.

✔ Communicate the company's message to middle managers, outside directors, lenders, and potential investors.

CHOOSING YOUR GOALS AND OBJECTIVES

The business plan serves as a blueprint for building a company. It is a vehicle for describing the goals of the business and how these goals can be reached over the coming years. Moreover, it is a means to:

✔ Raise capital for a business.

✔ Project the sales, expenses, and cash flows of the business.

✔ Explain to employees their responsibilities and company expectations.

✔ Improve and assess company performance.

✔ Plan for a new product development.

The single most important reason for preparing a plan is its use in securing capital. Investors agree that an effectively prepared business plan is requisite for obtaining funding for any business, whether it is a new business seeking *start-up capital* or an existing business seeking financing for expansion or a turn-around situation.

 start-up capital
money needed to launch a new venture during the pre-start-up and initial period of operation.

The business plan, in many ways, is a first attempt at strategic planning. You should use it as a tool for establishing the direction of your company and setting the action steps to guide the company through this period. Many entrepreneurs say that the pressure of the day-to-day management of a company leaves them little time for planning. However, without the plan, they run the risk of proceeding blindly through a rapidly changing business environment. Of course, writing a business plan is not a guarantee that problems will not arise. But, with a thoroughly thought-out process, you can better anticipate a crisis situation and deal with it up front. Further, a well-constructed plan can help avoid certain problems altogether. All in all, business planning is probably more important to the survival of a growing start-up company than to a larger, more mature one.

SETTING PERFORMANCE BENCHMARKS

A business plan can also be used to develop and document milestones along your business's path to success. In the heat of daily operations, you may find that taking an objective look at the performance of your business is difficult. A business plan can provide you and your management team with an objective basis for determining if the business is on track to meet the goals and objectives you have set.

START THE PROCESS: FIVE STEPS

Your company's story must be told and retold many times to prospective investors, new employees, outside advisers, and potential customers. The most important part of the story is the part about the future, the part featured in a business plan. The plan should show how all the pieces of your company fit together to create a vibrant organization capable of meeting its goals and objectives. It must also be able to communicate your company's distinctive competence to anyone who might have an interest. The five steps in preparing your business plan are:

Step 1—Identify Your Objectives

Before you begin writing a successful plan, you must determine your audience, what they want to know, and how they intend to use the information. The needs of your target audience must be established and communicated to your readers.

Step 2—Set Up the Outline

Once you have identified the objectives and know the areas to emphasize, prepare an outline based on these special requirements. The outline should be detailed so that it will be more useful to you and your audience.

Step 3—Review

Review your outline to identify any other areas that should be presented in detail form. Keep in mind that your business plan should also describe your company at a high level of detail as well. Detailed support for your statements and assumptions should also be available.

Step 4—Write the Plan

You will probably find it necessary to research many areas before you have enough information to start writing. Most entrepreneurs begin by collecting historical financial information about their companies and/or industries and completing their market research before beginning to write any part.

Initial drafts of proposed financial statements and projections are often prepared next, after the basic market research and analysis are completed. By preparing these statements, you will know which strategies will work from a financial perspective before investing many hours in writing a detailed description. Also keep detailed notes on the assumptions so that later the use of footnotes will accompany the statements.

The last element to be prepared is the executive summary. Since it is a summary of the plan, its contents are contingent on the rest of the document and cannot be finished until the other components of the plan are essentially complete. As you write each section, refer to the detailed outline in this chapter to make sure you cover each area thoroughly.

Step 5—Have the Plan Reviewed and Updated

Once a draft is done, have a professional review it for completeness and effectiveness as a document. The plan must be updated every six months. As your objectives change, update the plan to reflect these changes. Refer to this chapter each time it is updated to be certain that all areas are properly covered.

WHAT KIND OF PLAN IS BEST FOR YOU?

There are three major types of plans:

1. A total business plan is necessary when you need a significant amount of funding and to describe the business in detail to potential investors, strategic partners, or buyers.

2. A summary plan is a short format that contains the most important information about the business and its direction. It is usually about 10 to 15 pages long and is used to gauge investors' interest and in seeking strategic partners. It can also be

used to attract key employees or for persuading friends to invest in the business.

3. An operational plan is a document used internally. It should focus toward a common goal and be used by the management team.

Functions of Your Business Plan

A business plan serves three major functions:

First, it can be used to develop new ideas or products about the venture. It is a way to refine the business strategy and examine the company from all perspectives (e.g., marketing, finance, and operations).

Second, it is a tool for you to use to assess the performance of the company over a period of time. For example, the financial part of a plan can be used as the basis for a budget and can be monitored to see how well the business is on track.

Third, it facilitates the raising of capital. Most lenders and investors will not put money into a business without first seeing a business plan.

Targeting Your Business

Some investors invest only in certain types of business such as technology, the Internet, or e-commerce. Therefore, send a plan to the appropriate group. This can include:

- ✔ Bankers—to provide loans for expansion and equipment purchases.
- ✔ Business brokers—for selling the business.
- ✔ New employees—to enlist and join the company.
- ✔ Investors—to invest in the company.
- ✔ Small Business Administration (SBA)—to approve business loans.
- ✔ Investment bankers—to prepare a prospectus for an IPO.
- ✔ Suppliers—to establish credit for purchases.

Start by Answering the Top 10 Questions

1. Is there a market? Has the opportunity been well defined?
2. What is the primary product or service?
3. Who are the target customers?
4. Who is the competition and what are the barriers to entry?
5. Who comprise the management team?
6. What is the pricing structure model?
7. What are the risks and market constraints?
8. What sales distribution channels will you need to sell the product or service?
9. What is the current financial cash flow and break-even plan?
10. What are your financial needs?

WRITING THE BUSINESS PLAN

There are usually eight components, excluding the title page and table of contents:

1. Executive summary.
2. Marketing analysis.
3. Company description.
4. Marketing and sales strategies.
5. Products and services.
6. Operations.
7. Management and ownership.
8. Financial plan.

Title Page and Table of Contents

The title page provides the name, address, and phone number of the company and the CEO. The table of contents includes a sequential listing and pagination of the sections.

Executive Summary

The executive summary must be able to stand on its own. It should be merely an introduction to the rest of the business plan. Investors may read only the executive summary. Therefore, it must gain the investor's confidence, or the plan will be rejected.

Four Elements in the Executive Summary

1. *Marketing Concept.* Describes the business, its product, and the market it will serve. It should point out exactly what will be sold, to whom, and why the business will hold a competitive advantage.

2. *Services.* Details any developments within the company that are essential to its success. Major achievements include patents, prototypes, location of a facility, any crucial contracts that need to be in place for product development, or results from any test-marketing that has been conducted.

3. *Current Position.* Furnishes relevant information about the company, its legal form of operation, when it was formed, the principal owners, and key personnel.

4. *Financial Features.* Highlights the important financial points of the business, including sales, profits, cash flow, and return on investment.

The executive summary should be no more than two to three pages and convince the reader that the business will succeed.

Marketing Analysis

The marketing analysis describes how the business will react to market conditions and generate sales to succeed. It should explain the marketing goals and describe the business itself as an attractive investment. Bear in mind that the marketing challenge is most critical to a

venture capitalist
an investor who provides early financing to new ventures—often technology-based—with an innovative product and the prospect of rapid and profitable growth.

company's success. Therefore, potential investors give a great deal of attention to this section. *Venture capitalists* feel that the most important criteria for predicting the success of a new company are those factors that establish the demand for the product or service. If a real market need is not presented, all of the talent and financing in the world will not make a company successful.

Some of the most important issues are:

1. *Market Opportunity.* The marketing section must establish a demand or need for the product or service and should define both the market and opportunity. The secondary target market should also be addressed.

2. *Competition.* Describes the market conditions that exist in the business. The degree of competition and what impact this competition is likely to have on the business is a critical factor. It is also important to address other forces such as government regulations and outside influences.

3. *Marketing Strategy.* Defines how the business will use its marketing tools. This can include factors such as distribution, advertising and promotion, pricing, and selling incentives. The mission and vision will vary depending on the stage of development.

4. *Market Research.* Describes market research as a separate section by itself, or add this section to the marketing plan.

5. *Sales Forecasts.* Usually financial projections are presented in the financial section of a business plan. However, it is useful to present sales projections in the marketing section. These might include projected sales growth, market share, and sales by customer.

6. *Support Material.* Include in the appendix materials that will make the plan more credible—industry studies, letters of support, brochures, and reviews or articles related to the product or service.

While there is a great deal of flexibility in the writing of the marketing section, you should focus the plan to fit the characteristics of the proposed business.

Company Description

The company description provides an overview of how all of the elements of the company fit together without going into detail, since most of the subjects will be covered in depth elsewhere.

The section begins with a general description of the company, which should take no more than a few pages. It should present the fundamental activities and nature of the company. A fine level of detail is not appropriate in this section because you will have the opportunity to offer further detail in the other sections.

Address questions such as: What is the company's business? What customers will you serve? Where is the company located and where will it do business?

Some further insight should also be offered as to what stage the company has reached. Is it a "seed"-stage business without a fully developed product line? Has it developed a product line but not yet begun to market it? Or is it already marketing its products and anxious to expand its scale of activity?

Articulate the business's objectives. Maybe the company is seeking a certain level of sales or geographic distribution. Will it become a publicly traded company or an attractive acquisition candidate? A statement of such objectives is important and may succeed in generating significant interest.

Marketing and Sales Strategies

Marketing and sales strategies describe how the business will implement the marketing plan to achieve the expected sales performance. This analysis will guide you to establish pricing, distribution, and promotional strategies that allow the business to become profitable within a competitive environment.

Distribution Strategy Distribution describes the process of getting the product to customers. The type of distribution network you select will depend on the industry and the size of the market. Analyze the distribution channels of your competitors before deciding to use similar channels or alternatives such as:

✔ *Web E-Commerce.* Sell your products and services on your web site or through Internet partner alliances.

✔ *Direct Sales.* This is the most effective distribution channel. Sell the product directly to the end user.

✔ *OEM (Original Equipment Manufacturer) Sales.* Your product is sold to an OEM and is incorporated into the finished product and distributed to the end user.

✔ *Manufacturer's Representatives.* These sales reps handle an assortment of complementary products and divide their selling time accordingly.

✔ *Brokers.* They buy directly from the distributor and sell to retailers or end users.

✔ *Direct Mail.* Sell to the end user using a direct-mail campaign.

Pricing Strategy Pricing is an important element in the marketing strategy since it has a direct impact on the success for the business. The policy regarding discounting and price changes should also be addressed as well as the impact on gross profit (revenue less cost of goods sold). Consider these methods:

✔ *Cost-Plus Pricing.* All costs, both fixed and variable, are included and a profit percentage is added on.

✔ *Demand Pricing.* Sell the products or services based on demand.

✔ *Competitive Pricing.* Enter a market where there is an established price and it is difficult to differentiate your product from another.

✔ *Mark-up Pricing.* Calculate the price by adding your estimated profit to the cost of the product.

Advertising, Public Relations, and Promotion
Many start-up or early-stage companies do not have large advertising budgets. However, a public relations campaign is often within reach. Although public relations campaigns can be more expensive than advertising campaigns, they can be done on an ad hoc basis and shoestring budget.

Related Budgets Use PowerPoint pie charts, graphs, tables, and other graphics to effectively present how the marketing effort will be organized and business resources will be allocated among various marketing tools.

Products and Services

This section describes the characteristics and the appeal of the products or services. This can include a prototype, sample, or demonstration of how the products work. Include:

1. *Physical Description.* A description of physical characteristics usually includes photographs, drawings, or brochures. In the case of a service, a diagram sometimes helps to convey what is being provided by the business.

2. *Use and Appeal.* You should comment on the nature of its various uses and what constitutes its appeal. This is an opportunity to emphasize the unique features of the product or service and establish the potential of the business.

3. *Stage of Development.* Focus on the stage of development of the product or service. Include how the company's offerings have changed to their present state and may evolve in the future.

4. *Testimonials.* Provide a list of experts or prior users who are familiar with the products or services and who will comment favorably on them. Such testimonials may be included in letter or report form in an appendix.

Operations

This section is a detailed, in-depth operational plan. It will provide an opportunity to work out many potential problems on paper prior to commencement of operations. The importance will depend on the nature of the business. An e-commerce production site will probably require significant attention to operational issues. In contrast, most retail businesses and some service businesses will probably have less operational complexity. Issues addressed are:

1. *Product Development.* It is not unusual to prepare a business plan before a business's full range of products and services is developed. This is especially true of a start-up company. Even after the product has been developed, it is often necessary to continue its development effort in order to maintain its competitive position. Usually, it is worthwhile to present a summary of the product development activities that the company will undertake.

2. *Manufacturing.* In the case of a production facility, it is important to discuss the process by which a company will manufacture its products. This usually involves some description of the plant, equipment, material, and the labor requirements. The techniques that may be employed in combining these resources could include assembly lines and robotics, as well as the capability of the business in terms of production rates and constraints on production capabilities.

3. *Maintenance and Support.* In some instances, it is important to define the support that will be provided. Specifically, the plan should address the level of support a company will provide after a customer has purchased a product or service. This is particularly important in the case of a software or technical product.

Management and Ownership

The management team's talents and skills should be detailed is this section. If you are using the plan to attract investors, this section must emphasize the management's talents and indicate why they are a part of your company's distinctive competence advantage. Remember that individuals invest in people, not ideas. Issues that should be addressed:

1. *Management Team/Principles.* Describe the management team and the backgrounds of those individuals expected to play key roles in the venture. This includes investors, members of the *board of directors*, key employees, advisers, and strategic partners.

2. *Organizational Chart.* After introducing the key participants, it is appropriate to offer an organizational chart that presents the relationships and divisions of responsibility within the organization. In some instances, a brief narrative instead of, or in addition to, a chart may be helpful in providing further detail.

3. *Policy and Strategy.* Include a statement as to how employees will be selected, trained, and rewarded. Such background can be important for investors to give them a feel for the company's culture. A brief reference to the type of benefits and incentives planned may further help define the company's spirit.

 board of directors the people elected by stockholders of a corporation who are responsible to that group for overseeing the overall direction and policy of the firm.

Financial Plan

This section should formulate a credible, comprehensive set of projections reflecting a company's anticipated financial performance. If these projections are carefully prepared and convincingly supported, they become one of the most critical yardsticks by which the business's attractiveness is measured.

While the overall business plan communicates a basic understanding of the nature of the business, projected financial performance addresses itself most directly to the bottom-line interests. This is where the investor discovers the return on investment, performance measures, and exit plans.

The financial plan is the least flexible part of a business plan in terms of format. While actual numbers will vary, each plan should contain similar statements—or schedules—and each statement should be presented in a conventional manner. There should be enough information in these statistics for the reader to know not only the business but also how it relates to similar businesses. In general, the information that should be presented includes the following:

- ✔ The set of assumptions on which projections are based should be clearly and concisely presented. Numbers without these assumptions will have little meaning. It is only after carefully considering such assumptions that you can assess the validity of financial projections.

- ✔ Projected income statements, typically for three to five years, should be included. Prepare first year projections by month and second year projections by quarter. These statements most often reflect at least quarterly performance for the first year, while years two through five are often annual.

- ✔ Projected cash flow statements for the first two years should be developed in as great detail as possible. Quarterly or annual cash flows, corresponding to the period used for the income statements, are sufficient for years three through five.

- ✔ A current balance sheet reflecting the financial position of the company at its inception and projected year-end balance sheets, typically for two years, should be included.

- ✔ Other financial projections may include a break-even analysis that will demonstrate the level of sales required to break even at a given time.

The financial section can also be used to assess performance after the business actually starts. In some instances the plan may be the basis for a detailed operating budget. It can become a guiding document, detailing how and when the capital should be expended and listing objectives that must be achieved if the business is to be successful.

HOW LONG WILL IT TAKE?

The complete plan could take more than 200 hours to prepare, depending on your experience and knowledge of the business. The hardest part about writing a plan is getting started. Most beginning entrepreneurs incorrectly estimate the length of time it will take. Once the process has begun, however, you will realize that it is invaluable in sorting out the business functions of your company. To help you get started and make the process easier, here are tips to follow:

Executive Summary

✔ The executive summary should take up no more than three pages.

✔ This is the most crucial part of your plan because it must capture the reader's interest.

✔ What, how, why, where, when, and so on, must be summarized.

✔ Complete this part after all sections have been written.

Company Overview Segment

✔ Describe the name of the business.

✔ A background of the industry with history of the company should be included.

✔ The potential of the new venture should be defined. List key customers, major products, and applications.

✔ Any unique or distinctive features of the venture should be spelled out.

Marketing Strategy Segment

✔ Convince investors that sales projections and competition can be met.

✔ Market studies should be used and disclosed.

✔ Identify a target market and market share.

✔ Evaluate all competition and specifically cover why and how you will be better than the competitors.

✔ Describe the pricing strategy to penetrate a market and maintain a market share.

✔ Identify your advertising plans and give cost estimates to validate the proposed strategy.

Products and Services Segment

✔ Describe the features and benefits of the services or products.

✔ Detail the current stage of development.

Research, Design, and Development Segment

✔ State the costs involved in research, testing, or development.

✔ Explain carefully what has already been accomplished (prototype, lab testing, early development).

✔ Mention any research or technical assistance that has been provided for you.

Operations Segment

✔ Provide the advantages of your location (e.g., zoning, tax laws, wage rates).

✔ List the production needs in terms of facilities (plant, storage, office space) and equipment (machinery, furnishings, supplies).

✔ Describe the access to transportation (for shipping and receiving).

✔ Explain the proximity to your suppliers.

✔ Mention the availability of labor in your location.

Management Segment

✔ Provide resumes of all key people.

✔ Carefully describe the legal structure (sole proprietorship, partnership, S corporation, LLC, or C corporation).

✔ Cover the added assistance of advisers, consultants, and directors.

✔ Provide information on current ownership and options for an exit strategy such as selling the business or going public.

Financial Data Segment

✔ Convince investors that the business makes sense from a financial standpoint.

✔ Prepare three- to five-year financial projections.

✔ Prepare first-year projections by month.

✔ Prepare second-year projections by quarter.

✔ Include income statement and balance sheet.

✔ Provide cash flow statements for years one and two.

✔ Include three-year annual forecast.

UNDERSTANDING WHY BUSINESS PLANS FAIL

Generally, a poorly prepared business plan can be blamed on one or more of the following factors. Consider these items and make sure they are addressed in your presentation.

✔ The goals set are unreasonable and cannot be met. Setting goals requires you to be well informed about the type of business and the competitive environment. Goals should be specific and not be generic.

✔ The owner has no real commitment to the business. You should make a total commitment to the business. For example, it is difficult to operate a business on a part-time basis while holding down a full-time position. Investors will not be favorably inclined toward a venture that does not have a full-time commitment. Investors may also expect you to make a financial commitment to the business even if it means a second mortgage or a depletion of savings.

✔ The owner has no experience in the planned business. Generally, a lack of experience will result in failure unless you can either attain the necessary knowledge or team up with someone who already has it.

✔ There is no sense of potential threats or weaknesses.

✔ No customer need has been established for the proposed product or service.

SUMMARY

This chapter has established the value of a business plan and the step-by-step procedure involved in its preparation. The business plan for a start-up company is usually your first attempt at strategic planning. It is your tool for setting up the direction of the company and the action steps to guide you through this period.

Before starting, you will need information on the market, manufacturing operations, and financial estimates. This information should be evaluated based on the goals and objectives of the new culture, which provide a framework for writing the plan. The executive summary must be able to stand on its own. It should describe who is expected to purchase the product, how much money is required, and what the payback is expected to be.

The marketing section must establish the demand for the product or service and the potential for the business. Typically, this will include a summary of the industry growth potential, the sources of demand, and how demand is satisfied.

The company description section begins with a general description of the company, which should take no more than a few pages. It should present the fundamental activities and nature of the company. A fine level of detail is not appropriate in this section because you will have the opportunity to offer further detail in the other sections.

A marketing and sales strategy describes how the business will implement the marketing plan to achieve the expected sales performance. This analysis will guide you to establish pricing, distribution, and promotional strategies that allow the business to become profitable within a competitive environment.

The operations section is a detailed plan that defines the potential problems prior to starting the operation. The importance will depend on the nature of the business. An e-commerce production site will require significant attention to the operational issues of outsourcing versus performing the operations internally.

In the management section, the team's experience should be detailed. If you are using the plan to attract investors, this section must emphasize the management's talents and their distinctive competence advantage. Investors always look for a strong management team before making investments.

The financial plan section should demonstrate a set of projections that reflect the company's financial goals and performance. They are one of the most important yardsticks if not exaggerated and they are prepared correctly.

As is often the case in the preparation of a business plan, the quality of information included is dependent on the amount of energy devoted to gathering it. Good sources for such data include trade associations, trade literature, industry studies, and industry experts.

Many businesses fail because the proper talent has not been assembled. This issue is addressed by describing the objective assessment of the team's strengths and weaknesses as well as the company's requirements for growth. It includes how employees are selected, trained, and rewarded.

The business plan is essential in launching a new business. The result of many hours of preparation will be a comprehensive, written, and well-organized document that will serve as a guide and an instrument for you to raise the necessary capital and financing.

ADDITIONAL RESOURCES

Biz Plan Software: www.jian.com

Biz Women: www.bizwomen.com

Business Plans: www.bplans.com

Business Plans Made Easy: www.entrepreneur.com

Entreworld: www.entreworld.org

Small Business Advancement National Center: www.sbanet.uuca.edu

$$\mathcal{C}hapter$$

Getting the Funding

Objectives

1. Understand the problems in raising capital.
2. Identify the different methods of funding and know which one is best for you.
3. Know the process of finding investors.
4. Know how to select a venture capitalist.

INTRODUCTION TO FUNDING

If you are planning to launch a new business, you will encounter the issues of where to find start-up capital. In most cases, you will not be aware of the many choices of locating financing options that best suit your business needs.

Therefore, it is important to know the expectations and requirements of these sources as well as the options available for financing. Angel investing, commercial loans, private placements, and venture capital are just a few of the terms used to raise capital. Each potential source has certain criteria for providing financing, and they will be the focus of this chapter.

In this chapter, we will summarize the various sources of capital available to new and growing businesses. We will also explain why the ability to obtain funding depends on a number of factors (i.e., management team, collateral, cash flow, earnings, and marketability of the product). Plan ahead and do not let the financial

Profile: Mati Weiderpass—Funding Watch World International

Mati Weiderpass, founder of Watch World International, has come a long way from his youth on a chicken farm in Rhode Island to being the country's premier retailer of sports and fashion watches. He earned a degree in management engineering from Worcester Polytechnic Institute in 1981 and fulfilled the requirements of his ROTC scholarship by serving four years in the military, achieving the rank of captain. While he was a MBA candidate in Lausanne, Switzerland, he was asked to select a company and create a marketing plan for it. He chose Swatch. And so began his career in the watch industry. After studying and presenting his findings to Swatch, he so impressed the executives that they asked him to join the company.

After nine years with Swatch, Mati presented Swatch with his plan for a Swatch retail site; however, the company was not interested. Acting on impulse, Mati decided to pursue his retail site independent of Swatch. In 1994, Mati opened his first Watch World International store in New York City on the corner of Houston Street and Broadway. Five years later, there were over 100 Watch World International stores throughout the United States.

The fashion watch segment was born with the introduction of Swatch in 1981. Fashion brands such as Guess, Fossil, and Anne Klein followed shortly thereafter. This segment grew in department stores, which were not service-oriented, but was eschewed by jewelry stores and traditional watch stores that concentrated on high-end watches. Watch World International was developed to fill this niche in a fun gallery-like environment. Mati initially invested approximately $1 million of his own money to launch the business. Fortunately, this money came from his previous business ventures in real estate. The financial plan was to grow the company to the next level, approximately eight to nine stores, and then seek venture capital financing. Two companies, Traveler's Insurance and Global Retail Partners (affiliated with Donaldson, Lufkin & Jenrette (DLJ), invested over $10 million to provide the resources and funding for expansion.

Today, Watch World International has over 100 locations nationwide and a strong Internet presence. It is one of the top three retailers for most of the watch brands it carries among retailers.

requirements be a surprise. Arranging financing takes time, and rush decisions can be costly.

FUNDING SOURCES

Sources of Funding

1. Nonbank creditors:
   ✔ Venture leasing.
   ✔ Insurance.
   ✔ Credit cards.
2. Self-funding.
3. Family and friends.
4. Angels.
5. Private equity:
   ✔ Venture capital.
   ✔ Private placements.
   ✔ Preferred stock.
   ✔ Web sites.
6. Public equity.
7. Corporate support.
8. Bank loans.
9. Joint venture.
10. Moonlighting.
11. Bootstrapping.

Nonbank Creditors

Venture Leasing Venture leasing is available to companies that have been granted financing. The advantage is not raising additional capital for equipment. Venture leasing deals typically require payments of 100 percent of principal, plus 8 percent to 12 percent in interest charges over a 24-month to 60-month lease horizon (plus the leasor gets the equipment when the lease period ends). For leads, contact your accounting firm or bank representative.

Insurance This type of loan is becoming more popular for obtaining early financing. Insurance companies have allowed policyholders to borrow against the value of their policies or cash in their life insurance policies.

Credit Cards Credit cards have always been popular. If your bank turns you down, contact all the major credit-card suppliers to compare prices and options. As you would with a bank, make sure you'll have opportunities to increase your borrowing limit (and add on other financing sources, such as equipment leasing) as necessary, once you've proved that your company is a good customer.

"Pulling out the plastic" for fast funding of the business is more viable now than ever before. MasterCard or Visa cardholders with good credit now often receive credit limits of $10,000 and above. By being able to carry more than one credit card, the entrepreneur can considerably boost the total amount tapped into at any one time.

Credit card interest rates on cash advances vary considerably, from as high as 21 percent to 15 percent or lower. Annual fees can also range from over $50 down to zero. This means it is wise to investigate getting the best deal when obtaining credit cards. It may be advantageous to close out one or more high-interest cards and transfer the balances to lower-cost credit cards.

Remember that obtaining funds through credit cards costs much more than bank loans. If the enterprise is not successful, the credit card payments will continue and may place the entrepreneur in a personal financial squeeze.

Self-Funding

Most new businesses (close to 90 percent) start with less than $100,000, and close to a third start with less than $10,000. This kind of money is usually available to the motivated entrepreneur by looking at his or her personal resources. The vast majority of new businesses are started with the main source of funding coming from personal savings or various forms of personal equity of the founder(s). This capital reflects the degree of motivation, commitment, and belief of the founder in the enterprise. This type of investment also takes the shape of sweat equity, where individuals either donate their time or provide it at below market value to help the business get established. Many times entrepreneurs use profits from previous endeavors to pour into their new enterprises.

Family and Friends

This is a very popular source for start-up capital. Friends and family are not as worried about quick profits as professional investors. However, there are problems associated with this method. Usually friends and family do not investigate the business very well and are not familiar with all the risks of the business. The best method is to provide the same disclosure to a friend or relative that you would provide to the most sophisticated investors. Resist the temptation to keep things loose and undocumented.

Angels

Angels are an excellent source of capital and sometimes the best source for you to seek. Banks are not in a position to fund a new business, and some businesses are too small to get venture capital. Usually angels are willing to fund a business and will put up as much as $20 million—that's how much angel, Michael Egan, former chairman of Alamo Rent-A-Car, put into TheGlobe.com's start-up. If you need or require a limited amount of money, angels are a good alternative. Over a million angels invest over $40 billion of equity in small businesses each year. The investment is usually in the $25,000 to $100,000 range. However, if you deal with several angels at once you can get a better deal, since they sometimes prefer to invest as a group. Angels want an equity stake, a return of 20 to 35 percent, and some ask for a board seat. To find an angel, check out the chamber of commerce and any entrepreneurs groups in your state. Angel networks and matchmaking services set up by universities and state development agencies are another great source. These networks charge a fee—generally between $150 and $300—to list an organization in their database. Investor contacts and angel networks are:

 angel
a private investor who often has nonmonetary motives for investing as well as the usual financial ones.

Investor Contacts and Forums

Alliance Forum (New York State)
(415) 742-0757

Annual Venture Finance Conference
Minneapolis, MN
(612) 338-3826

The Great Midwest Venture Capital Conference
Indianapolis, IN
(317) 264-2820

Information Industry Association's Investor
    Conference
Washington, DC
(202) 639-8260

New York Venture Group
(212) 832-NYVG

Oklahoma Investment Forum
(918) 585-1201

Pennsylvania Private Investors Group's Monthly
    Showcase
(215) 975-9430

Angel Networks
Georgia Capital Network
(404) 894-5344

Investors' Circle
(708) 876-1101

L.A. Venture Network
(310) 450-9544

Mid-Atlantic Investment Network
(301) 681-0162

Northwest Capital Network (only serves businesses
    located in Oregon)
(503) 282-6273

Pacific Venture Capital Network
(714) 856-8366

Seed Capital Network, Inc.
(615) 573-4655

Technology Capital Network (formerly the Venture
    Capital Network at MIT)
(617) 253-7163

Texas Capital Network
(512) 794-9398

Venture Capital Network of Minnesota
(612) 223-8663

Venture Line
(518) 486-5438

Washington Investment Network
(206) 389-2559

Private Equity

Venture Capital Venture capital firms also are a source of equity capital for start-up firms. However, while some venture capital firms specialize in very early-stage funding, this is the exception rather than the rule.

Most often, venture capital is not available until the firm has reached the demonstration phase and possibly not until the firm is ready for commercialization. Many venture capital firms want to invest where the time horizon is relatively short, since they must liquidate their investments and provide cash return to their investors over a finite period.

The average investment made by venture capital companies has doubled from $3.5 million in 1992 to more than $7 million today. Total venture capital investments (in seed money plus primary and secondary financing) now average around $24 million, up from $9.5 million seven years ago, according to a survey by *The Economist*. A third of all venture capital raised around the world—$5 billion a year—is invested in companies in Silicon Valley.

The payoff is potentially as great. The return on investment on American business in general over the past 30 years has averaged 16 percent. The return on investment on entrepreneurial high-tech companies averages well over 50 percent, according to *Red Herring* magazine. Venture capital firm Sequoia Capital put $2 million into Yahoo! Today, that stake is worth $4.4 billion, a 2,200-fold return on Sequoia's investment.

The potential for failure is even greater, however. Fewer than one in 100 new businesses ever manage to break even, according to the Small Business Administration (SBA), much less increase its worth 2,000-fold. Fewer than one in 1,000 start-ups ever manage to go public, according to the SBA.

A *public offering* of stock is an option for raising capital for a firm undergoing rapid expansion after the initial commercialization phase. A firm may need added equity to finance the rapid growth stage, and the image of being a public company adds credibility to the firm. As a general rule of thumb, a firm should have profits after taxes of $1 million before it considers *going public*.

Also, a firm could be acquired in this phase, and the acquirer may provide cash to the firm. The acquirer may also provide marketing skills or production know-how to help in expansion. The more identifiable corporate name of the acquirer, the more credibility with potential customers. If the firm is acquired by a public company, the founding entrepreneurs may receive shares from the sale of equity and obtain liquidity, just as if the firm had gone public.

The year 1998 proved to be another record year for the venture capital industry. Some $25.3 billion was raised, according to the National Venture Capital Association (NVCA). Venture capital investments as a whole increased 24 percent from 1997 to 1998. That brings the total funds raised by VCs to $84.2 billion.

Whatever the dollar amount, knowing where venture funds originate gives entrepreneurs insight into the methods and motives of venture capitalists. For example, institutional investors may allocate 2 percent to 3 percent of assets in venture capital funds, but this comprises 50 percent of the funds available to VCs, according to the NVCA.

Also, venture capital firms specialize in different stages, seed investing, early-stage investing, and expansion-stage investing. In addition to providing capital money, VCs lend management assistance and typically require a seat on the funded company's board. VCs expect compounded annual returns of 30 percent or higher. Most have a five- to seven-year time horizon.

Getting into a Venture Capital Firm Despite claims to the contrary, getting a VC firm's attention is not easy.

public offering

the sale of a company's shares of stock to the public by the company or its major stockholders.

going public

the process by which a corporation offers its securities to the public.

One venture firm, Draper Fisher Jurvetson, of Redwood City, California, reportedly receives 10,000 proposals yearly. Only about 170 companies (1.7 percent) actually get funded. The odds are even steeper at San Francisco-based 21st Century Internet Venture Partners. It receives 1,600 proposals a year, but funds only four to five companies.

With so many business plans being submitted, VCs no longer insist that entrepreneurs spell out their company's business model in exacting detail. According to *Forbes* magazine, many VCs would rather pore over an abbreviated document specifying the business strategy for controlling a market. *Forbes* reports that VCs believe that time and talent are scarcer resources than money. Far more important is how well company founders and the management team present their plan.

LBOs and Early Buyouts If things don't work out as planned, a growing number of VCs stand ready as secondary funding providers. Secondary funds purchase the investment portfolios from VCs, providing the original investors with some welcome liquidity. Other firms create a "fund of funds," a pool of capital doled out to various venture firms.

Silver Lake Partners of Menlo Park, California, put a new spin on the secondary funding trend when it created the first leveraged buyout firm focused on early-stage technology companies. The fund leverages the cash of institutional investors with bank loans. Start-up companies rarely can produce sufficient cash to pay off the debt resulting from a leveraged buyout. Most require a steady stream of cash to continue growing and stay in business.

Growing at a Steady Pace Most entrepreneurs prefer growing slowly and steadily right from the start rather than retrenching following a disastrous, and sometimes deadly, market setback.

Sequoia Capital, also of Menlo Park, has made a specialty of handing out $50,000 to $100,000 to first-time entrepreneurs. Smaller investments mean less *dilution* of ownership for the entrepreneurs. Ironically, the firm goes after entrepreneurs who have failed their first time out. A

dilution
the reduction of a stockholder's percentage of ownership in an enterprise, usually done by selling more common stock to other parties. Sometimes called watering the stock.

stunning failure makes those entrepreneurs all the more determined to prove themselves and their business the second time around.

Small investors may also influence private equity markets in the future. In 1998, Technology Funding Venture Capital (TFVC), a San Mateo, California–based VC firm, began soliciting small-time investors over the Internet. To qualify, investors must have $60,000 in assets (excluding home and automobile) and a gross annual income of at least $25,000. TFVC is not alone. The VC firm joins other web-based equity funding sites such as Witcapital.com of New York, which give average investors a shot at early-stage financing.

On the Web Companies looking for funding or to get inside the heads of venture capitalists have plenty of places to look on the Internet. For starters, bookmark these sites:

- ✔ www.vfinance.com—A comprehensive venture capital resource library.
- ✔ www.upside.com—Electronic site for *Upside* magazine that covers high-tech venture capital network.
- ✔ www.redherring.com—Site for *Red Herring*, which covers high-tech venture capital. Online material is tailored more toward the venture capital community itself.
- ✔ www.nvca.org—Headquarters for the National Venture Capital Association.
- ✔ www.techcapital.com—Online magazine dealing with venture capital.
- ✔ www.witcapital.com—Leader among a number of sites creating a market for IPOs.
- ✔ www.garage.com—Assists start-ups wishing to acquire funding.

Private Placements A *private placement* involves selling stock to private investors in a private corporation. Federal and state laws regulate these activities and determine how the offerings are done. The investors are solicited with a private placement memorandum that involves the completion of a business plan and a prospectus explaining

private placement
the sale of stocks or bonds to wealthy individuals, pension funds, insurance companies, or other investors, done without a public offering or any oversight from the Securities and Exchange Commission.

the risks, issues, and procedures of the investment. Private placements should be done with the advice of an attorney who knows the federal laws and those of the state you plan to start in. Private placements are less costly and take less time than public offerings. Each state has standardized disclosure and offering documents.

The Securities Act of 1933 states that securities may not be issued unless they are *registered stock* or an exemption from registration is available. The typical exemption would be Regulation D, adopted by the Securities and Exchange Commission (SEC) to simplify the private offering process for investors who meet the requirements.

 registered stock stock that has been somehow registered with the SEC, and thus can be sold publicly.

1. *The Rule 504.* Up to $1 million limit in 12 months' time can be sold to the number of investors, whether they are sophisticated or not. There is no requirement of disclosure and no advertising restrictions on resale of stock. "Sophisticated" refers to any investor who has a net worth of $1 million or received a salary over $250,000 annually for the previous two years.

2. *The Rule 505.* Allows up to 5 million in 12 months of unregistered securities to be sold. There can be no more than 35 unaccredited investors. *Accredited investors* are defined as having individual income in excess of $200,000 in each of the two most recent years or joint income in excess of $300,000. Additionally, any person whose individual net worth or joint net worth exceeds $1,000,000 qualifies as an accredited investor.

 accredited investors individual or institutional investors who meet the qualifying SEC criteria with respect to financial sophistication or financial assets.

3. *The Rule 506.* There is no limitation to selling stock. There is a maximum of 35 nonaccredited investors (nonaccredited investors must be able to evaluate merit and risks) and no requirement of disclosure to accredited investors.

Preferred Stock Preferred stock is another technique for investors. Giving preferred stock was a way to give investors guaranteed credit status in case a company went bankrupt. Now it's used to give investors an incentive when a company has an *initial public offering (IPO)*. The

 IPO the initial public offering process.

preferred stock may be structured so that if an IPO takes place in three years instead of two, investors will receive the full value of their original investment plus stock at exit time.

Web Sites The wide world of the Internet offers many options for raising capital. The biggest player, Wit Capital (www.witcapital.com), has concluded more than 40 offerings so far, including IPOs and public and private venture capital as well as other equity deals.

Public Equity

The expanding stock market and venture capital firms are changing the way America does business and the way it defines success. This is true across the high-tech spectrum of companies, from wireless telecom to software development, hardware to handsets, and multimedia to virtual reality. Nowhere is it more true, however, than on the Internet. But as with all high-tech enterprises, the Internet means banking on the unknowable outcome.

High tech is a volume business. Building market share and outmaneuvering the competition in the early stages are the best routes to longer-term success. This means raising huge amounts of money and knowing that the second or third rounds of capitalization will follow.

See Chapter 7, "The IPO Process," for detailed discussion of going public.

Corporate Support

Strategic partnerships are an excellent alternative for many companies that find themselves either shut out of traditional financing deals or unwilling to swallow the equity valuations or interest charges required to make those deals happen. Cash infusions connected with strategic partnerships are usually much smaller than they might have been with a traditional financing deal (and sometimes investments aren't a factor at all). When a partnership's synergy clicks, the resulting growth can often yield far greater capital options later on.

Bank Home Equity Loans

This may be the fastest-growing method of raising money for individuals. Banks generally are willing to lend up to 70 percent (or more) of a home's appraised value, minus any existing mortgage(s).

Home equity loans are generally offered through commercial banks or savings and loan associations. Interest rates for second mortgages in 2000 were below 10 percent. In some instances, an approved home equity loan can be structured like a bank line of credit at slightly lower interest rates.

For tax purposes, you should deduct interest on up to $100,000 of debt on home equity loans, regardless of how the money is used. This makes a home equity loan attractive when looking for start-up capital. But remember that since this money is secured by a home, the bank could foreclose if the entrepreneur falls behind in payments.

See Chapter 6 for detailed discussion of bank loans.

Joint Venture

A *joint venture* with another firm with a synergistic fit is also a possibility. The joint venture partner, an established firm, would provide an investment in cash or in marketing, manufacturing, or other services to assist the entrepreneurial firm in its early phases.

joint venture usually refers to a short-lived partnership with each partner sharing in costs and rewards of the project; common in research, investment banking, and the health-care industry.

Suppliers or customers can be an important source of funds for a developing business. Suppliers may provide goods at low initial cost or extend payment terms. Customers may provide a down payment or cash advance against future deliveries. These actions ease cash advances against future deliveries as well as ease cash flow constraints and lower the amount of cash the firm must obtain from other sources.

Moonlighting

Many home-based businesses are begun while the founder is still working a regular job. The income from the job can both help support the owner during negative or low cash flow of the business set-up phase and provide working capital to augment the business's cash flow. Usually when the business begins paying as well or better than the regular job, the entrepreneur can jump ship from his or her job and devote full time to building the new business.

Bootstrapping

Often the best money to go after is the money that can be saved from the current costs and overhead of an ongoing business. This is a commonly overlooked source to business owners and managers.

The process of analyzing the operation for opportunities of savings and improved efficiencies will also allow the entrepreneur to learn more about the details of the company. The benefit is that by becoming more efficient and cost conscious, the entrepreneur will be in a stronger position to qualify for additional refinancing.

Choosing Your Funding Source

Entrepreneurs have many ways to raise funds for their companies. See box for options to match the company you plan to start with funding sources.

	Home-Based Business	Franchise	Buying an Existing Business	Start-Up Venture
Self-funding	X	X	X	X
Friends and family	X	X	X	X
Angels	X	X	X	X
Private placement				X
Venture capital		X		X
Joint venture			X	X
Debt/home equity loans	X	X	X	X
Public stock offering				X

FINDING INVESTORS

Once you have prepared a business plan and executive summary and secured a few good leads, it is time to contact potential investors to see if they may be interested in funding your business.

Contacting the Investor

You should first call the potential investor after you have completed the plan. Your initial conversation with the investor is to present a "five-minute summary" of your plan that describes your business and the type of deal that you are attempting to get financed.

Preparation

You should prepare for this session and cover the following points:

- ✔ A brief description of your business (i.e., product/service, target market).
- ✔ The unique features of your business or product/service.
- ✔ The management team.
- ✔ The type of funding desired (i.e., common stock, preferred stock).
- ✔ The general terms of the deal.

Meeting

Arrange a meeting to send the business plan or the executive summary before the investor chooses to meet with you.

Mail the Plan

Send the plan or summary with a cover letter. Try to be as specific as possible in the letter and refer to matters discussed in your earlier telephone conversation so that the letter is not perceived as a mass mailing.

Follow Up

Give the investor two weeks and then follow up to answer any questions.

Oral Presentation to the Investor

due diligence

the responsibility of those preparing and signing the registration statement to conduct an investigation in order to provide a reasonable basis for their belief that statements made in the registration statement are true and do not omit any material facts. Proper due diligence can help protect these parties from liability in the event they are sued for a faulty offering. The company, on the other hand, has strict liability for errors or omissions in the registration statement.

After a review of the plan, investors will usually require you to make an oral presentation. The oral presentation should summarize the key features of the written plan. In addition, the members of your management team should be prepared to answer questions asked by the investor. You should strengthen the oral presentation with the use of presentational aids such as PowerPoint presentations, prototype of products, web sites, and so on.

Investors want to know if your management team has the capability to make critical decisions and to function as a team. They will determine the expertise of your key members' skills in finance, marketing, and operations. All members of your management team should be prepared to provide input during the presentation to demonstrate the capabilities of a management team rather than of a single entrepreneur. Investors will also want the key managers to have stock in order to foster growth.

Evaluation

Usually over 80 percent of the proposals (i.e., executive summaries) are rejected immediately. After the business plan is written and evaluated by the investor, a large percentage of those plans are rejected, too. Further rejections are made after the oral presentation.

A final evaluation is generally made three to six months following the oral presentation, after the investors have conducted background checks on the management team and discussed the business with experts in the field as well as with suppliers, customers, and competitors of the business. This process is called *due diligence*.

Dealing with Failure

You can use this experience as a positive opportunity, even if you are turned down because of the early stage of the business. Also, the investor may know another interested party. Always ask:

- ✔ Who else may be interested?
- ✔ Do you have a contact name?
- ✔ If we do not receive funding now, can we count on you for later financing?

Your Agreement

Once accepted, you will begin to negotiate the final financing agreement that includes ownership, control, and financial objectives.

Ownership ranges from 10 percent (profitable companies) to 90 percent (financially troubled firms). Most investors, however, do not want to own more than 50 percent of a business. They want the new business to be managed as an entrepreneurial concern by its current managers.

Control usually remains with you and your management team. However, the investor will generally ask for representation (occasionally, major representation) on your board of directors or for your board of directors to have some say in important decisions.

Profits realized are by either a corporate acquisition or a public stock offering. This is done within three to seven years of the investment. Such provisions are discussed when you negotiate your long-term financial objectives with the investor.

Your Equity Deal

Finally, negotiate the equity positions for you and the team. This is always subject to negotiation.

Two key concerns in equity:

1. Determining the valuation of the business.
2. Determining the return for the investor, which is actually dictated by the value of the business.

You want the investor to value the company for what it will be worth in three to seven years (i.e., a corporate acquisition or an initial public offering). This is important in order to determine how an investment today will be worth more tomorrow. Obviously, all investors are interested in maximizing the return on their investments. The larger the ownership position, the greater the potential return. See Chapter 7 for valuation methods.

GUIDE TO SELECTING A VENTURE CAPITALIST

1. *Scrutinize the business with a critical eye.* Can it give the returns that a venture capitalist demands? Work out solid financial projections to prove the results to the venture capitalist.

2. *Beef up management.* Venture capitalists invest in start-ups, but they don't want unseasoned executives. Everyone has strengths and weaknesses. Hire staff who can make up the deficits.

3. *Keep a high profile so the VCs will visit.* For example, Edison Venture Fund, a venture capital firm in Lawrenceville, New Jersey, initiates contact with about 35 percent of the companies it funds. "We've already heard good things about the company and have researched their potential," says managing partner John Martison, who also serves as chairman of the National Association of Venture Capitalists.

4. *Target the search.* Look for firms that specialize in the industry and the size of investment.

5. *Keep a lookout.* Look for smaller VC firms that may be more flexible and more receptive to investing in a company.

6. *Investigate possible venture partners.* Treat the method of locating venture capitalists as if they were customers. Find out what the needs are for the venture capitalist so when a visit is made, the meeting can be more successful.

Timing

Timing is critical, and it is important that the business not delay looking for capital by waiting until it has a serious cash shortage. For a start-up, especially one with no experience or success in raising money, it is unwise to delay looking for capital since it is likely to take six months or more to raise capital. In addition to the problems with cash flow, the lack of planning implicit in waiting until there is a cash shortage can undermine the credibility of a management team and negatively impact its ability to negotiate with investors.

On the other hand, do not try to obtain capital too early, because doing so may cause the equity position of the founders to be unnecessarily diluted, and the discipline instilled by financial leanness may be eroded.

The right investor can add value in a number of ways, such as:

- ✔ Identifying and helping recruit key management team members and providing key industry and professional contacts.
- ✔ Serving as a mentor, confidant, and sounding board for ideas and plans to solve problems or quicken growth.
- ✔ Helping to establish relationships with key customers or suppliers, or both.
- ✔ Having "deep pockets" to participate in and syndicate subsequent rounds of financing.

Your Exit Plan—Being Acquired

Every high-tech entrepreneur dreams of being the next Bill Gates. That means going public. But in the world of high tech, even that is changing. The preferred exit strategy has shifted from an IPO to an acquisition. Silicon Valley's top venture capital firm, Kleiner, Perkins, Caufield & Byers, managed only six IPOs last year, compared with 11 the year before.

Entrepreneurs increasingly start enterprises with the express purpose of being bought out, often without having to demonstrate sound fundamentals first. So how does an entrepreneur sustain a business as it loses money?

✔ Some high-tech companies classify new equipment as upgrades so the customer can maintain its depreciation schedule. Depreciation is an accounting entry, not a cash burner.

✔ Real growth in the high-tech sector comes from acquiring stock in other companies. As earnings rise, this gets cheaper. If the share price dips, this system falls apart.

✔ Any successful company, whether based on ideas or on goods, needs a sound business model, strong market position, good management, and a low cost of attracting and keeping customers. It's the least that companies should offer potential investors.

Due Diligence Process

This involves the investor completely investigating and evaluating the risks of the investment. The process for the investor takes from 90 to 120 days so that all aspects of the product, market, management, financial, and exit strategies can be examined. The following checklist for a proposed transaction identifies the complexity of the process.

CHECKLIST FOR EVALUATING A COMPANY

Corporate Organization

✔ Incorporation documents and other organizational papers.

✔ List of places in which the company is qualified to transact business.

✔ List of directors and officers, including brief description of current duties and current compensation.

✔ Minutes books, including all shareholder, director, and committee minutes and written consents.

✔ List of stock options, *warrants*, and purchase plans, including copies of any agreements.

Real Property

✔ List of all owned property and locations (and mortgages or trust deeds related to them).

✔ List of all leases and subleases of real property.

✔ List of all *liens* or encumbrances against real property.

✔ Copies of any appraisals of real property owned or leased.

✔ Copies of any assignment of leases made for security purposes or otherwise.

✔ Copies of any engineering reports prepared regarding real property owned or leased.

✔ Copies of any guarantees or warranties relating to improvements on real property.

✔ Copies of any outstanding notices of violation.

✔ List of condemnation or eminent domain proceedings pending or threatened against real property.

Plant and Equipment

✔ List of machinery and equipment, motor vehicles, office furniture, fixtures, and inventory, and locations where kept, including a complete list of motor vehicles used or operated by the company.

✔ Copies of all contracts or options to purchase, sell, or lease material personal property.

✔ Copies of all installment contracts for the purchase of personal property or equipment.

Contracts

✔ Copies of all agreements for the purchase or lease of capital equipment, in excess of $5,000 for any one agreement.

✔ Copies of all agreements for their performance of services.

warrant
an option to buy a certain amount of stock for a stipulated price that is transferable—it can be traded.

lien
an interest of a creditor in any real assets or property as security for repayment of credit. A legal claim against property.

✔ Copies of all agreements relating to the borrowing of money or extension of credit, promissory notes, indentures, lines of credit, letters of credit, security agreements, and guarantees.

✔ Copies of all sales agency or representative, manufacturer representative, distributorship, and franchise agreements.

✔ Copies of all requirements, output, and supply contracts.

✔ Copies of all product development contracts.

✔ Copies of all joint venture agreements.

✔ Copies of all stockholder agreements, voting trust agreements, and other voting agreements.

✔ Copies of any acquisition or merger agreements.

Litigation

✔ List of all pending or threatened lawsuits, claims, and assessments, as well as unasserted claims and assessments, indicating those for which insurer has accepted liability.

✔ Copies of all judgments, decrees, final orders, rulings, injunctions, and temporary orders.

✔ List of all patent infringement claims or other claims with respect to intellectual property asserted by or against the company.

Insurance

✔ List and copies of all current insurance policies and commitments, including personal injury, property, product liability, casualty, key person, and directors/officers.

Intangible Property

✔ Copies and a list of all pending applications for patents, trademarks, trade names, copyrights, and other intellectual property rights.

✔ Copies and a list of all inventions and invention disclosures.

Tax

✔ Copies of any notices from state or local authorities regarding returns deficiency claims with regard to income, sales, property, or other taxes.

✔ List and brief description of any ongoing tax disputes, together with copies of revenue agents' reports, correspondence, and so on.

Financial

✔ List of bank accounts and average balances.

✔ Copies of credit reports from banks and Dun & Bradstreet.

✔ List of statement of inventories.

✔ List of offices where records relating to receivables are kept.

✔ List of aged accounts receivable and description of credit and collection policies.

✔ Copies of feasibility studies, strategic planning documents, and financial forecasts.

SUMMARY

Depending on your funding needs, you face a number of options to use for funding. To increase your chances of success, you must know what sources are available and understand the procedures of the financial partners. Preparing a business and financial plan before beginning the search helps you to determine which sources would be most likely to assist in capitalizing the business.

This chapter examined the many sources of capital. Initial attention was given to debt and equity financing in the form of bank home equity loans and various forms of equity instruments.

Venture capital has advantages and disadvantages as a source of equity capital. Although large amounts of money can be raised in short periods of time, you will sacrifice a degree of control and ownership.

The venture capital market has grown dramatically. Billions of dollars are now invested annually to seed new ventures or help fledgling enterprises grow. The individuals who invest these funds are known as venture capitalists.

Venture capitalists use a number of different criteria when evaluating new-venture proposals. In the main, these criteria focus on two areas: the entrepreneur and the investment potential of the venture. The evaluation process typically involves four stages: initial screening, business plan evaluation, oral presentation, and final evaluation.

Recently, the informal risk capital market has begun to play an important role in new-venture financing. Everyone with money to invest in new ventures can be considered a source for this type of capital. Some estimates put the informal risk capital pool at more than $5 billion. Entrepreneurs who are unable to secure financing through banks or public stock offerings typically turn to the informal risk capital market by seeking out friends, associates, and other contacts who may have (or know of someone who has) money to invest in a new venture.

Private placements are an alternative means of raising equity capital. This source is often available to entrepreneurs seeking venture capital in amounts from $2 to $5 million.

ADDITIONAL RESOURCES—
VENTURE CAPITAL GUIDES

Association of Venture Capital Clubs
P.O. Box 3358
Salt Lake City, UT 84110
(801) 364-1100

The Capital Network, Inc.
3925 West Braker Lane, Suite 406
Austin, TX 78759
(512) 305-0826

National Venture Capital Association (NVCA)
1655 North Fort Meyer Drive, Suite 400
Arlington, VA 22209
(703) 351-5269

Pratt's Guide to Venture Capital Sources
Stanley E. Pratt
Venture Economics, Inc.
75 Second Avenue, Suite 700
Needham, MA 02194

Seed-Capital Network, Inc.
8905 Kingston Pike, Suite 12
Knoxville, TN 37923
(423) 573-4655

Chapter

Bank Loans and Debt Financing

Objectives

1. Know how to use commercial banks to acquire a loan.
2. Understand how to write a loan proposal.
3. Know how to apply for a loan.
4. Build a relationship with your banker.
5. Understand the other sources of debt financing and government loan programs.

INTRODUCTION

Entrepreneurs face few choices of where to find start-up capital. Usually, the company starts by raising capital from personal savings of the owners and/or from family or friends. Bank loans come at a later point. However, it is important to understand in this chapter debt financing and the financial possibilities appropriate for the business. Bank loans, commercial banks, loan proposals, and government sources are some of the major terms used in the search for *debt capital*. If you need debt financing from a commercial lending institution, this section will provide a range of credit options from which to make a choice. Not all of these sources are equally favorable. From a bank's perspective, the most important consideration is the degree of certainty that

 debt capital
funds or assets acquired by borrowing.

Profile: Lisa Abrams, Founder of Music Sounds Inc.— Shopping for a Loan

Lisa Abrams started her first company out of her dorm room in college 13 years ago and landed her first line of credit for $50,000 four years later. It took Lisa a long time to realize that the bank was really interested in supporting her only because of her public-relations value to the bank as a minority and female business owner. It wasn't because the bankers really understood or believed in her business concept.

The more aggressively she pursued growth, the more the bank rejected her demands for a loan. The company, a mail-order house for instruments, grew in sales dramatically to $4 million in revenues, but the margins were slim. Six years ago she established a new market in the instrument-rental business that serves local schools. This time the margins were much higher, so she decided to apply for a loan and received approval for a $1 million-plus loan package. The approval was based on the track record of her first company, personal commitment to secure assets, and signing personally on the note. Her advice: "If you're unhappy with your banker, move on quickly. If he or she only wants to support you because you're a woman, minority, or whatever, don't waste your time. And above all else, don't expect a bank to know what's best for your business. You've got to know that and how to communicate it to them."

a loan will be paid back on the agreed schedule of intent and timing. Additionally, in this chapter we will describe what lenders look for in preparing a loan proposal and the guidelines to improve your chances for a loan approval.

HOW TO USE COMMERCIAL BANKS

Most commercial loans are made to small businesses and are either unsecured or secured loans. An unsecured loan is a personal or signature loan that requires no collateral. The loan is granted on the background and strength of the borrower's reputation. Loans are made at fair market interest rates if you can demonstrate that the business is sound. To most banks, that will mean having an operating history of at least two or three years. Banks often require that the borrower maintain appropriate deposits with them. In addition, most banks will require personal guarantees for newer companies. Secured loans are those with security pledged to the bank that the loans will be paid. There are several types of security and collateral used in loans:

- ✔ Comaker: person who signs as secondary principal.
- ✔ Endorser: person who pledges to back loan.
- ✔ Guarantor: person who personally guarantees loans.
- ✔ Real property: real estate, leaseholds, and land.
- ✔ Securities: stock and bonds that can be pledged.
- ✔ Equipment: capital assets that include machinery, computers, and instrumentation.
- ✔ Inventory: usually finished goods.
- ✔ Accounts receivable: items receipted as sold with verifiable credit outstanding.
- ✔ Insurance policies: cash surrender value of policies.

Not all commercial banks are willing to loan to early-stage businesses. In most instances, you must seek loans through community banks that make it their business to serve the small business sector. Community banks are independently chartered and serve local clients; consequently, they thrive on small businesses. You should first find out which banks are most active in making loans in your state. If no local institutions are available, reference the Small Business Administration Publication for friendly out-of-state banks. Many of the 567 banks that make business loans of less than $100,000 cross the state lines in the process. Also, you should reference the SBA's report on small business lending in the United States, which ranks about 9,000 commercial banks by state based on their lending practices. Other reports are available at www.sba.gov/adov/ lending/nusz or at (800) 827-5722. You may also want to visit www.entrepreneur/money/bestbank for a recent listing of the banks friendlier to small businesses.

HOW TO WRITE A LOAN PROPOSAL

All bankers want to hear how the loan they will provide will improve the worth of the company. Address your presentation to this question and you will improve your chances of coming away with the loan. A loan proposal consists of eight parts. Using the information from your business plan, shift the emphasis toward your new audience to convert it to a loan proposal. Here are some guidelines to prepare a loan proposal:

1. *Summary.* On the first page, give your name and title, company name and address, nature of business, amount sought, purpose, and source of repayment.

2. *Management Team Profiles.* Prepare a biography on yourself and the management team with background, education, experience skills, areas of expertise, and accomplishments. Bankers seek their ultimate security in experienced management.

3. *Business Description.* Provide details on the legal structure, number of employees, union status, and current business assets. Define the products and markets as well as customers and competitors. Describe your inventory in terms of size, rate of turnover, and market ability. Report the status of your accounts receivable and accounts payable.

4. *Projections.* Show the projections on your current share of the market and describe how you plan to exploit these opportunities for the next three years. List your alternative and fallback plans. Prepare a realistic timetable for achieving your goals. Bankers judge your plans and goals in terms of your industry's practices and trends.

5. *Financial Statements.* Prepare a balance sheet and income statement for the past three years (if available). Bankers are more comfortable with audited statements. If you can't afford a full audit, ask your accountant for a financial review. While less convincing than an audit, this new intermediate procedure gives your banker more assurance than an unaudited statement. Prepare two sets of projected

balance sheets as well as income and cash flow statements, one predicated on receiving the loan and the other on going forward without it. Although critical to proving your claim that the loan will increase company worth, your projections must be realistic. Bankers match projections against published industry standards, searching for padded earnings and meager cost estimates. Personal financial statements, including tax returns for the past three years, must also be submitted, since your own net worth is a factor. Bankers check your personal credit rating in addition to your company.

6. *Purpose.* State your purpose for the loan. A request for working capital will elicit questions, not money. Instead, explain what the working capital is for (e.g., to build up Christmas inventory by increasing production starting in late summer).

7. *Amount.* Ask for the precise amount needed to achieve your purpose, and support your figures with estimates or previous cost figures. Do not ask for a high amount, expecting your request to be negotiated. Bankers know costs. They will verify all requested amounts.

8. *Repayment Plans.* The asset must match the loan. Any asset you want to finance must last at least as long as the loan period. Also, the asset should generate the repayment funds by increasing sales, slashing costs, or heightening efficiency. Weaving these into a repayment schedule is a complex task, but you won't be required to do it all yourself. Lending officers anticipate calls for advice on this and all other elements of your loan proposal. They look to you to be an expert only on your business; however, you will be expected to come in with all the requisite financial data.

HOW TO APPLY FOR A LOAN

When lenders consider a loan request, they concentrate on what are sometimes referred to as the "four Cs" of credit: character, cash flow, collateral, and (equity) contribution.

Lenders are looking for the ability of a company to repay its debt. No matter how big a hit a company is, usually a lender has only the promise of being rewarded with steady payments of principal and interest. While a borrower may become a better customer of the bank as the business grows, the bank will not necessarily prosper in direct proportion to the company's success.

Character

Character is a crucial element in an individual's attempt to secure a loan. Character is of course a subjective, "soft" criterion that enters into the lender's decision process. But, nonetheless, the lender must have confidence in the individual he or she is dealing with or the lender won't go forward with the venture. Such traits as talent, reliability, and honesty are used as they try to describe character.

One slice of character that is always used is credit history. Credit history in terms of a commercial loan is a one-way street. A bad credit rating will often eliminate a potential new business out of the credit-obtaining box. A good credit history, on the other hand, will do little on the positive side.

In the final analysis, even with your positive credit history, a banker's decision comes down to intuition. How capable is this individual? Will he or she run the business ethically and keep the bank honestly appraised of the real status of the business? How much faith can the bank have that this individual can successfully run a business and pay the monthly debt service?

Cash Flow

Banks need to be satisfied that cash flow will be adequate to cover debt service throughout the term of the obligation. Most loans are structured with interest and principal payments due every month beginning in month one. In some instances principal payments can be deferred, but usually no more than a year.

The business must be solid to meet debt service and

operating obligations, and still have enough available cash to address uncertainties. You must remember that projections are imperfect and must therefore provide for deviations. Lenders will want to be assured that the margin for error has been considered and provided for amply.

Effectively projecting cash flow requires sound judgment and intuition. However, you should project cash flow with sensitivity to industry norms and standards, and give a logical explanation if the plan shows a projected departure from these norms.

Collateral

No good lender will make a decision to loan money based solely on strong collateral. But every good lender will try to get the best collateral possible on the loan. This normally involves securing the lender's interest by liens or mortgages against tangible assets such as real estate or equipment. In addition, most lenders will require your personal signature as evidence of the borrower's real commitment to the business.

As an example, one may keep personal assets in the name of other family members, most often a spouse or child. Also, a lender cannot take assets held jointly by spouses unless the lender has both spouses' signatures on the note. Incidentally, most lenders will ask for both signatures if the collateral is insufficient. The issues related to personal liability and loan repayment are complex, and it is often important to have advice from a lawyer when making borrowing arrangements.

You will generally be required to have some type of collateral to support the loan. The types of securities that are used for collateral include:

- ✔ Endorsers or comakers (cosigners).
- ✔ Accounts receivable.
- ✔ Assigned leases.
- ✔ Real estate.
- ✔ Stocks and bonds.
- ✔ Life insurance.
- ✔ Personal savings.

Contribution

Almost all lenders require a significant commitment by you to ensure the success of the financing. Your financial contribution also serves to reduce the lender's exposure relative to the deal's total size. This provides a cushion to allow the lender to come out "whole" in the event of default.

In addition, different industries customarily have different ratios of debt to equity, commonly known as leverage. Some industries have traditionally been highly leveraged with debt three to four times greater than equity, often because of high success rates and good collateral. Real estate and the apparel industries are good examples of highly leveraged businesses. An unusually high failure rate and/or poor collateral may result in relatively low leverage in an industry, as exemplified by the restaurant business. Because of these varieties it is difficult to generalize as to how much you must contribute to a venture.

ESTABLISHING THE TERMS OF DEBT

The term of the debt (the length of time over which the obligation is amortized or paid off) usually depends on the life of the asset financed. A lender who really wants to make a deal can give some latitude in order to structure the debt so that the deal makes sense economically and cash flow is sufficient to amortize the debt. Working capital loans are usually paid off over the shortest periods of time, and real estate loans are usually paid off over the longest. Remember, the longer the term is, the lower the monthly payment (principal and interest) will be, but there will be more monthly payments, more interest accruing, and more money paid in total to meet the debt requirements. Failure to meet interest payment typically constitutes loan default. Normally, on default, the entire principal amount outstanding becomes immediately due.

Rates

Most business debt today is provided at a variable interest rate, usually fluctuating with the prime rate (the rate banks charge their best customers). This rate is usually quoted as "prime plus" multiplied by percentage points, often 0.5 percent to 2 percent, but it can be as much as 3 percent or even 4 percent above prime, depending on risk and other variables that motivate the lender. This rate can change as often as the prime rate changes; therefore, each monthly payment can be different.

There will also be other covenants, rules, and restrictions to the loan, which may restrict your freedom of management. This can include not giving raises to senior management without lender's approval or not obtaining further financing without the lender's approval.

The loan officer will make a determination of your financial position based largely on your earnings statement and balance sheet, which measure growth potential and financial stability. The lender will be particularly interested in the company's net worth or *equity* as well as general information on:

equity
total assets minus total liabilities equals equity or net worth.

Receivables and Payables

✔ Accounts receivable turnover.

✔ Percentage of total accounts owed by your largest account.

✔ Reserve for doubtful accounts.

✔ Condition of your clients' payables.

✔ Ratio of debt to net worth.

Inventories

✔ Need for markdowns.

✔ Amount of raw material versus work in process versus finished goods.

✔ Obsolescence of inventory.

Fixed Assets

✔ Condition of equipment.

✔ Depreciation policy.

✔ Future plans for additional purchases.

BUILD A RELATIONSHIP WITH A BANKER

Setting up a checking account at a bank is one of the first steps in getting started. This will provide the opportunity to meet a loan officer who can be crucial in the development of the business. The best borrowing relationships often depend on a loan officer who knows your business and will take a personal interest in you and the company. You should consider the following questions before making a choice:

✔ How much lending authority does the banker have, and what is the approval process?

✔ Can the banker understand your business? Is there any interest in your business?

✔ What experience does the banker have with companies similar to yours?

Issues to Avoid

The following pitfalls are important for you to identify prior to building a relationship with your banker:

✔ *Picking the wrong bank and banker.* Some banks are much more aggressive in their lending practices, focusing on small companies. Others will do everything possible to avoid small business loans. Find a bank—and a banker—who understands the financial needs of small companies, especially those in your industry.

✔ *Being inadequately prepared to make loan requests.* Bankers expect more than just a handshake and a "Hi, I'd like to borrow $50,000 for my business" from entrepreneurs. They want to see a complete business plan and forecasts showing how the loan will benefit your company and exactly how you intend to repay it.

✔ *Paying too little attention to financial details, especially cash flow.* Even though financial projections are sometimes best guesses of what is likely to happen, they are an integral part of any loan request. Your banker wants to be sure that you understand the tools of financial management and cash flow analysis, because they are essential to business success.

✔ *Omitting a marketing plan.* An idea for a great product or service is meaningless without a solid marketing plan. You must include a customer-focused marketing plan as part of your loan request. It must explain how you plan to sell your product, how you will price it, to whom you will sell it, and why they will want to buy it.

✔ *Being overly optimistic.* Entrepreneurs are famous for being optimistic; bankers are equally famous for being pessimistic, especially when reading business plans and loan requests. Your business plan should be based in reality, not fantasy, and your financial projections should show this. "When you're looking at a business plan and someone projects astronomical growth in five years, you tend to think they're not someone that you really want to put a lot of faith in," counsels one bank executive.

✔ *Failing to sell the strengths of the management team.* Every banker would rather see a strong, experienced team of managers working together to make a company successful than a strong entrepreneur trying to do everything all alone. A solid business plan is essential, but you must have the management team to carry it out.

✔ *Failing to recognize problems and weaknesses.* Too often, entrepreneurs are tempted to gloss over or to omit totally their businesses' problems and weaknesses. Bankers, however, are very good at finding them. Omitting problems and weaknesses is a surefire way to lose all of your credibility with a banker. Emphasize your strengths, but be straightforward about your weaknesses, too.

OTHER SOURCES OF DEBT CAPITAL

As previously mentioned, banks are usually the first stop for entrepreneurs in search of debt capital, but they are not the only lending game in town. We now turn our attention to other sources of debt capital.

Factoring

Factoring is similar to asset-based lending. The only major difference is that the lender agrees to buy the account receivables. The factor advances 60 percent to 80 percent up front and takes over the responsibility of collecting from the borrower's clients. Factors charge a fee, commonly known as a discount. The fee varies from 2 percent to 4 percent and can increase to 15 percent or more if payments are overdue or not payable for several months.

The advantage of factoring is that money can be raised quickly and without other collateral. Also, since the factoring company acts as the accounts receivable department, costs can be cut in terms of hiring personnel who will be responsible for receivables.

The disadvantage is that it is more expensive than traditional financing because of the risk involved to the lender. The higher the risk, the more expensive the interest rate and the more expensive the financing. There is a direct correlation between risk and the cost of borrowing.

Purchase Order Financing—Venture Banks

When a company receives an order that requires the purchase of specific quantities of raw materials, the venture bank buys the needed materials and provides them to fill the purchase order. Unlike commercial banks that typically advance no more than 50 percent of inventory, venture banks are privately funded and often finance up to 100 percent of the cost of materials. Once the merchandise is shipped, the venture bank normally exits the transaction, turning the financing to a receivables lender.

Asset-Based Lending

This is similar to commercial bank lending. Similar to banks, asset-based lenders provide loans based on the collateral. Acceptable collateral includes accounts receivable, inventory, equipment, and real estate. The cost and timing factors of the loan depend on the type of collateral, the credit history of the firm, length of time in business, plus financial performance. Asset-based lenders are more flexible than banks and are cheaper than factor companies. Typically, asset lenders provide up to 80 percent financing against accounts receivable, 60 percent against inventory, or 75 percent against machinery and equipment. The more common types of *asset-based financing* are discounting accounts receivable and inventory financing.

 asset-based financing
financing an enterprise by using its hard assets for collateral to acquire a loan of sufficient size with which to finance operations. Widely used in leveraged buyouts (LBOs).

Discounting Accounts Receivable The most common form of secured credit is accounts receivable financing. Under this arrangement, the business pledges its accounts receivable as collateral. In return, the commercial bank advances the owner its loan against the value of approved accounts receivable. The amount of the loan tendered is not equal to the face value of the accounts receivable, however. Even though the bank screens the firm's accounts and accepts only qualified receivables, it makes an allowance for the risk involved, because some of them will be written off as uncollectible. A business can usually borrow from 55 percent to 85 percent of its receivables, depending on the quality. Generally, banks hesitate to finance past-due receivables, and no bank will accept accounts that are as much as 90 days past due.

As the firm receives payment from customers on accounts receivable, it transfers them to the bank. The bank subtracts an agreed-upon percentage of the proceeds, applies it to the loan balance, and then deposits the remainder in the firm's account. If an unusual number of accounts are uncollectible, the firm must make up the deficit to satisfy the loan.

The interest rate the bank charges on accounts receivable financing is normally higher than that charged on unsecured loans. But when the accounts receivable are pledged as collateral, no compensating balances (which raise the actual cost of borrowing) are required. Although the cost differential between the two methods appears to be substantial, a closer inspection shows it to be quite small. So, by pledging a security interest to its receivables to the bank, the firm is able to convert unpaid customer accounts into immediate cash, thus improving its liquidity and cash flow.

Inventory Financing A firm's inventory—raw materials, work in process, and finished goods—can serve as collateral for a small business loan. If the owner defaults on the loan, the bank can claim the firm's inventory, sell it, and use the proceeds to satisfy the loan (assuming the bank's claim is superior to the claims of other creditors). Because inventory is not a highly liquid asset in most cases, banks are willing to lend only a portion of its worth—usually no more than 50 percent of the inventory's value. Most asset-based lenders avoid inventory-only deals; they prefer to make loans backed by inventory and more secure accounts receivable.

GOVERNMENT PROGRAMS

There are more than 300 federal government programs that provide direct loans, grants, subsidiaries, and loan guarantees to small businesses. We will describe a few of these here. Our focus is on government agencies that account for a majority of small business assistance.

Small Business Administration (SBA) Loans

For a business that is looking for start-up funds, applying for an *SBA loan* is considered an alternative approach. Today the SBA is making loans for start-up businesses, most of which are for minorities and in special industries. The approach for SBA financing is first to locate a commercial or savings bank that is a certified SBA lender. The SBA does not directly fund the loan. What it does is guarantee up to 80 percent of the loan for the lending institution. The key advantage is to repay the note over an extended period of time. The SBA is not in the business of guaranteeing bad loans. Once the institution accepts the credit, it recommends the company to the SBA.

 SBA loan
loan providing SBA guarantee for 90 percent of a loan obtained from banking sources.

There are several types of financial assistance to obtain through private lenders and then guaranteed by the SBA. These programs, which vary somewhat from state to state, include regular loans and special loans.

Regular Loans Most of the regular SBA loans are made by private lenders (such as commercial banks, savings and loans, insurance companies, etc.) and then guaranteed by the SBA. The average size of a guaranteed loan is approximately $100,000 with a maturity of less than 10 years.

Special Loans   There are several types of these loans:

✔ *Local development company loans* to groups who want to improve the economy in their areas. The loan can be used to assist small businesses in the construction, expansion, and acquisition of plant or equipment.

✔ *Small general contractor loans* to assist small construction firms with short-term financing. Funds can be used to finance residential or commercial construction or rehabilitation.

✔ *Seasonal line of credit* guarantees to provide short-term financing for small firms with seasonal loan requirements.

✔ *Energy loans* to companies engaged in the manufacturing, selling, installing, servicing, or developing of energy measures.

✔ *Handicapped assistance loans* to owners of small businesses who are physically handicapped and to private nonprofit organizations that employ handicapped persons.

Qualifying for an SBA loan requires that the borrower meet the criteria for being classified as a small business. Usually any business will qualify if it has fewer than 25 employees and if its sales do not exceed $1 million; manufacturers and health service enterprises can qualify as long as they have fewer than 500 employees. However, SBA guidelines include numerous exemptions.

Borrowers must have appropriate collateral as security; the SBA does not accept unsecured applications. Collateral includes assets normally considered as security by lenders, including real estate, machinery, inventory, equipment, personal property, and receivables. The SBA will also consider as security cosigned endorsements by the guarantors. These are evaluated in the same manner they are evaluated by commercial lenders. The application must be accompanied by cash flow projections and several other documents together with a description of how the business will use the loan proceeds. See box for a summary of SBA application requirements.

When the loan is approved, the SBA will restrict the use of the money. For example, SBA loans cannot be used to repay past-due executive salaries or consolidate personal liabilities. They must underwrite operations or business expansion. As a result, the ability of the business to generate cash flow to repay the loan is the single most important consideration in the loan application.

Small Business Innovation Research (SBIR) Program

One of the best opportunities for loans is participation in the federally founded SBIR program. This program allocates in excess of $50 million annually to businesses with proposals for developing scientific innovation and has three phases:

✔ Phase I—There is a grant award up to $100,000 for the purpose of investigating the feasibility of an innovation. The award recipient has six months to

---

The SBA Loan Application

1. *Applicant Information.* Names of owners, backgrounds, addresses, business name, date started, and other statement of business.
2. *Use of Loan Proceeds.* Description of how the loan will be used in business operations.
3. *Collateral Pledged.* List of all business and personal assets to secure the loan.
4. *Disclosures.* List of existing or previous government financing, personal and business debts, bankruptcies, and lawsuits.
5. *Personal Balance Sheet.* Balance sheet on borrower(s).
6. *Financial Statements.* Cash flow, income, and use-of-funds statements.

prepare a feasibility plan that includes prototypes, market research, and developing a report.

✔ Phase II—The report is reviewed and, if feasible, an award of $1 million can be awarded for operating expenses. There is a two-year deadline to complete this phase, which can include further testing and market research. A report must be prepared to review the results that were achieved and how the funds were spent.

✔ Phase III—This is not a funded stage of the program. Funding for development and commercialization must be obtained through private financing.

How to Qualify To begin the process, remember that the SBIR receives more than 8,000 proposals each year with fewer than 1,000 grants being approved. Under the Small Business Innovation Development Act, applicants must be independently owned companies with 500 or fewer employees and be able to demonstrate the capability for scientific or technological research. Through the first eight years of SBIR grants, award recipients have had, on average, fewer than 35 employees with nearly half of all initial Phase I awards going to companies with fewer than 10 employees. The SBIR grant program provides operating money to companies and is not a loan. There is no assumption to repay the amount of the loan.

For more information on the SBIR program, contact:

Small Business Administration
Office of Innovation Research and Technology
1441 L Street, NW
Washington, DC 20416
(202) 653-6458

Other Government Financing Sources

The Farmers Home Administration (FmHA) provides guaranteed long-term loans for rural development. These loans are limited to applicants who reside in cities or rural areas with less than 50,000 population. Although FmHA is viewed as a farmer's program, it exists to help any rural enterprise with start-up working capital, equipment purchases, and expansion. The Department of Housing and

Urban Development (HUD) provides loans and grants for rehabilitation of city areas. HUD operates predominantly in metropolitan areas, and funds are administered through local authorities. Funds are used for remodeling downtown stores and refurbishing historic sites, as well as converting older buildings for residential and commercial use.

Small Business Investment Companies (SBICs) and Minority Enterprise Small Business Investment Companies (MESBICs) are licensed by the SBA and may provide management assistance as well as equity funding to emerging businesses. These loans are arranged through lenders, and regulations vary from state to state. They are targeted to businesses capable of enhancing economic growth within the state.

SUMMARY

In general, there are two types of funding sources: lenders and investors. The lenders we are generally referring to are commercial banks.

Commercial loans are given to small businesses that are called either unsecured or secured loans. An unsecured loan requires no collateral and is either a personal or signature loan. The unsecured loan is granted on the background and strength of the borrower's reputation. Loans are made at market interest rates or 1–2 percent above the prime rate. Most banks require that the company have operating and financial history of at least two or three years. Banks will also require personal guarantees for newer companies, and the borrower should maintain their business with the bank. In either case, banks tend to be cautious about lending and carefully weigh the four Cs of lending: character, cash flow, collateral, and contribution.

Banks always look for the ability of a company to repay its debt. Regardless of size, a lender has only the promise of being repaid with principal and interest. Banks want companies to become a better customer. However, as the business grows, the bank will not necessarily prosper in direct proportion to the company's success.

Opening a checking account at a bank is the way to begin. Establish a relationship with a loan officer who can be crucial in preparing a financial plan for the business.

The loan officer relationship should be based on knowing your business and taking a personal interest in you and the company.

You must also include a customer-focused marketing plan as part of your loan request. The plan must detail how you will sell the product, set the pricing, and why customers will buy the product or service. Also include a strong management group to demonstrate how the team will implement the plan.

The only difference between factoring and asset-based lending is that the lender agrees to buy the accounts receivable. Factors charge a fee, commonly known as a discount and will advance up to 80 percent up front. The fee varies from 2 percent to 4 percent and can increase to 15 percent or more if payments are not made on a regular basis.

Asset-based lenders provide loans based on collateral. Acceptable collateral includes accounts receivable, inventory, equipment, and real estate. The cost of the loan depends on the type of collateral, credit history of the company, number of years in business, and financial performance. Asset-based lenders are usually more flexible than banks and are cheaper than factors.

Accounts receivable financing is the most common form of secured credit. Usually, the business pledges its accounts receivable as collateral. In return, the commercial bank advances the owner its loan against the value of approved accounts receivable.

Not every entrepreneur will qualify under the bank's careful scrutiny. When this occurs, an alternative for an entrepreneur is the SBA-guaranteed loan. The SBA guarantees 80 percent of the loan, allowing banks to lend money to businesses that might otherwise be refused.

The Small Business Administration is the most active federal agency in assisting small businesses. Loans guaranteed by the SBA are the prevalent means of obtaining government support, but direct loan assistance is available under certain programs. The Small Business Innovation Research (SBIR) program provides direct grants to businesses engaged in scientific development. With an SBIR Phase I grant, entrepreneurs are provided up to $100,000 for development of feasibility plans; Phase II grants can be $1 million for commercialization of their innovations.

In the next chapter we will focus on the IPO process and how you can establish a valuation and price for your business.

ADDITIONAL RESOURCES— BANKING REFERENCES

American Bankers Association (ABA)
1120 Connecticut Avenue, NW
Washington, DC 20036
(800) 338-0626

Annual Statement Studies
Robert Morris Associates
1650 Market Street, Suite 2300
Philadelphia, PA 19103
(800) 677-7621

Dun & Bradstreet Corporation
3 Silvan Way
Parsippany, NJ 07054
(201) 605-6000

National Association of Small Business Investment
    Companies (NASBIC)
666 11th Street, NW
Suite 700
Washington, DC 20001
(202) 628-5055

Polk World Bank Directory
Polk Bank Services
Thompson Financial Services
1321 Murfreeboro Road
Nashville, TN 37217
(615) 889-3350

Thompson Bank Directory
Thompson Financial Services
4709 West Golf Road, 6th Floor
Skokie, IL 60076-1253
(847) 676-9600

The IPO Process (Going Public)

Objectives

1. Learn the process of launching an initial public offering (IPO).

2. Understand the advantages and disadvantages of going public.

3. Apply the techniques used in a valuation of a business.

4. Know when to use the various methods for valuations and what approach is best.

INTRODUCTION

Going public can mark a turning point in the life of a company by providing capital to fund fast growth, expanding through acquisition or merger, and having the ability to attract valuable employees. However, going public represents a rite of passage for a company and provides both benefits and obligations that should be carefully considered. The IPO process is a difficult task, because the pitfalls are numerous and stakes are high. Poor market timing and inadequate planning can jeopardize an IPO. The success stories we hear about are counterbalanced by many companies whose shares are dropping and that are experiencing management shakeouts. To increase the chances of successfully obtaining capital, you must know what sources are available and understand the operations of the various financial institutions. All of these issues will be addressed in this section.

This chapter is a management guide for going public. It contains discussions of a company's stages of growth, factors that determine success, and the IPO process. The IPO procedure is described together with information on working with the underwriters, registration statements, process road show, and professionals.

The key issue to confront when going public or raising private equity funds is to determine the company's value. The prepared valuation will determine the percentage of ownership of a company and the investment criteria.

EVALUATING HIGH-GROWTH BUSINESSES

In the discussions and evaluations of high-growth entrepreneurial businesses, Ernst & Young has segmented successful business models into five stages, driven by five key "accelerators of value." These accelerators are infrastructure, capital, e-business continuous strategy, talent, and alliances/acquisitions.

The accelerators help determine what stage of growth the company is positioned for and what issues need to be addressed. The accelerators for each stage are listed in Figures 7.1 through 7.5. You should match your stage of growth with the value accelerators and determine what key activities are required for your company.

Three commonly referred to growth stages that entrepreneurial companies progress through are:

✔ Emerging (or start-up).

✔ Rapid growth.

✔ Market leader.

At each stage of growth certain key activities and issues need to be addressed. These are the length of time in business, number of employees, rate of revenue growth, sources of financing, and market penetration. Consider your stage of growth and use these factors when answering the following questions:

✔ What activities do you need to address to move to the next stage of growth?

✔ Does your business strategy address each of these five accelerators?

Profile: Laurence N. Charney of Ernst & Young— The IPO Process

If the liquidity of an alternate currency (common stock) is your goal, Laurence Charney and his team at Ernst & Young, LLP can substantially improve your chances of achieving an IPO success. This experienced team of professionals is dedicated to helping entrepreneurial growth companies succeed. Larry qualifies his "go to market" targets as "gazelles," which are quick-moving companies poised for success. He also states that an experienced management team and its discipline to periodic planning will significantly contribute to the company's prospect of outperforming the market. Entering the public marketplace at the appropriate time in a company's life cycle is also crucial to predicting success. Whether a firm is owner-managed, venture-backed, or publicly held, Larry and his team work to help achieve the owner's goals.

Ernst & Young has led the charge for the past 15 years in providing services to companies journeying through the IPO process. Its entrepreneurial culture has fostered an environment to empower its professionals to align their thinking with that of the entrepreneur. As director of entrepreneurial services for Ernst & Young's metropolitan New York area and now as its area director of sales, Larry and his team have supported the marketplace and hundreds of clients in understanding the issues and challenges in their journeys.

Larry's current clients in the computer software, Internet services, retail/wholesale and media and advertising industries include Marvel Entertainment, Amdocs Inc., Computer Outsourcing Services Inc., and Donovan Data Systems Inc. Professional advice for these companies includes shareholder values and successes, strategy in evolving into the public marketplace, and defining the relevant procedures and issues. As specialists in SEC compliance, compensation, and management growth issues, he and his team have also assisted clients with succession and strategic planning.

The team of professionals will advise you on a winning methodology for financing alternatives, operating strategies, acquisitions, and divestitures along with personal wealth building. In today's economic environment, it is important to be linked to a company with the commitment, capabilities, and worldwide network of Ernst & Young.

Ernst & Young LLP (www.ey.com) provides assurance and advisory business services, tax services, and consulting for domestic and global clients. The firm has 30,000 people in 87 U.S. cities and is the founder and producer of the Entrepreneur of the Year awards program (see end of chapter). The firm is dedicated to accelerating the success of the world's best entrepreneurs.

FIGURE 7.1 Infrastructure.

Valuation Accelerators	Emerging	Rapid Growth	Market Leader	Sustained Market Leader/Reinvented
Infrastructure	Scalable Architecture	Connected Capacity	Connected Competitive Advantage	Extended Network Connections
Operations, Technology, and Facilities Build-Out Strategy ■ **Physical environment** (scalability, location optimization, lease vs. own) ■ **Systems and technology** (communications platforms: reliability, scalability, availability) ■ **Back office personnel and systems** (in-source vs. outsource) ■ **Logistics/supply chain arrangements** (connectivity, trust, reliability) ■ **Custom relationship management systems** (capacity, reliability, personalization)	■ Developing infrastructure critical to supporting the business model. ■ Designing a scalable infrastructure platform. ■ Estimating transaction volume and scaling for growth. ■ Make vs. buy decisions. ■ Outsourcing. ■ Use of incubation center. ■ Identifying strategic vs. nonstrategic infrastructure. ■ Best use of time and capital.	■ Forecasting and ensuring infrastructure adequacy to handle transaction volumes (i.e., technology, sales and marketing, supply chain, customers, and stakeholders). ■ Focusing on gaining more efficiency in business. ■ Building capacity ahead of the growth curve. ■ Optimal design location and ownership of physical (B&M) environment.	■ Leverage infrastructure for enhanced-platform competitive advantage. ■ Adapting infrastructure to identified new markets and opportunities. ■ Offer the leading connectivity experience (e.g., Amazon's one-click purchase capability). ■ New alliance/outsource models—partners want to work with the leaders (AOL and Wal-Mart, Ameritrade and Sprint). ■ Customer intimacy through data/technology convergence. ■ Rational experimentation. ■ Should have capital available to invest in R&D. ■ Ease and speed as competitive advantage—"nimbleocity."	■ Creating the necessary touch points in the market to broaden your infrastructure to include new delivery methods, new technology (i.e., wireless, live customer service, etc.). ■ Leader in coupling new technologies together to enhance position in market. ■ Capability anytime/anyplace.

FIGURE 7.2 Capital.

Valuation Accelerators	Emerging	Rapid Growth	Market Leader	Sustained Market Leader/Reinvented
Capital	Value for Idea	Value for Execution	Value for Leadership	Value for Innovation
Sourcing (alternative sources, accessibility, value-added) **Structure** (debt/equity mix, dilutions) **Leverage Intellectual Property** (identify, protect, value, consideration of tax jurisdiction) **Allocation** (dilution vs. funding, resource allocation, long term vs. short term) **Exit Strategy** (sale, IPO)	▪ Robust/unique and evolving business model. ▪ Business plan has attracted external interest and validation. ▪ Intellectual property strategy (e.g., identification, valuation, monetization, and protection). ▪ Product/service in development or operational stage. ▪ Early round(s) financing obtained. ▪ Target capital structure developed. ▪ Tax-advantaged structures considered. ▪ Capital allocation challenges balanced against ownership retention objectives.	▪ Assess next-stage capital requirements—fuel efficiency vs. speed. ▪ Capital sources/alternatives evaluated (e.g., equity joint ventures, public/private markets, merge/acquire, sell out). ▪ Value-added capital sources selected. ▪ Agreed-upon execution milestones. ▪ Build track record of achievement—perform.	▪ Established financial relationships. ▪ Significant cash flow. ▪ Sophisticated—combination of equity/debt. ▪ Tax-advantaged structure implemented. ▪ Strong financial brand (e.g., effective market awareness, investor relations, leading market capitalization). ▪ Financial engineering and staying power—stock viewed as a "long-term hold." ▪ Full/partial exit plan developed to provide required investor liquidity.	▪ Capital sourcing for reinvention: Utilize internal funds. Issue further stock offering in parent. Evaluate spin-offs and divestiture of noncore businesses; carve out new entity and finance independently. ▪ Enhance financial brand through continuous successful innovation. ▪ Leverage competencies and intangibles (e.g., brand, alliance network, knowledge, speed, and customer base).

FIGURE 7.3 e-Business Continuous Strategy.

Valuation Accelerators	Emerging	Rapid Growth	Market Leader	Sustained Market Leader/Reinvented
eBusiness Continuous Strategy	First-Mover Advantage	Market Creation/Capture	Brand Power	Network-centricity
Connectivity ▪ **Customers** (customer relationship management) ▪ **Suppliers, business partners, employees, shareholders** ▪ **Web presence** (user experience and quality) **Distribution** ▪ **Logistics, site selection, transportation, customs, shipping currency** **Relationship Transformation** ▪ **Efficiencies** ▪ **Speed** ▪ **Innovation** ▪ **New value creation** **Globalization** ▪ **Language, culture, distribution, regulatory**	▪ Align e-business efforts with corporate vision and core competencies. ▪ Create/reinvent new business model/value chain that incorporates e-business throughout all areas of the organization. ▪ Exchange information with suppliers, employees, customers, and business partners. ▪ Build e-business capabilities through acquisitions, technology, and people. ▪ Transfer trust-enabled environment to the Internet.	▪ Be recognized as a "category killer" (i.e., capture energy, attention, and market buzz). ▪ Capture and secure mind-share of market players. ▪ Expand market share and business opportunities through the creation of new business channels. ▪ Focus on customer/supplier attraction and satisfaction. ▪ Invest in and build on flexibility and scalability of business model. ▪ Expand use of web-based networks to complete buy/sell or data record transactions (i.e., create new sales channels, broaden supplier relationships, communicate with employees).	▪ Create ubiquitous brand. ▪ Be confident in the reliability of your infrastructure to support high volume and efficiency. ▪ Focus on retention of customer and supplier relationships through customization/unique identifiers. ▪ Extend business activities beyond the traditional enterprise boundaries (i.e., expand new competencies to extend to new market opportunities).	▪ Leverage brand and presence to create new markets (i.e., cobranding). ▪ Power other companies with your business models. ▪ Conduct business as participant in open marketplace environments; facilitate customer-centric solutions. ▪ Innovation—"Bringing the Silicon Valley Culture Inside."

FIGURE 7.4 Talent.

Valuation Accelerators / Talent	Emerging / Dream Team and Advisers	Rapid Growth / Impact of Players and Depth	Market Leader / Mission-Driven Culture	Sustained Market Leader/Reinvented / The Best Is Not Good Enough
Building the Best Team ▪ Assessment of skills needed ▪ Selection and recruiting ▪ Skill development ▪ Recognition, reward, and compensation (cash vs. equity) ▪ Retention ▪ Winning culture	▪ Assess mission-critical skills to launch the business. ▪ Identify alternative talent sources ("make vs. buy"). ▪ Attract initial team possessing passion, energy, innovation, commitment, and track record. ▪ Implement results-based compensation plan. ▪ Build culture and shared vision for future of the company. ▪ Establish board of directors and external advisory board. ▪ Select team of professional advisers (e.g., accountants, lawyers, etc.).	▪ Growth in business requires greater depth in team and delegation by founders. ▪ Recruiting web extends beyond relationships and referrals. ▪ Formalized human resources practices. ▪ Commitment to skill building, leadership, and people development. ▪ Protect, nurture, and evolve culture. ▪ Promote/reward innovation and risk. ▪ Sculpt responsibilities and compensation to retain "A" players.	▪ Assess capability of existing talent within new environment—retrain or replace as needed. ▪ Develop "bench strength" of leaders. ▪ Implement performance measurement systems. ▪ Assist management and employees to build and protect wealth. ▪ Your team becomes "the prey." ▪ Promote personal growth. ▪ Continue to cultivate the culture and communicate the vision.	▪ Acquire new skills necessary for reinvention (internal and external). ▪ Founder's ongoing role in company may evolve. ▪ Cultural change may be imperative. ▪ Prioritize and reinforce risk taking, innovations, and entrepreneurial spirit. ▪ Promote "nimbleocity." ▪ Free best employees to work on reinvented projects.

FIGURE 7.5 Alliances/Acquisitions.

Valuation Accelerators / Alliances/Acquisitions	Emerging — Mission-Critical Connections	Rapid Growth — Synergistic Acquisitions	Market Leader — Industry-Defining Alliances	Sustained Market Leader/Reinvented — Dynamic Information Partnerships
Valuation Accelerators ■ Make vs. Buy ■ Speed, Scale, Connectivity, and Intangibles ■ New Markets, Channels, and Solutions ■ e-Business Transformation Synergy ■ Cost Sharing/ Efficiency **Alliances/Acquisitions**	■ Establish business partner connections that are fundamental to the business model by design. ■ Scope boundaries of opportunity and clearly define competitive advantage. ■ Develop proactive alliances that credentialize and accelerate business model ("price of admission"). ■ Establish access to people, capital, information, technology, innovation, channels, and markets. ■ Compress time to market. ■ Share costs.	■ Acquire strategic/complementary organizations to build team, achieve scale, and fill gaps. ■ Broaden offering and enhance market position—faster. ■ Create new opportunities. ■ Use intellectual property leverage. ■ Reduce marketing and operating costs. ■ Accelerate R&D through acquired technologies. ■ Consolidate market position by acquiring competitors.	■ First-mover advantage—difficult for competitors to replicate. ■ Create unique and valuable capability (reshape/create new categories). ■ Help to redefine customer connections and loyalty (e.g., airline code sharing and frequent flier alliances). ■ Move to one-stop shopping. ■ 1 + 1 = 5. ■ Converge multiple mediums to create new channels. ■ Consolidation and roll-up.	■ Evaluate business model: raison d'être. ■ Seek appropriate strategic transaction. ■ "Company" as a destination. ■ Leverage market intelligence, customer information, and technology—networked "nimbleocity." ■ Bold moves/quantum leap(s). ■ Re-create value chain. ■ Continuous adaptation of business model to market dynamics. ■ Real-time customer-specific relationships identify competitive regimes.

    ✔ What other value accelerators—outside of these five—do you believe have a strong impact on the success of your business?

    ✔ How would you prioritize the issues identified today?

No company remains as a dominant market leader for long unless it is proactive in reinventing or extending its business model to serve new customers and markets or it delivers products and services in a new and innovative way. This is true of technology, dot-com companies, as well as the traditional bricks-and-mortar type of businesses. (See Figures 7.6 and 7.7)

DECIDING WHETHER TO GO PUBLIC

The number of initial public offerings exploded from 498 in 1998 to nearly 600 in 1999. Despite initial positive performance after the offerings, many companies discovered that the values recede soon after going public and underperform in both profits and share price.

The following questions need to be addressed in making an IPO decision:

    ✔ Are you ready to share the ownership of your company with the public?

    ✔ Are you prepared to disclose your company's most closely held secrets?

    ✔ Can you live with the continued scrutiny of investors and market analysts?

    ✔ Can you devote the 100 percent required of your time for six to eight months that it takes for a typical IPO?

    ✔ Are you prepared to take on the issues, challenges, and responsibility to go public?

FIGURE 7.6 Analysis of Figures 7.1 to 7.5.

Valuation Accelerators	Emerging	Rapid Growth	Market Leader	Sustained Market Leader/Reinvented
Infrastructure	Scalable Architecture	Connected Capacity	Connected Competitive Advantage	Extended Network Connections
Capital	Value for Idea	Value for Execution	Value for Leadership	Value for Innovation
e-Business Continuous Strategy	First-Mover Advantage	Market Creation/Capture	Brand Power	Network-centricity
Talent	Dream Team and Advisers	Impact of Players and Depth	Mission-Driven Culture	The Best Is Not Good Enough
Alliances/ Acquisitions	Mission-Critical Connections	Synergistic Acquisitions	Industry-Defining Alliances	Dynamic Information Partnerships

INFRASTRUCTURE
Operations, Technology, and Facilities Build-Out Strategy
- Physical Environment
- Systems & Technology
- Back Office Personnel and Systems
- Logistics/Supply Chain Arrangements
- Customer Relationship Management Systems

CAPITAL
- Sourcing
- Structure
- Leverage Intellectual Property
- Allocation
- Exit Strategy

ALLIANCES/ACQUISITIONS
- Make vs. Buy
- Speed, Scale, Connectivity, and Intangibles
- New Markets, Channels, and Solutions
- e-Business Transformation
- Synergy
- Cost Sharing/Efficiency

Business Model

e-BUSINESS CONTINUOUS STRATEGY
- Connectivity
- Distribution
- Relationship Transformation
- Globalization

TALENT
Building the Best Team
- Assessment of Skills Needed
- Selection and Recruiting
- Skill Development
- Recognition, Reward, and Compensaion (Cash vs. Equity)
- Retention
- Winning Culture

FIGURE 7.7 Business model.

BENEFITS AND OPPORTUNITIES

The benefits of going public are many and diverse. To determine whether they outweigh the drawbacks, you must evaluate them in the context of personal, shareholder, and corporate objectives. Some of the most attractive benefits include the following:

✔ *Improved financial condition.* Selling shares to the public brings equity money that does not have to be repaid, immediately improving the company's financial condition.

✔ *Benefits to the shareholder/investor.* Going public offers liquidity to existing investors despite the sales restrictions imposed on the major investors and officers and directors of the company. Underwriters will restrict founding stockholders and management from selling their sales through lock-up agreements for a specific period of time (normally 180 days); eventually they can convert their shares into cash. The value of the stock may increase remarkably, starting with the initial offering. Shares that are publicly traded generally command higher prices than do those that are not. There are at least three reasons why investors are usually willing to pay more for stock in public companies: (1) the marketability of the shares, (2) the maturity/sophistication attributed to public companies, and (3) the availability of more information.

✔ *Diversification of shareholder portfolios.* Going public makes it possible for shareholders to diversify their investment portfolios. IPOs often include a secondary offering (shares owned by existing shareholders) in addition to a primary offering (previously unissued shares). You must ensure that potential investors and shareholders do not perceive the secondary offerings as a bailout for shareholders. Underwriters frequently restrict the number of shares that can be sold by existing shareholders in a secondary offering.

✔ *Access to capital.* Accessing the public equity markets enables you to attract better valuations, accept less dilution of ownership, and raise more money. The money from an IPO can repay debt, fund special projects, and be used for acquisitions. For example, the proceeds can be used to acquire other businesses, repay debt, finance research and development projects, and acquire or modernize production facilities. Another plus is that raising equity capital through a public offering often results in a higher valuation for your company, through a higher *multiple* of earnings (or price-earnings ratio), as compared with many types of private financing. Thus, it often results in less dilution of ownership than with some other financing alternatives, such as venture capital. Raising capital in this way also avoids the interest costs and cash drain of debt financing.

 multiple a firm's price-earnings ratio. Used for quick valuations of a firm; for example, a firm that earns $5 million a year in an industry that generally values stock at 10 times earnings (multiple of 10) would be valued at $50 million.

✔ *Management and employees incentives.* The company can issue stock options to management and employees. This can be motivating and rewarding to employees and will attract and retain the key executives.

✔ *Enhanced corporate reputation.* The company's public status and listing on a national exchange can provide a competitive advantage over other companies in the same industry by providing greater visibility and enhanced corporate image. This can lead to increased sales, reduced pricing from vendors, and improved service from suppliers.

✔ *Improved opportunities for future financing.* By going public, a company usually improves its net worth and builds a larger and broader equity base. The improved debt-to-equity ratio will help you borrow additional funds as needed or reduce your current cost of borrowing. If your stock performs well in the continuing aftermarket, you will be able to raise additional equity capital on favorable terms. With an established market for your stock, you will have the flexibility to offer future investors a whole new range of securities with liquidity and an ascertainable market value.

✔ *A path to mergers and acquisitions.* Private companies often lack the financial connections and resources to assume an aggressive role in mergers and acquisitions. Well-conceived acquisitions can play a big part in corporate survival and success. A merger can be the route to instant product diversification and quick completion of product lines. It also can provide technical know-how, greater executive depth, economies of scale, improved access to financing, entry into otherwise closed markets, vertical integration of manufacturing operations, and new marketing strength. Going public enhances a company's financing alternatives for acquisitions by adding two vital components to its financial resources: (1) cash derived from the IPO and (2) unissued equity shares that have a ready market.

Public companies often issue stock (instead of paying cash) to acquire other businesses. The owners of an acquisition target may be more willing to accept a company's stock if it is publicly traded. The liquidity provided by the public market affords greater flexibility and ease in selling shares and using shares as collateral for loans.

DRAWBACKS OF A PUBLIC COMPANY

The benefits must be weighed against the drawbacks of going public. Here again, you must view the possible drawbacks in the context of your personal, company, and shareholder objectives. In many cases, you can minimize the impact of these drawbacks through thoughtful planning backed by the help of outside advisers.

✔ *Loss of control.* Depending on the proportion of shares sold to the public, you may be at risk of losing control of your company now or in the future. Retaining at least 51 percent of the shares will ensure control for now, but subsequent offerings and acquisitions may dilute your control. However, if the stock is widely distributed, management usually can retain control even if it holds less than 50 percent of the shares. You can also retain voting control by having a new class of *common stock* with limited voting rights. However, such stock may have limited appeal to investors and may therefore sell for less than ordinary common stock.

✔ *Sharing your success.* Investors share the risks and successes of your business when they contribute capital. If you realistically anticipate unusually high earnings in the next two or three years and can obtain bank or other financing, you may wish to temporarily defer a public offering. Then, when you do go public, your shares will command a higher price.

✔ *Loss of privacy.* Of all the changes that result when a company goes public, perhaps none is more troublesome than the loss of privacy. When your company becomes publicly held, the Securities

 common stock shares that represent the ownership interest in a corporation. Both common and preferred stock have ownership rights, but the preferred normally has prior claim on dividends and, in the event of liquidation, assets. Both common and preferred stockholders' claims are junior to claims of bondholders or other creditors. Common stockholders assume greater risk, but have voting power and generally exercise greater control. They may gain greater rewards in the form of dividends and capital appreciation. Common stock and capital stock are terms often used interchangeably when the company has no preferred stock.

and Exchange Commission (SEC) requires you to disclose much information about your company—information that private companies don't ordinarily disclose. And some of those disclosures contain highly sensitive information such as compensation paid to key executives and directors, special incentives for management, and many of the plans and strategies that underlie the company's operations. These disclosures rarely harm your business. For the most part, employee compensation and the price you pay for materials and receive for your products are governed by market forces—not by your disclosed financial results.

✔ *Limits on management's freedom to act.* By going public, management surrenders some degree of freedom. While the management of a privately held company generally is free to act by itself, the management of a public company must obtain the approval of the board of directors on certain major matters; and on special matters, it must even seek the consent of the shareholders. The board of directors, if kept informed on a timely basis, can usually be counted on to understand management's needs, offer support, and grant much of the desired flexibility.

✔ *The demands of periodic reporting.* Management is required to comply with SEC regulations and reporting requirements. These requirements include quarterly financial reporting (*Form 10-Q*), annual financial reporting (*Form 10-K*), and reporting of current material events (Form 8-K). Reporting requirements of a registrant demand significant time and financial commitments. Securities analysts will also demand management's time.

✔ *Initial and outgoing expenses.* Going public can be costly and will result in a tremendous commitment of management's time and energy. The largest single cost in an IPO ordinarily is the underwriter's discount or commission, which generally ranges from 6 percent to 10 percent of the offering price. In addition, legal and accounting fees, printing

Form 10-Q
the quarterly report required to be filed with the SEC.

Form 10-K
the annual report required to be filed with the SEC.

costs, the underwriter's out-of-pocket expenses (generally not included in the commission), filing fees, as well as registrar and transfer agent fees can typically add another $300,000 to $500,000. Costs depend on such factors as the complexity of the registration statement, the extent to which legal counsel must be involved, management's familiarity with the reporting requirements for a public company, and the availability of audited financial statements for recent years. These expenses generally are not deductible for income tax purposes. On the other hand, they also do not affect your reported net income because under generally accepted accounting principles (GAAP), they are treated as part of a capital transaction and thus deducted from the proceeds of the offering.

✔ *New fiduciary responsibilities.* As the owner of a private business, the money you invested and risked was your own. However, as the manager of a public company, the money you invest and risk belongs to the shareholders. You are accountable to them, so you must approach potential conflicts of interest with the utmost caution. It also will be necessary to work with your board of directors to help them discharge their fiduciary responsibilities when acting on corporate matters.

THE IPO EVENT

The IPO event follows many months of careful preparation. During the IPO, the president/CEO will serve as the company's major representative, delivering the company's story to the financial market. The CEO will be involved in setting the strategic direction for the SEC registration statement. As the registration statement is being drafted, the CEO can spend time providing high-level direction to the presentation of the upcoming road show.

The road show is your opportunity to tell the company's story to the people who will help sell your securities and influence potential investors. It will also allow you to meet many of the people who will follow your company after the public offering. This includes analysts and market makers that issue buy, sell, or hold recommendations on the company. The show is so challenging that no one can ever be completely prepared. The plan is to present a balanced view of your business, market, and competition, and why the company will be a huge success.

The IPO event usually lasts between 90 and 120 days, but some take up to six months. It includes preparing and filing your registration statement (and one to three amendments—responding to *comment letters* from the SEC), going on the road show, and the closing and buying of the company stock by the underwriting syndicate. Other events will include your first periodic reports, proxy solicitation, and dealing with restricted stock.

comment letter

a letter from the staff of the SEC describing deficiencies noted in its review of a registration statement. Comment letters request additional information or changes that must be made before the offering can become effective and the shares offered to investors.

Example of Timetable for an IPO

Day 1	First meeting ("all hands")
Day 45	Draft of registration statement
Day 55	Second meeting—revisions and agreement
Day 60	Filing of registration statement with the SEC
Day 90	Receipt of SEC comment letter
Days 70 to 100	The road show
Days 90 to110	Revisions and pricing
Day 115	Effective date
Day 120	Closing

REGISTRATION PROCESS

The registration process begins when you have reached an understanding with an underwriter on your proposed public offering. From this point on, you become subject to SEC regulations on what you may and may not do to promote your company. The center of the process is preparing the registration statement, which includes:

✔ A complete description of the company, its business, the market for its products, and the regulatory environment in which it operates. This entails establishing the appropriate internal accounting policies for the business, systems, management, and preparing the required financial data, including highlights and timing. The financial statements must be audited and should reflect income statements for the preceding three years, balance sheets for the prior two years, and interim financial statements for the applicable periods.

✔ The company's officers and directors, and their biographies, compensation, and stock ownership. Other factors to consider are employment contracts, compensation, and board of directors.

The first step in preparing the registration statement is the initial meeting or "all hands," which includes company executives, attorneys, auditors, underwriters, and underwriters' attorneys. At this meeting, responsibility is assigned for gathering information and for preparing the various parts of the registration statement. Typically, the attorneys play a coordinating role in directing this team effort.

The registration statement is usually approved by company counsel and has comments from the underwriter, management, and company accountants. The prospectus, which is a part of the registration statement, becomes the marketing document for the IPO.

EDGAR online
Electronic data gathering for SEC filings.

Filing the Statement

When outstanding issues have been resolved and the company officers and majority of the board of directors have signed the registration statement, it is filed with the SEC (normally electronically) on the SEC's *EDGAR* system. In addition to filing with the SEC, the statement is also filed with any state in which the securities will be offered and with the National Association of Securities Dealers (NASD). At closing, documents are executed and *stock certificates* are exchanged. Usually company officers, counsel, transfer agent, and managing underwriters attend the final closing. The rules also require a final prospectus be delivered to all purchasers of the company stock.

stock certificate
a document issued to a stockholder by a corporation indicating the number of shares of stock owned by the stockholder.

THE ROAD SHOW

After your registration statement has been filed, the underwriters generally will take representatives of your company on a traveling road show, also referred to as a "dog-and-pony show," to meet with interested investors. These meetings give prospective members of the underwriting syndicate, institutional investors, and industry analysts an opportunity to meet your company's management team and ask questions about your offering and your company.

The participants probably will be the company's chief executive officer and chief financial officer, whose major task will be to generate interest in the investors, and the investment bankers, who will manage the tour and monitor the book, or computerized log of orders. Typically, the road show consists of between five and seven back-to-back meetings every day for two weeks. The question-and-answer period is equally important and requires extensive preparation. If you anticipate the most challenging questions and welcome them, you will have a chance to turn what might have been an issue into a nonissue.

The preparation for the road show should include:

- ✔ Development of a precise, 20- to 25-minute slide presentation. Detail the company's business, strategy, financial history, management, growth prospects, market, and regulatory environment.
- ✔ Determination of which management personnel will present material and field questions.
- ✔ Education of the underwriters' team.
- ✔ Dry run of the road show presentation before institutional sales and corporate finance presentations are given at selected locations.

EXPENSES OF GOING PUBLIC

Dealing with the SEC

Be prepared to discuss and answer the current hot topics in dealing with the SEC:

✔ Revenue recognition policies.

✔ Stock option accounting and valuations.

✔ Accounting for intangible assets.

✔ Accounting for acquisitions.

✔ Restructuring charges.

✔ Depreciation and amortization.

Underwriters' Compensation

The underwriters will receive a discount (spread) between the price at which they buy stock and the price at which the underwriters sell the same stock to the public. The amount of the spread is negotiated based on the size and risk of the offering. A typical firm commitment offering discount is approximately 7 percent of the public offering price of the stock.

Underwriters may also be granted warrants as partial compensation for an offering. Other compensation may include reimbursement of expenses, rights of first refusal on future underwriting, directorships, and consulting arrangements.

Accounting and Legal Fees

The lawyers' and accountants' fees depend on the amount of work involved in preparing the registration statement and reviewing the financial statements and other financial data. The company should endeavor to do as much of the work of preparing the registration statement as possible in order to cut costs.

Directors' and Officers' Insurance

Before going public, a company needs to take out a personal liability insurance policy that will protect the officers and directors from being held personally liable if a shareholder suit is brought based on incorrect information in the registration statement.

Printing Costs and Filing Fees

Printing expenses will depend on the extent and frequency of revisions in response to SEC comments and the number of printed prospectuses needed for circulation. The SEC filing fee for fiscal 1999 was $278 per million of the maximum aggregate price at which the securities were proposed to be offered, and the NASD fee is $500 plus 0.01 percent of gross proceeds of the offering. The listing fee varies depending on the exchange.

Selecting the Underwriter

The underwriter that manages the offering will play a critical role in the success of the IPO. The role is to prepare the company's registration statement and sell the company's securities. In selecting an underwriter, the following factors are important:

1. *Experienced Industry Analyst.* The underwriter should have an experienced analyst in IPOs and the industry you are in.
2. *Synergy.* The company should feel comfortable with the individual bankers. The right synergy between the bankers and management is important.
3. *Distribution.* The investment bank should have the resources of a retail sales force to sell the stock.
4. *Post-IPO Support.* The underwriter should have a strong record of post-IPO price performance of companies it has recently taken public. A solid track record will indicate how well the investment bank priced recent transactions.

Leading the IPO Market

The major venture capital and investment banks for 1999 that lead the IPO market are described in Figures 7.8 and 7.9. Figure 7.8 details the aftermarket increase by percentage and the revenue worth in billions for the number of IPOs. Figure 7.9 details the proceeds derived and the number of IPOs for each of the major investment firms.

FIGURE 7.8 Venture capital firms/capital gains of 1999.			
Name	Aftermarket Increase (%)	Aftermarket Increase ($B)	Number of IPOs
Lucent Technologies	2,636.6	71.8	3
Crosspoint Venture Partners	1,773.5	117.6	8
Institutional Venture Partners	1,440.4	91.1	11
VantagePoint Venture Partners	1,195.8	33.7	6
AT&T Ventures	1,170.2	60.5	9
H&Q Venture Associates	1,011.4	31.8	7
New Enterprise Associates	955.0	66.4	20
Weiss, Peck & Greer Venture Partners	953.8	27.4	7
Cisco Systems	869.6	35.0	5
Amerindo Investment Advisors	810.0	66.3	10

Source: Red Herring. Reprinted with permission.

FIGURE 7.9 Investment banks of 1999.		
Manager	Proceeds ($M)	Tech Issues
Morgan Stanley Dean Witter	4,754.8	34
Goldman Sachs	4,297.4	34
Credit Suisse First Boston	3,846.6	45
Donaldson, Lufkin & Jenrette	2,341.6	28
Robertson Stephens	2,289.2	39
J. P. Morgan	2,103.1	4
Merrill Lynch	2,088.3	17
Lehman Brothers	1,579.7	19
Deutsche Bank Alex. Brown	1,562.8	22
Bear Stearns	1,403.1	19

Source: Red Herring. Reprinted with permission.

PREPARING A VALUATION FOR YOUR COMPANY

The key issue you will confront when going public with an IPO or raising equity funds is determining a value of the company. This valuation will determine how much the new investors will receive for funding the company. This is first considered by understanding the factors that make up valuation.

Key Factors in Valuation

The main factors in any valuation are the history, characteristics, and industry in which the business operates. This provides the strength and weakness of the company and risks in investing in the business.

Another financial factor to consider in the analysis is comparing your company to other companies in the industry. This can include the price-to-earnings ratio of similar companies and understanding the financial condition of the company. Usually, future earnings capacity is calculated by weighing the most recent earnings higher than previous year's earnings.

The last valuation factor is the stock price of similar companies in your industry. This valuation factor is used in the earnings valuation as described in this chapter.

WHAT IS THE BUSINESS WORTH?

There are several methods used for valuing a business: asset valuation, earnings valuation, and cash flow valuation. Let's examine each of these.

Asset Valuation

Asset valuation involves the worth of the assets of the business. This is a useful starting point for negotiations, as it constitutes the minimum value of the business. It is important to note that it would not be appropriate to value most companies using an asset-based approach, especially in the case where the company is a typical earnings-based concern. The asset approach is most appropriate when used in a liquidation scenario and/or in valuing an asset-based company such as a real estate holding company or investment holding company. Assets can be valued as follows:

- ✔ *Book value.* This equals the total net worth or *stockholders' equity* of the company, as reflected on the balance sheet.
- ✔ *Adjusted book value.* This adjusts for discrepancies between the stated book value and the actual market value of assets, such as machinery and equipment, which have depreciated, or land, which has appreciated the book value.
- ✔ *Liquidation value.* This adjusts for the value of assets if the company had to dispose of those assets in a quick sale.

> **stockholders' equity**
> the portion of a business owned by the stockholders.

Asset	Liquidation	Book Value	Value
Cash	100%	$ 7,000	$ 7,000
Accounts receivable	70	200,000	140,000
Inventories/computers	50	100,000	50,000
Land and buildings	100	250,000	250,000
Equipment	80	100,000	80,000
Other assets	50	80,000	40,000
Total		$800,000	$630,000
Less: Liabilities			(400,000)
Net liquidation value			$230,000

Earnings Valuation

This approach involves valuing the business based on:

- ✔ *Historical earnings.* Valuation is based on the future performance of the business based on how profitable it has been in the past.
- ✔ *Future earnings.* The most widely used method of valuing a business that provides the investor with the best estimate of the probable return on investment.

Once you have decided on the time frame (i.e., historical versus future earnings), you must multiply the earnings figure by a factor to determine its value. Generally, a price/earnings (P/E) multiple is used. For example, if the company is expected to have earnings of $1.5 million in five years and if similar companies are likely to go public at a price-to-earnings ratio of 10, the company is projected to be worth $15 million five years from now.

The appropriate price/earnings multiple is selected based on norms of the industry and the investment risk. The search for a similar company must be classified in the same industry, share similar markets, and have similar products and earnings. A higher multiple is used for high-risk businesses and lower multiple for low-risk businesses. Higher multiples are typically applied to companies with higher earnings growth. Growth is directly tied to multiples. Higher-growth companies receive higher market multiples (high-tech, etc.), and lower-growth companies or cyclical companies whose earnings have peaked typically receive lower multiples (basic industries or airlines). For example, a low-risk business in an industry with a five times earnings multiple would be valued at 7.5 million in the preceding example.

Valuation is a judgmental process involving trial and error. There are several techniques of valuation, no single one of which can provide the right answer. The best is a combination of methods that may apply to a given situation. For example, start-ups usually rely heavily on the discounted cash flow (DCF) method. In one of the following fixed price examples, you weigh the asset approach value of $2 and the multiple of earnings value of $10 equally. An appraiser who would weigh such different indications of value equally would be incorrect in doing so. When using the valuation process, there are several reasons to consider that play important roles in establishing the value for the company.

✔ *Sale of a business.* A valuation to determine net worth is required when asking a price for a business. If you are buying a business, you will want to know how much the company is earning, its projected cash flow, and the exact fair market (or replacement) value of the assets.

✔ *Increase credit line.* An increased credit line may be added by a valuation that presents lenders with the fair market value of the equipment, or a favorable patent or franchise position.

✔ *Tax value.* The value of an ownership interest may need to be valued for gift tax purposes. A valuation also can establish a fair market value of a business that may be needed in the future to settle an estate.

✔ *Buy-sell agreements.* Under a *buy-sell agreement*, a valuation may be required to buy out an interest of an owner in the event of employment termination, retirement, or dispute.

✔ *Stock option plan.* Employee stock plans require valuations of the stock. These methods can include the usual stock options, as well as profit sharing or stock bonus.

✔ *Raising equity capital.* Valuations are a must when raising public or private capital. The valuations can cover securities such as common stock, preferred stock, warrants, and convertibles.

✔ *Stockholders.* Sometimes stockholders want the business to purchase their stock, referred to as a "right of appraisal." This can occur when a stockholder strongly objects to a major transaction for which the company needs stockholder approval.

 buy-sell agreement contracts between associates that set the terms and conditions by which one or more of the associates can buy out one or more of the other associates.

Here are examples of methods used in the valuation process.

Fixed Price This approach is typically incorporated in a buy/sell agreement and is also referred to as a formula approach. For example, you and your partner equally own a company and each own 100,000 shares of common stock (a total of 200,000 shares outstanding). The company's net income is $200,000. Here are two basic values to consider:

Example 1

Assets	$1,000,000
Liabilities	$ 600,000
Net book value	$ 400,000
	$1,000,000
Book value per share	$2
Earnings per share	$1

Example 2 If we assume a price-earnings multiple of 10 on the earnings per share of $1, the value of each share of stock is $10. You and your partner can agree to place a 50 percent weight on your book value per share and 50 percent on your multiple of earnings value. Based on these two assumptions, the weighted value per share would be $6, computed as follows:

Method	Value	Weight	Weighted Value
Book value	$ 2	50%	$1
Multiple of earnings	$10	50%	$5
		100%	$6

Tangible Book Value Another method of valuing a business is to compute its net worth as the difference between total assets and total liabilities. This value uses balance sheet position. It's the book value (net worth) of the business—total assets less total liabilities, adjusted for any intangible assets such as deferred financing costs, partners, and *goodwill*. Most companies use the book value as reported by their accountants.

> **goodwill**
> the difference between the market value of a firm and the market value of its net tangible assets.

	Book Value	Fair Market Value
Inventory	$200,000	$225,000
Plant and equipment	$500,000	$600,000
Other intangibles		$ 50,000
Total	$700,000	$875,000
Excess		$175,000

Other balance sheet and income statement adjustments are (1) bad-debt reserves, (2) long-term debt securities, and (3) loans and advances of officers, employees, or other companies. Additionally, earnings should be adjusted. You should also consider whether the company's net income has benefited from a reduction in its income tax provision due to net operating losses in prior years.

Multiple of Earnings: Price/Earnings Ratio The price/earnings (P/E) ratio is a method used to value publicly held corporations. Many start-up companies have no earnings and therefore do not have price-to-earnings ratios. In fact, though, this P/E approach is a primary method for valuing privately held companies. To value a private company in a particular industry, seek out a set of comparable publicly traded companies by which to benchmark the private company. Compute the P/E and other valuation ratios for the public comparables. After comparing many financial measures and growth prospects of the private company versus the public comparables, choose an appropriate P/E multiple based on the public company P/Es. This multiple chosen for the private company is the estimate of the P/E that the market would apply to this company if it were public. This is basically the same process that investment bankers/underwriters undertake for an IPO company.

Also, valuation is determined by dividing the market price of the common stock by the earnings per share. In the case of a company with 300,000 shares of common stock, trading at $5 per share and net income of $1 share, the P/E would be 5 ($5 divided by $1). Additionally, since the company has 300,000 shares of common stock, the valuation of the enterprise would now be $1,500,000 (300,000 shares times $5).

When determining valuation of a company that is not publicly held, a market price must be determined. One method is to use the capitalization rate assumption. For example:

Shares of common stock	$100,000
1999 net income	$100,000
Assume 15% capitalization rate	6.7 price/earnings multiple (derived by dividing 1 by 0.15)
Price per share	$6.70
Value of company ($100,000 × $6.70)	$670,000

Net income for the prior year is determined and then capitalized using a P/E multiple. A 15 percent capitalization rate is often used, which is equivalent to a P/E multiple of 6.7 (1 divided by 0.15). If a business has an excellent growth rate, a low capitalization rate can be used, say 5 percent (a multiple of 20).

In contrast, if the business is stable (low growth rate), a capitalization rate of 10 percent can be used (a multiple of 10). Whichever capitalization rate and multiple you use, the resulting value is then divided by the total number of shares outstanding to get a value per share.

Discounted Cash Flow The real value of any ongoing business is its future earning power. Accordingly, this approach is most often used to value a business. The discounted cash flow (DCF) method projects future earnings over a 5- or 10-year period and then calculates their present value using a certain discount or present value rate (e.g., 15 percent). The total of each year's projected earnings is the company's value. The basic principle underlying this method is that a dollar earned in the future is worth less than a dollar earned today. Thus, it is not only the amount of projected income (or net cash flow) that a company is expected to generate that determines its value but also the timing of that income.

It is critical to note that if you are to use this approach in valuing a company, you must decide how to value the cash flows after the forecast period is over. If you were to limit your DCF calculation to just the 5 or 10 years in the forecast, you would omit any value that would accrue from years 11 and beyond. The way this "terminal value" is typically captured is by using some terminal P/E to indicate what the selling value of the business would be after year 10.

Let's assume that you will receive $100,000 today and then $100,000 a year over the next four years. What is today's value (present value) of the total $500,000 income stream? To determine the value of the transaction, you must use present value factors. Now, let's construct a table that would show you how the total $500,000 payments would be valued today and over the next four years. To compute the value, simply lay out the amounts by year and apply an 18 percent present value factor to each amount.

Today's Value of Income

Year	Inflow	18% PV Factor	Value Today
Today	$100,000	1.000	$100,000
1	$100,000	.847	$ 84,700
2	$100,000	.718	$ 71,800
3	$100,000	.609	$ 60,900
4	$100,000	.516	$ 51,600
	$500,000	3.690	$369,000

As shown, the total income of $500,000 over five years is worth (today) $369,000. That represents 30 percent less than the $500,000 that you thought you were going to receive over the five-year period.

DETERMINE THE INVESTORS' SHARE

The approach to use to estimate the desired ownership a venture capitalist will seek for a given amount of investment is indicated by the following formula:

$$\text{Venture capitalist} = \frac{\text{VC \$ investment} \times \text{VC investment rate of return}}{\text{Ownership (\%) company's projected profits in year 5} \times \text{price/earnings multiple of comparable company}}$$

Steps in Determining Investors' Share

1. Estimate the earnings after taxes based on sales in the fifth year.
2. Determine an appropriate earnings multiple, based on what similar companies are selling for in terms of their current earnings.
3. Determine the required rate of return.
4. Determine the funding needed.
5. Calculate, using the following formulas:

$$\text{Present value} = \frac{\text{Future valuation}}{(1 + i)^n}$$

where:

Future valuation = Total estimated value of company in five years

i = Required rate of return

n = Number of years

and:

$$\text{Investors' share} = \frac{\text{Initial funding}}{\text{Present value}}$$

Example 1 Let's assume that you need $1 million of venture capital money. The projection is $300,000 in net income, and the investment multiple is 4 times. Your analysis has indicated that the price/earnings of a similar company is a multiple of 10. Therefore, you would have to give up 13 percent of the company to obtain the needed funds, as calculated here:

$$\frac{\$1,000,000 \times 4}{\$3,000,000 \times 10} = 13\%$$

A detailed method for determining this percentage is given in the box. The step-by-step approach takes into account the time value of money in determining the appropriate investors' share.

Example 2 You estimate the company will earn $1 million after taxes on sales of $10 million. The company needs $500,000 now to reach that goal in five years. A similar company in the same industry is selling at 15 times earnings. An investor wants a 50 percent compound rate of return on investment. What percentage will you give up?

$$\text{Present value} = \frac{\$1,000,000 \times 15}{(1 + 0.50)^5} = \$1,975,000$$

and

$$\frac{\$500,000}{\$1,975,000} = 25\%$$

Thus, 25 percent will have to be given up.

SUMMARY

An IPO (initial public offering) can mark a turning point in the life of a company. With this one event, the company can accelerate its growth, launch new products, enter new markets, and attract valuable employees. Those who consider the IPO as just a short-term financial transaction underestimate its far-reaching impact. The IPO itself is only one component of this journey. This event generally lasts 90 to 120 days, whereas the journey begins at least a year or two before the IPO and continues well beyond it. It is up to the CEO (chief executive officer) to anticipate the leadership challenges and lead the management team through the major operational, transactional, and people milestones.

The IPO process is a difficult task, because the pitfalls are numerous and the stakes are high. Poor market timing and inadequate planning can jeopardize an IPO. The success stories we hear about are counterbalanced by many companies whose shares are dropping and that are experiencing management shakeouts. To make a decision, the benefits of accessing the public equity markets are that doing so enables you to attract better valuations, accept less dilution of ownership, and raise more money. The money from an IPO can repay debt, fund special projects, and be used for acquisitions. For example, you can use the capital to acquire other businesses, repay debt, finance research, develop projects, and acquire or modernize production facilities. Another plus is that raising equity capital through a public offering often results in a higher valuation for your company, through a higher multiple of earnings (or price-earnings ratio), as compared with many types of private financing. Thus, it often results in less dilution of ownership than with some other financing alternatives, such as venture capital. Raising capital in this way also avoids the interest costs and cash drain of debt financing.

Depending on the proportion of shares sold to the public, you may be at risk of losing control of your company now or in the future. Retaining at least 51 percent of the shares will ensure control for now, but subsequent offerings and acquisitions may dilute your control.

Management is required to comply with SEC regulations and reporting requirements. These requirements include quarterly financial reporting (Form 10-Q), annual financial reporting (Form 10-K), reporting of current material events (Form 8-K), and other reporting. The SEC's reporting requirements demand significant time and financial commitments. Securities analysts will also demand management's time.

The IPO event follows many months of careful preparation. During the IPO, the president/CEO will serve as the company's major spokesperson, delivering the company's story to the financial market. The CEO will be involved in setting the strategic direction for the SEC registration statement. As the statement is being drafted, the CEO can spend time providing high-level direction to the presentation of the upcoming road show.

The registration process begins when you have reached an understanding with an underwriter on your proposed public offering. From this point on, you become subject to SEC regulations on what you may and may not do to promote your company. The center of the process is preparing the registration statement.

The underwriters will receive a discount (spread) between the price at which they buy stock and the price at which the underwriters sell the same stock to the public. The amount of the spread is negotiated based on the size and risk of the offering as well as other factors. A typical firm commitment–offering discount is approximately 7 percent of the public offering price of the stock.

The key issue you will confront when going public with an IPO or raising equity funds is determining a value of the company. This valuation will determine how much the new investors will receive for funding the company. The main factors in any valuation are the history, characteristics, and industry in which the business operates. They provide the strength and weakness of the company and risks in investing in the business.

Another financial factor to consider in the analysis is comparing your company to other companies in the industry. This can include the price-to-earnings ratio of similar companies and understanding the financial condition of the company. Usually, future earnings capacity is calculated by weighing the most recent earnings higher than the previous year's earnings.

The last valuation factor is the stock price of similar companies in your industry. This valuation factor is used in the earnings valuation as described in this chapter.

To increase the chances of successfully obtaining capital, you must know what sources are available and understand the operations of the various financial institutions. Preparing a solid business and financial plan before beginning the capital search enables the entrepreneur to determine which sources would be most likely to assist in capitalizing the business.

ERNST & YOUNG'S ENTREPRENEUR OF THE YEAR AWARDS PROGRAM

Each year the most successful entrepreneurs vie for the most prestigious honor in this class: the Ernst & Young Entrepreneur of the Year (EOY) award. EOY winners represent virtually every industry—from the traditional to the newly created. Many have become household names: Jeff Bezos of Amazon.com, Andy and Jack Taylor of Enterprise Rent-a-Car, Steve Case of America Online, and

Howard Schultz of Starbucks Corporation. Other note-worthy award winners include names such as Kenneth Cole of Kenneth Cole Productions, Jay Walker of Priceline.com, Bill Daugherty and Jonas Steinman of iWon.com, Tim and Nina Zagat of Zagat Survey, Kevin O'Connor of DoubleClick, Jeff Dachis of Razorfish, and Charles Wang of Computer Associates International.

Tim and Nina Zagat—Zagat Survey, LLC

What began as an informal survey of New York area restaurants in 1979 has evolved into an official guide for dining out not only in New York but also in dozens of other cities around the world. After asking friends to rate the food, decor, and services of some 75 local restaurants, Tim and Nina compiled the results and found themselves besieged by requests for additional copies. The annual survey eventually took on a life of its own with distribution reaching some 10,000. It was at this point that Nina recommended recouping costs by publishing their survey in book form for sale.

By 1986, the *Zagat New York Restaurant Survey* had become the number-one-selling guide in New York. Guides are now available for 45 major markets, domestic and abroad, as well as hotels, resorts, spas, airlines, and nightlife destinations. The launch of zagat.com has enjoyed much of the success of its offline sibling. Tim and Nina are committed to strengthening their publishing business, while a steady stream of partnerships and alliances are being formed to continue the rapid growth of their online business.

Jeffrey Dachis—Razorfish

Jeff founded Razorfish in 1995 with Craig Kanarick and launched the company from an apartment on Manhattan's Lower East Side. He has been spearheading and shaping Razorfish as well as the digital communications landscape ever since. As CEO, Jeff leads the strategic development of Razorfish, defines its vision, and sets the strategic initiatives required to realize that vision.

Jeff's contributions have been recognized by publications including the *Silicon Alley Reporter*, which placed him in "The Silicon Alley 100," and *The New York Post*, which dubbed him as one of "Silicon Alley's Top 20 Movers and Shakers." Viewed as an industry expert, Jeff is frequently quoted in leading publications—including *The New York Times*, *Wired*, the *Silicon Alley Reporter*, the *Industry Standard*, and *Information Week*—and is an active speaker at conferences around the world.

The Entrepreneur of the Year Award Process

Each individual and company nominated for Entrepreneur of the Year has a unique and interesting story—a story that illustrates courage, imagination, and perseverance—everything it takes to pursue the entrepreneurial dream. These stories have remained largely untold, and that is why Ernst & Young executives assemble each year to honor these outstanding entrepreneurs. By recognizing their accomplishments, they hope to encourage and contribute to the kinds of activities and environments that foster and support the entrepreneurial spirit.

The awards program was created 14 years ago to recognize and celebrate this elite group of entrepreneurs, whose vision, innovation, and hard work have established and sustained successful and growing businesses. Creating jobs and fostering social and economic benefits across the country, these men and women represent the very best in business.

It all begins with the nomination process. A nominee must be the owner/manager primarily responsible for the recent performance of a company that is at least two years old and excels in the following areas: individual commitment, leadership, vision, innovation, performance, community spirit, empowerment of management, and perseverance. Founders of public companies are eligible, provided the founder is still active in top management.

Seven to 10 award recipients are selected in several award categories in each of 46 regions by independent panels of judges comprised of local business, financial, academic, and media figures. Winners are honored at regional award banquets during the month of June and inducted into the elite Entrepreneur of the Year Hall of Fame at the international conference held each November in Palm Springs, California. All regional award winners become eligible for the national awards. An independent panel of judges selects winners and finalists in several national categories as well as one individual who is named the Ernst & Young Entrepreneur of the Year.

In 1999, 498 individuals were named Entrepreneur of the Year award recipients. These EOY award winners ran companies that averaged 786 employees and $197 million in sales, and grew at an average rate of 33 percent.

Nominations can be submitted by anyone who is associated with a successful entrepreneur—family members, employees, bankers, attorneys, public relations managers—or the entrepreneurs themselves. Interested in nominating someone for the preeminent award in business? A copy of the nomination form and complete information on the Entrepreneur of the Year award program is downloadable free from the web site at www.ey.com/eoy. You can also call Ernst & Young toll-free at 1-800-755-AWARD.

Chapter

8

Launching an Internet Business

Objectives

1. Determine if the Internet is right for your business.
2. Launch an effective Internet business.
3. Know why some Internet companies fail.
4. Establish an Internet web presence.
5. Explore Internet e-commerce and business-to-business opportunities.

INTRODUCTION

L et's assume you are interested in starting a business and exploring e-commerce as your start-up venture. After all, you have heard the stories: dot-com companies going public and raising millions of dollars; everyday folks starting Internet businesses and making a fortune; e-commerce being touted as the great economic revolution of our time. The question is, how much of this is true? And, more importantly, how much business opportunity does the Internet present for a company?

This chapter focuses on the enormous business opportunities on the Internet. The Internet is growing at a staggering rate. In the past five years, it has revolutionized how people communicate, how information is dispersed, and how business is conducted. Consider that nearly 13 million people browse the World Wide Web regularly and just under two million have purchased something through

Profile: Donn Rappaport of Impower—Starting an e-Marketing Solutions Company

In the mid 1970s, Donn Rappaport began working as a copywriter for an advertising agency in New York City. He recognized an opportunity to improve direct mail response by applying sophisticated market research and data analysis to the process of list targeting and segmentation. When the agency was sold in 1978, Donn started his career as an entrepreneur. With $40,000 in savings, he and his wife formed American List Counsel (ALC), a full-service mailing list, database brokerage, and management company.

Over the next 20 years, ALC built its business by helping clients attract, cultivate, retain, and leverage the value of customers through traditional direct marketing methods and techniques. Today, the company's gross sales are over $130 million, and it employs some 200 people operating in four regional offices. The company provides database-marketing services to hundreds of clients around the country, including many blue chip corporations, such as American Express, MCI, Time Warner, Neiman Marcus, and other leaders in virtually every category of business.

In 1995, Donn realized that his clients were beginning to struggle with how to develop an Internet strategy. Clients, who were extremely successful direct marketers, were building web sites for their products and services but failing to transfer their direct mail marketing expertise to the Internet world. He wanted to create a value proposition that would allow clients to cost-effectively acquire new customers and maximize their lifetime value. As a result, Donn launched an Internet direct marketing company called Impower. His strategy was to offer a comprehensive portfolio of products and services to leading Internet publishers, marketers, and e-tailers. The services would offer highly targeted and cost-effective solutions to fulfill marketers' online customer development needs. His belief was that the Internet was the ultimate direct response medium, bringing buyers and sellers together in ways that were more immediate, intimate, and interactive than any medium before. What was needed, he decided, were tools to facilitate faster, more efficient and profitable e-commerce.

The launch of Impower enjoyed rapid success, so much so that in 1999, the company took in $15 million in private equity from a venture capital firm. The funding is helping to build the technology, infrastructure, and staff to support the business growth.

In late 2000, Impower acquired Datamark Technologies, Inc., a loyalty and stored value provider, as part of their platform to enhance the value proposition of a profitable customer acquisition and the leveraging of lifetime values.

Impower's success to date is an excellent benchmark for its future accomplishments. Among them is the application of a cost per action (CPA) paradigm to Internet advertising, allowing marketers to pay for performance. Donn embodies the leadership, spirit, and vision of an entrepreneur; he identifies the opportunity, creates the solution, and executes better than his competition.

it. Even more staggering are the projections. In 1998, consumers spent more than $2.5 billion buying goods and services over the Internet. For the year 2000, this figure could grow to $18 billion. With each day bringing more people to e-commerce, this chapter will assist you in considering if the Internet is the way to go for your business. Any way you look at it, e-commerce (commercial transactions handled over the Internet) is becoming less a novelty and more a viable alternative to how people interact and use transactions in the world. The future is indeed bright.

IS THE INTERNET RIGHT FOR YOUR BUSINESS?

Nearly everyone agrees e-commerce brings great opportunities (see Figures 8.1 and 8.2), but that doesn't really matter unless the Internet is suited to your business. To understand if e-commerce is good for your business, you should consider the following issues.

What Are You Selling?

Some products and services, such as software and music, can be downloaded directly from your site and onto the consumer's hard drive. One site, for example, might allow you to compare a range of prices on particular software and then download it upon payment. These sites do not have to rely on shipping since their product can be transferred electronically, saving the consumer time and money. Likewise, web sites offering specialized information, such as comparing insurance rates, require no fulfillment or delivery of the product, as the information is readily available to the consumer.

Investigate Your Competition

Are your competitors engaging in e-commerce or e-business, or are their web sites mere marketing tools that simply give an overview of their company? If so, you may be missing out by not taking your business to the next level online. This might include offering products to online visitors, collecting important customer information

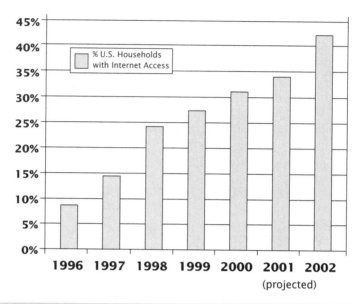

Source: U.S. Department of Commerce

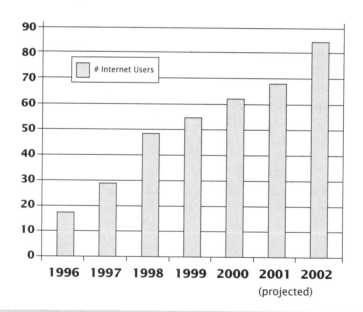

Source: U.S. Department of Commerce

in a database for marketing purposes, making the shopping experience more interactive, or establishing a rewards/incentive program on your site.

If they are not involved with e-commerce or e-business, ask why. Is what you are selling likely to be purchased online? According to a recent article in *The New York Times*, computer-related items and books are the two hottest products being sold online today. Specifically, 39 percent of shoppers surveyed showed a preference for buying these kinds of items online. Twenty-one percent showed a preference for buying clothing and music online.

Where Are Your Customers Located?

Are your customers located in one region or are they scattered geographically? The Internet is far more powerful in the latter case, for people around the world could potentially become customers. This is one of the greatest advantages of having a business on the Internet—its ability to find a worldwide customer base. On the other hand, if your business is a restaurant that relies on customers in the nearby region, much of the Internet's power is undermined. By its nature, the number of people who can be influenced to shop at your restaurant is limited to those who live nearby and the occasional tourist. Products and services that can be sold throughout the world benefit the most from the Internet. Generally speaking, the more geographically scattered your customer base, the more effective a business web site can be.

ADVANTAGES TO AN INTERNET BUSINESS

Let's say you believe your business is compatible to the Internet. You should consider some of these advantages of taking your business online:

✔ By having a business online, you could attract international customers in a way undreamed of before the Internet. Since the World Wide Web is used in almost every industrialized country, the potential pool for customers is extremely large.

This is especially true for specialty products with international appeal that might attract a small following in the United States but can mushroom when sold worldwide.

✔ People who buy products online tend to be in a higher income bracket than consumers buying the same goods in retail stores. According to a profile published in *USA Today* (February 2000), 7 percent of people making purchases online earn $101,000 or more; 39 percent earn $51,000 to $100,000 per year; and 36 percent earn between $30,000 and $50,000. This means that nearly 80 percent of consumers making purchases online earn more than the national median income for individuals.

✔ Males in their late teens and early twenties tend to be major Internet browsers and are a very desirable group for advertisers to reach. This can be important if you wish to add advertising banners to your site as a way of raising additional revenue.

✔ With an Internet business, your virtual store can be open 24 hours/7 days per week. Think of all the business a store may lose when it is closed on Sundays, major holidays, and late evenings— there are so many missed opportunities for sales. The beauty of an Internet company is that its products can always be sold. Likewise, you do not have to worry about time differences. Traditional stores selling to international customers or to the opposite coast of the United States may lose customers due to differing schedules.

✔ The Internet allows you to appear as a major player. Even if you have a home-based, small retail business and lack major start-up funds, your web site can appear as a well-established company. After all, customers are not coming to your physical site. How you appear on the Internet is how you appear to them. This crucial factor can give you credibility from the very beginning. In this way, the Internet has an equalizing influence that is quite helpful to the small entrepreneur.

✔ An Internet business's start-up costs are often much less than those of traditional businesses. The rent and overhead may be minimal. If what you are offering can be downloaded, such as software, you may not need an 800 number for customers to call, nor a fulfillment center to ship the orders, since all this can be taken care of on your web site. You can limit your start-up costs by designing the web page, enabling e-commerce with a secure server to transact credit cards, and having an Internet service provider host the site, administrative costs, and advertising.

WHY SOME INTERNET COMPANIES FAIL

You should be aware of potential pitfalls in making e-commerce your business. Many Internet start-up companies fail because they did not raise enough capital to carry them through the inevitably difficult start-up period. Those that have gone by the wayside had good ideas and effective ways of carrying them out, but without enough seed money, they ran out of time. The reality of business is that in most cases it takes time for a company to realize a profit. The company may have to deal with unexpected costs and an initial period of getting the kinks out. Most companies simply need time to build a customer base before they see their investment realized.

Many Internet companies today are overly focused on revenue and attracting customers rather than paying enough attention to the bottom line, which translates into a profitable venture. The outcome of this will result in a consolidation of Internet companies within defined markets and profitability becoming a key issue for survival and success.

Another common pitfall is that many would-be entrepreneurs begin an Internet start-up company without a well-defined business model or plan. Perhaps they think the Internet has changed the rules of business. It has not. Only the medium has changed. More than ever, you must fully understand the needs of the marketplace, the needs of your customers, and who your major competitors are. (See

Chapter 4 for writing a business plan.) Starting a company without a well-defined business plan is like a football team taking the field in the Super Bowl without a game plan.

LAUNCHING AN INTERNET SITE

Let's say you have done your research and found that the products and/or services you are offering are well suited to the Internet. You are ready to take the leap into launching an online business.

After you have written your business plan and have a firm grasp on your potential customers, competitors, and needs of the market, it is time to have your web page designed. Although there is software available enabling you to design a web site yourself, it is certainly worth the investment to hire a professional designer who will implement your design ideas. After all, if your business is to be e-commerce, it is vital for your site to have a professional look. If your web site appears amateur in any way, you will raise questions in your customers' minds as to the validity of your products and services.

If the Internet is to be your mode of business, you need to be up to speed with an Internet logo. See box for key Internet terms any entrepreneur should be familiar with.

FINDING A WEB PAGE DESIGNER

How do you find a good web page designer?

1. Start with the Yellow Pages. Speak with designers on the phone and if you are comfortable with their experience, ask to see their samples. Inquire if they have designed pages similar to yours. Ask for several of their clients and check with them to rate the quality of their work. You should also try newspapers specializing in the computer industry that may be local to your area in which computer designers tend to advertise.

2. Run a search on the Internet for designers in your area. Many Internet service providers (ISPs), in

ASP (*application service provider*): ASPs run and host software for other companies that access the applications over the Web for a monthly fee.

Bandwidth: A measurement showing the volume of information that can be transmitted over a network and is usually expressed in megabits per second. Home users accessing the Internet through a phone line can transmit information at only 56 kilobits per second.

Click & mortar: The integration of e-commerce with retail in store commerce.

Dial-up connection: Accessing the Internet using a telephone and modem.

Download: To transfer a copy of a file from a remote computer to the requesting computer by means of a modem, such as downloading from the Internet.

Graphical user interface (GUI): A more user-friendly screen that represents programs, files, and options through icons, menus, and dialogue boxes. The user employs the keyboard and/or mouse to select desired options.

HTML: Abbreviation for HyperText Markup Language, the language used for the World Wide Web. Documents read on the WWW are coded in this language.

Hyperlink: A word, phrase, symbol, or image in a hypertext document that connects the user to another place in the document or another site on the WWW.

Infrastructure: The equipment that powers the Web, from phone lines to data centers, routers, and servers.

Intranet: A private network contained within a business organization used for internal communications. Intranets are often linked to the Internet through gateway computers.

LAN: Stands for local area network, a group of computers and other devices dispersed over an area, connected by a communications link allowing any device to interact with any other on the network.

Portal: Generally understood to mean a starting point through which one enters the Web. Users are provided with news and value-added services related to the business or industry the marketplace serves. A marketplace

(Continued)

serving a particular industry might display commodity prices, searchable database, and discussion groups geared to the interests of purchasers it would like to attract.

Scale: The term used for growing at a fast pace. Businesses scale by adding customers quickly while limiting additional costs.

T-1: Leased telephone lines that allow very rapid movement of data (1.54 megabits per second) over the Internet.

Wireless application protocol (WAP): The communications standard for the wireless Web used for any mobile device.

Web browser: Client applications, such as Netscape or Explorer, which enable a user to view HTML documents as web pages and not as coded language. The browser first retrieves the web pages and then interprets them. It also allows for hyperlinks.

addition to supplying you with access to the Internet, will design your site and host it on their server. You may be more comfortable with a major company, such as a telecommunications supplier, that is used to dealing with expanding businesses.

3. Surf the Web and note the sites that impressed you the most. Perhaps these design companies are located in your area, or you could transact business long-distance.

4. Word of mouth can be a valuable resource. Are there certain designers that others would recommend? If you have business acquaintances that have had their sites designed, ask whom they would suggest.

WHAT MAKES A GOOD WEB PAGE?

Even if you're going to hire a designer to create the site, you should be familiar with basic design principles that make for a compelling site. After all, without a well-designed site, you will not attract or keep your customers.

1. *Navigability.* It is very important that each web page on your site maintains a consistent look and feel. The color pattern and design layout should have enough overlap that a unity is achieved. While your pages will have different content, the consistent design will remind users that they are at your site. Keep in mind that users always want to know where they are at all times and how to get back to the home page. To accomplish this, you should have a clearly defined navigation bar that gives users a sense of place and allows them to go wherever they want, in the order they choose. (A navigation bar is a series of icons or buttons leading to different pages. This tool for navigating through your site should appear the same on all your web pages for consistency.)

2. *Hyperlinks.* While the site needs to have structure, it should also give the user control in navigating the site. Include hyperlinks in your site that will allow users to go to different parts of your site or to another site on the Internet. Hyperlinks can be a word, phrase, symbol, or image that, when clicked on, brings the viewer to another page in the web site, to another part of the page (such as top or bottom), or to a web site outside your own. Hyperlinks are almost always another color than the rest of the text and are most commonly blue and underlined.

3. *Aesthetics.* If your site is pleasing to look at, more people will spend a greater amount of time there. An important principle in web page design, which is often violated, is simplicity. There are HTML editors on the market that can create dazzling effects and dizzying animations. But the bottom line is a cluttered page is unattractive and extraneous elements often detract. Don't include the bells and whistles just because you can. It's important that the screen not be cluttered. Clutter makes a site not only less attractive but often quite confusing. Certain studies have shown that typical Internet users spend little more than 20 seconds on a particular screen. Consequently, a typical screen should be limited to 30 lines of text.

4. *Graphics.* Interesting graphics can make for interesting sites. The WWW is largely a visual medium. The role of the graphic, whether a photograph or an illustration, can bring out key parts of the text and liven up a page.

5. *Download Time.* Download time must be short. If it takes too long to download your page (this number varies, but not more than 10 seconds), many impatient users will go to the next site. This is an unfortunate way to lose potential customers because it is so avoidable. There is actually a thriving business of companies that measure the time it takes for a web page to download from different locations, although you could measure this yourself, preferably from computers with different download speeds.

6. *Originality.* Not only should your site be logical and unified, it should be different. Otherwise it will fail to attract. Use interesting graphics. Humor is often a good tool to liven things up. Don't be afraid to look into animation, audio, and video. Animation, or programming things to move in a prearranged way, can make your page come to life. Audio and video files can add another dimension, although you should be wary of the additional download time. Users can hear the voice of the president of the company or an explanation of certain products. They can see the product in action rather than simply read about it in the text. In the past, download time for opening multimedia files made this option less attractive, but with the advent of streaming audio and video, user waiting time is minimal.

OBTAINING A DOMAIN NAME

While you are having the web site designed, you need to register for a domain name. This is the specific address or URL (Uniform Resource Locator) a user will type in to retrieve your web page.

As the WWW has grown incredibly fast, many domain names have been bought. You may need to be creative to make your name different. There is also the option of buying an existing domain name from the owner. In addition, you can try putting hyphens into your desired web address, if the address is already taken. For example, the web site for this book is www.start-a-company.com because the existing name without the hyphens was taken.

Once you have a name, you need to register it. As of late 2000, this will cost you about $70 for two years of using the name. Sites such as Register.com (www.register.com) or Network Solutions (www.networksolutions.com) can help you search for available domain names and register them for you.

Naturally, you want your domain name to relate to your company. If that is not possible, it should relate to the product you are selling. You will most likely take the suffix ".com," as your site is a for-profit company, as opposed to "org," which is for nonprofits; ".edu," for educational institutions; ".gov," for government entities; ".mil," for a military organization; or ".net," for a network administration.

WEB HOSTING

You also need to find a company that will host your web site in cyberspace. There are many companies that offer this service: major telecommunications companies and well-established firms such as Exodus and Globix. Many ISPs, in addition to offering you access to the Internet, will provide you with hosting space on their servers for a fee.

A good resource for ISPs that do web hosting is thelist. com, which provides a list of the various services offered. It is critical that you choose a reliable host site if you anticipate many hits and will offer e-commerce. The host's server must handle many requests at one time and will need to download quickly.

Free Web Hosting

There are sites that offer free web hosting. While this may sound appealing, there are a number of problems associated with it. First, these free sites often advertise on all your web pages, which can be distracting. Secondly, they do not support the domain name you choose but rather you are given an address under their name. Third, the amount of space offered is usually limited. In most cases, free hosting sites should be avoided.

SECURE METHOD FOR E-COMMERCE

E-commerce is fueled by technology that allows for the secure taking of credit card numbers online, thus allowing the point of sale on the web site itself. If you're going to start an Internet company that takes orders online, you will need a secure server capable of relaying your customers' credit card transactions and encrypting them as they speed through the phone lines. Encrypted electronic information is quite safe. An Internet company such as Amazon.com takes thousands of credit card numbers per day electronically and has never reported a problem.

Many of the same companies that offer web page design can design a secure method of receiving payment online and transacting the purchase. When choosing your service provider, make sure it has a strong record for handling e-commerce accounts.

In addition to payment information, you will need a form requesting the customer's name and address for shipping purposes and their e-mail for confirmation. Don't lose sight of the fact that interactivity is an important part of e-commerce. When a customer pays you online, you should confirm the order by e-mail. This will assure the customer that the order has gone through and that the product is on the way. A surprising number of e-commerce sites fail to do this.

FOUR MODELS OF REVENUE

Keep in mind you do not need e-commerce in order to run a profitable Internet site. That is just one option. There are other ways.

1. You can charge for advertising. In this model, banners appear on the top and/or beside your web page to lure the user to their web pages. The advertising model works only if you have many hits per day and can prove this to advertisers. You will need to show them the demographics of who is coming to your site and the numbers. To attract this number of hits, however, it requires highly specialized information, such as constantly updated news or a special feature like offering quick searches.

2. The second way is to charge the consumer for using your site, usually by registering. For the privilege of accessing your site, the user must pay. This can be either a one-time fee or a monthly charge. Such paying users are often called members. Successful sites that charge users have highly valuable information certain people are willing to pay for. For example, there is an apartment-listing company in New York City that charges each user $175 for access to its web site. In return for payment, users are given a user name and password that will entitle them to view apartment listings not listed in the newspaper and contact the landlord directly without a broker. As anybody who has ever looked for housing in New York knows, this information is highly valued, and the customers are constantly replenished since finding housing is an ongoing need.

3. Some sites charge you for becoming a member and advertising on their sites. This is certainly the most desired model as you now have two sources of revenue. However, this is out of reach for most web sites. To charge advertisers rates that will make you profitable, you need a proven, steady stream of visitors each day.

4. You may not expect to gain revenue from the Internet site itself. Instead, your web site can be a marketing tool to strengthen your existing business, as it acts as a vehicle to tell your story to clients and potential customers. It is also your chance to describe the company, the products and services offered, and how to improve the life of the customer or business. Many companies use their web sites to improve customer service. For example, instead of having customers wait endlessly on the phone in frustration, they can access the company web site and have their needs taken care of immediately. In addition, directing customers to a web site instead of having them call an 800 number for information (for which the company pays a fee per transaction) can save the company a significant amount of money.

A web site can deepen the relationship between company and customer by offering valuable information or informing them of your products in depth. It is a golden opportunity for your company to shine. Finally, if your site generates enough traffic, it can increase customer loyalty by building brand awareness. Recognizing this marketing and public relation potential, nearly all companies and organizations have some kind of web site today.

BUSINESS-TO-BUSINESS OPPORTUNITIES

Business-to-business (B2B) is an old concept, but what is different about the online B2B is the speed at which business connections can now be made. The web makes businesses smarter, faster, and more productive. Opportunities in B2B include companies that engage in marketplaces, enablers, and application service providers (ASPs). Marketplace opportunities exist in creating businesses that focus on online auctions. This will allow companies to submit sealed Internet bids that go through a site to win business from each other and create transactions to buy and sell supplies. Enablers are companies that help create marketplaces on the Internet. These companies supply software and expertise in content, procurement, transaction processing, and customer relationship management.

OPPORTUNITIES FOR APPLICATION SERVICE PROVIDERS

Initially e-commerce focused on selling simple products such as books and CDs and selling products for the same price to everyone. At present, buyers are changing how they buy products and services in two ways. The first is that customers will maintain loyalty to a specific company and visit that company's web site first to make a purchase. To preserve that customer relationship, companies must build selling sites that create a compelling Web experience that is consistent with its existing brand. Opportunities will exist in creating vertical marketplaces or shopping portals that will represent the new way customers will buy. In this marketplace, customers can visit one specialized web site to find a variety of products and services offered by multiple suppliers and negotiate the best terms available. These marketplaces offer new Internet business opportunities that combine customer value-added expertise, convenience, and cost efficiencies for consumers and businesses.

Application service providers (ASPs) are redefining the way businesses operate and making it easier to start a business online. An ASP is any company that remotely hosts a software application and provides access and use to clients over a network on a recurring fee basis. ASPs can provide the software tools and efficiencies you will need to launch your business venture. Offering software as a service provides real advantages: (1) applications can be deployed much more quickly with far fewer up-front costs; (2) ongoing operational and maintenance headaches are removed from the company to the ASP; and (3) advantages associated with outsourcing frees capital and internal resources, especially the information technology (IT) resources for other projects. The bottom line is that any software application can be rapidly implemented through an ASP in a fraction of the usual time and cost. This new opportunity will create many new businesses on the Internet.

ESTABLISHING AN INTERNET PRESENCE

Whether your company generates revenue from e-commerce, advertising, or registration, it will need many hits, or users visiting the site, to be successful. The result is that a well-designed web site is as good as your product is and how well you attract a critical mass of customers to your site.

Up to this point in our discussion, the process of placing a web site on the Internet could be done relatively inexpensively, depending on your specific needs. The task of attracting customers to your web site, however, quickly becomes expensive. There are so many web sites on the Internet and companies engaging in e-commerce that it's easy to get lost in the shuffle. You must find ways to lure potential customers.

Web Marketing

There are many ways to bring traffic to your web site, and most of them do not require expensive media budgets. Search engines, banner ads, opt-in e-mail, viral marketing, and affiliate networking are methods to develop customer loyalty, build brand awareness, capture market share, and generate more hits. Which marketing strategy will offer the most results? What are the shortcomings of a particular marketing method? How can I compete?

These are all questions currently being addressed by most businesses. Here are some of the answers.

Search Engines Registering with a search engine is an essential step in letting potential customers know of your web site. The Internet, while easy to use and fun, can be overwhelming because of the sheer quantity of sites available. A search engine is a way to make sense of it all. Acting like the Yellow Pages of the Internet, it enables the user to type a word or phrase in and receive a list of those companies matching that description. Search engines are the first place many users go to investigate products or services they are in the market for. Consider this: Of the 25 most visited web sites, nine are search engines. Following is a list of the more popular search engines:

- ✔ AltaVista (www.altavista.com).
- ✔ Excite (www.excite.com).
- ✔ InfoSeek (www.infoseek.com).
- ✔ Lycos (www.lycos.com).
- ✔ Webcrawler (www.webcrawler.com).
- ✔ Yahoo! (www.yahoo.com).
- ✔ Google (www.google.com).

Excite receives 16 million visitors per month, and Yahoo!, the most popular search engine, receives more than 32 million visitors each month. There is inexpensive software available that will register your site with hundreds of search engines around the world. To locate this software, conduct a search online. In addition, there are companies that specialize in analyzing your web site in terms of key words and potential rankings on search engines. Keep in mind that when building any web site, you need to identify both key words and a description (known as metatags) into the HTML code, which will enable the search engine to locate and rank your site.

Selecting inapplicable keywords, discounting the nature of search engines and directories, ineffectively using HTML tags, and failing to continuously monitor a web site's search engine position are all mistakes that can be avoided.

It's important for companies to register their sites with today's leading search engines such as Excite, Hot Bot, Yahoo!, InfoSeek, Lycos, Webcrawler, and Google. Although search engines are continually accepting submissions for new additions to their databases, it's unlikely that a site will appear in the top 10 list of every search engine. Spamming policies, source code readings, standards for relevancy, and the size of a search engine's database are all factors that can contribute to a particular site's ranking. Services such as Submit-it (www.submitit.com), Register-it (register-it.netscape.com), and Selfpromotion.com (www.selfpromotion.com) will submit information about a site to major search engines—for a nominal price.

Banner Ads Banner ads are another method of Web advertising but are beginning to have issues in attracting customers. Historically companies are spending aggressively using banner ads to acquire customers. Currently, the majority of advertising is priced on a cost per thousand (CPM) model. Marketers, however, are increasingly dissatisfied with the results of their advertising campaigns. They are discovering that response rates are often too low to support the CPM and find that few people even recall seeing their ads. Companies have started to move away from this model because of low returns on traffic and purchases. There is a steady migration away from CPM pricing and toward cost per click or cost per action. This shields companies from risk by requiring them to pay only when an ad or direct-marketing campaign results in a sale or some pre-specified action. Regardless of what approach you select, the importance of a successful banner ad campaign must include thorough detailed monthly reports and monitoring.

When contemplating using an ad banner, think through what your goals for the banner might be. Generally speaking, the goals of advertising fall into one of the following three consumer processes:

1. *Cognition.* The banner could be designed to facilitate awareness, knowledge, or active thinking about the brand. A banner could have this kind of benefit even if the consumer does not click on it.

2. *Effect.* The ad could focus on emotion, interest, feelings, or desire. It is difficult to achieve a change in a consumer's affect with just a banner ad; you need to draw the person to your site for a real influence.

3. *Behavior.* The ad might be designed to induce an action on the part of the consumer, such as an initial sale or an accelerated or repeated transaction. Most banner ads are designed simply to get the consumer to click through. After the consumer arrives at the site, the real advertising campaign begins.

Opt-In E-Mail Conducting an e-mail campaign to consumers who have agreed to accept correspondence is a new marketing method. It is called opt-in e-mail. Opt-in e-mail enables companies to send announcements and promotional offers to a captive audience that has already asked to be included on a mailing list. Opt-in e-mail campaigns can also be refined and messages can be customized to target the individual. These benefits provide increased traffic at a reasonable price. Amazon.com, for example, generates almost two-thirds of its sales from repeat buyers—many of whom are drawn to revisit the site with carefully crafted e-mail promotions.

Opt-in e-mail is an active medium requiring targeted e-mail lists. There are many third-party e-mail service bureaus that solicit consumers to grant permission to receive e-mail solicitations and then sell e-mail lists per price per solicitation. The market is beginning to recognize that the more compelling the offer for a consumer to give up his or her personal data and volunteer to receive unsolicited e-mail, the less qualified a prospect he or she may be. Therefore, you should consider using opt-in e-mail incentive programs because they have substantially more value as part of a larger e-marketing service offering that can include loyalty programs and other added features to attract and retain members.

Viral Marketing Equally inexpensive is viral marketing. Technology's answer to word-of-mouth advertising, viral marketing is the practice of encouraging consumers to pass on a marketing message to others. The beauty of viral marketing is that you turn your customers into your sales agents without their even realizing it.

Internet companies have generated endless exposure by giving away free e-mail addresses and services to consumers with a self-promotional tag attached at the bottom of every free message delivered. Consumers then spread the word by using this free service to e-mail an ever-increasing community of friends and associates. Piggybacking consumers is most powerful when a company is giving away products and services to attract attention.

Affiliate Networking Unlike viral marketing, which fosters a community of consumers, affiliate networking connects sites that need an additional revenue stream to businesses that want to improve sales or increase traffic. Here's how it works. A web site owner registers with a particular affiliate program, agreeing to post another company's promotional link and banners. When consumers click through these links and banners and complete a purchase, the web site owner is paid a commission for generating the sale.

By allowing the placement of advertising links on affiliated web sites, affiliate marketing enables retailers to expand their online presence, grow their Web business, and capture the attention of target demographics that would otherwise prove elusive. What's more, unlike viral marketing, affiliate networking enables companies to track the number of sales to determine visitors' buying preferences and to analyze their online behavioral patterns.

SUMMARY

E-commerce presents extraordinary opportunities for the entrepreneur. Every year brings millions more people to their computers searching for products and services. Even if the projected figure of $18 billion in e-commerce sales is not met in the year 2000, nobody can deny that e-commerce is growing at a dizzying pace, changing the way we live and do business.

As the entrepreneur, you should distance yourself

from the e-commerce frenzy, at least long enough to decide if it is right for your business. The following questions are important in making that decision: Who is your customer base and what are their buying habits? Is your competition engaged in e-commerce? If not, how are they using the Web to grow their business? Where are your customers located? Are they in one region or are they scattered geographically? What are you selling? Is it a product or service conducive to the Internet?

There are many strategic advantages to an Internet business. You will have the ability to attract international customers and open new markets. In general, the Internet population tends to be younger and wealthier than the general population and is more desirable for advertisers. Your virtual store can be open 7 days/24 hours without needing to hire employees around the clock. The Internet allows you to appear as a major player, even if you lack the start-up funds. This can be critical in establishing credibility with your customers. Finally, start-up costs tend to be far less than for traditional businesses.

Although there are a variety of factors as to why Internet companies fail, there are two dominant reasons. The first is that the company did not raise enough capital to carry it through the inevitably difficult start-up period. Although the company could have made a profit later, it ran out of time. The second is lack of a business plan or model. With Internet companies there is sometimes a rush to get to market without thoroughly thinking through all the aspects of the business. This lack of focus quickly leads to lack of direction.

In launching an Internet site, it is essential to find a talented web page designer, ideally with experience in building e-commerce sites similar to yours. A well-designed web page adheres to certain principles: navigability, hyperlinks, aesthetics, appropriate graphics, quick download time, and originality. In general, you want your site to stand out and be extremely user-friendly, always concentrating on what the customer wants.

The domain name you want may be difficult to obtain, as many names have been taken. Yet there are sites that specialize in helping you find an appropriate name and registering it. Naturally, you want your domain name to relate to your company. In choosing a web host, make sure it can handle many transactions at once and offer a secure method for e-commerce.

Three models of revenue for generating income on the Internet include advertising, charging to use of advertise on your site, or a combination of these. The fourth is more abstract. Many sites are marketing tools used to further communication between the company and customers and can lead to increased sales down the road.

Application service providers (ASPs) are redefining the way businesses operate and making it easier to start a business online. An ASP is any company that remotely hosts a software application and provides access and use to clients over a network on a recurring fee basis. It can provide the software tools and efficiencies you will need to launch your business venture.

Discovering Value in Intellectual Property: The Competitive Edge

Objectives

1. Know the different forms of intellectual property and how they differ.

2. Discover the purpose of trademarks, the business value, and how to register, select, and protect your trademark.

3. Learn about copyrights, their importance, and the process.

4. Learn the various forms of patents and how to apply for, promote, and harvest the value of one's patent.

5. Know the guidelines for selecting professional assistance, such as legal services, in pursuing your intellectual property rights.

6. Discover the important roles of reverse engineering and trade secrets in intellectual property.

INTRODUCTION

The realm of intellectual property (IP) deals with a range of usually legally defensible rights conferred upon individuals and companies that have produced original work of some potential value. The work itself may fall in any part of a broad spectrum including such diverse forms as software processes, oil painting, music composition, and computer chip design. The forms of protection are defined as trademark, copyright, and patent. In addition to the foregoing is another form of intellectual property known as a trade secret. Trade secrets are not afforded the same assurance of legal protection as their counterparts (laws vary from state to state), but are sometimes a more effective way of securing property rights.

The provision of specific legal rights for the creators of intellectual property is made in the U.S. Constitution, whereby it reads:

> *The Congress shall have the power to . . . promote the progress of science and useful arts, by securing for limited times to authors and inventors the exclusive right to their respective writings and discoveries.*—The U.S. Constitution: Article I, Section 8

The importance of intellectual property to the entrepreneur is in its ability to provide profit or some other form of competitive advantage. Where it is prudent to do so, the creator of a piece of intellectual property may wish to share it with the community, whether it be his or her specific technical community, country, or the world at large. By sharing, it is meant that the creator makes the intellectual property available for public or private use or consumption in some form, usually in a manner that generates profit for the owner of the intellectual property. In exchange, the government will usually confer some form of ownership rights, allowing a possible financial benefit from the sale or use of that creation by others, provided that the creation is properly presented and registered, and meets specific criteria.

This chapter will provide an explanation of these forms of intellectual property and guide you toward effectively developing, protecting, and promoting your own IP. A variety of tools and resources can be found throughout the chapter and in the additional sources offered at the end of the chapter.

Before going any further, it is important to point out that the laws governing intellectual property are complex and frequently subject to change. It is advised that entrepreneurs pursuing the advancement of their

IP consult the appropriate code early in their endeavors to minimize the possibility of wasted time and effort, especially given the importance of timely registration in seeking competitive IP rights. Professional legal advice and assistance may constitute the most appropriate means for efficiently pursuing IP rights for many entrepreneurs.

TRADEMARKS

What Are Trademarks?

Trademarks are highly useful tools employed by commercially active entities to distinguish their products and the sources of these products from one another. Trademarks are akin to and in some cases synonymous with brands. Because of their function, trademarks are one of the most familiar forms of intellectual property.

A trademark can take a number or some combination of forms including name, symbol, motto, or jingle, just to name a few, and represents a company and/or product it is associated with. The red triangle on a bottle of Bass Ale is a trademark for the Bass Brewing Company. The slogan "Quality is Job #1" is one of Ford Motor Company's trademarks. The three-note call sign of the National Broadcasting Company (NBC) is a well-known example of a trademark in the form of sound.

A lesser-known cousin of the trademark is the "service mark," which differs only by way of applying to services and their sources. Other lesser-known marks include the "collective mark," which is used by organizations, often to designate membership, and for use in commerce. The "certification mark," is used by entities other than the owner of the mark and requires the owner's permission. Because of its association with nonowner entities, the certification mark may be indicative of their identities and the attributes of the products, such as elements of quality and composition.

The following information focuses most specifically on trademarks. For additional information on the other marks, consult the proper federal authorities.

Value in Trademarks

The key to trademarks is in the association they render in the mind of the consumer. They are important forms of intellectual property affecting decisions in the minds of consumers or users. Based on personal experience, word of mouth, advertising, and other means of acquaintance, consumers form impressions about different products or services offered. Those impressions guide the consumer in making decisions about spending time and money when given a choice between competing products or services. Based on these associations, these consumers gain expectations on the products or services they will use. It is specifically the power of the trademark to convey such positive associations that imparts its value.

Even a catchy jingle or attractive design used as a trademark is unlikely to provide a business entity with much value unless that entity takes steps to create the positive associations described. Such associations are built initially with good advertising and promotional trials and reinforced by such practices as providing good quality, value, user-friendliness, and customer service, among others. In order to achieve the favorable trademark awareness it needs, a business entity will likely have to invest a substantial amount of capital, effort, and time in development. Once a trademark has been reliably established, it can be a highly effective tool for communicating a broad amount of information at a glance and for promoting use among consumers.

Registering a Trademark

Simply by using a mark in the course of public commerce the entrepreneur establishes a common law right to that mark, and may be considered its legal owner. Nonetheless, given the potential for different parties to concurrently use the same or similar mark, the challenge to one's common law right to a mark has the potential to surface and interfere with some or all future rights associated with its use. In order to safeguard one's trademark rights, it is recommended that the user of a mark apply to have it registered with the United States Patent and Trademark Office (USPTO) in Washington, D.C.

Only the owner of a trademark may apply for registration, although an attorney may initiate the application on behalf of an owner. Attorneys are not essential to this process but they can provide invaluable guidance to the aspiring trademark registrant for avoiding pitfalls and safeguarding the fruit of labor. With or without an attorney, the owner must submit an application along with supporting documentation. If the applicant's mark is already in commercial use, you must submit a "use application" that includes a drawing of the trademark on a separate sheet of paper, a filing fee corresponding with the class of product to which the trademark applies, and three specimens of the trademark. Where possible, specimens ought to be actual commercial-grade material bearing the trademark. Where specimens are impractically unwieldy, $8^{1}/_{2}$-by-11-inch photostats or photographs of actual specimens may be supplied instead.

When an applicant's trademark is not yet in commercial use at the time of application, an intent-to-use application must be filed. Submit a drawing of the trademark on a separate sheet of paper with a filing fee corresponding with the class of product to which the trademark applies. Also send either an amendment to allege use or a statement of use depending on whether the trademark has been published in some form and issue a notice of allowance by the USPTO. Owners filing an amendment to allege use form must also file an additional request for an extension of time to file a statement of use if the trademark is not used within the six months following their submission of application. Failure to make commercial use of the mark without an extension filing will result in disavowal of the application by the USPTO.

Applications should be sent to:

Assistant Commissioner for Trademarks
Box New App/Fee
2900 Crystal Drive
Arlington, VA 22202-3513

The USPTO also offers the Trademark Electronic Application System (TEAS) for easy online application printing that can be sent to the above address via mail. For further information, interested parties should start by calling the USPTO's automated message system at (800) 786-9199. Live operators are available if needed.

The USPTO will grant registration approval to the first party to commercially use or file an intent-to-use application. Because registration of a trademark with the USPTO confers upon the registrant's particular legal privileges, it is recommended that entrepreneurs seek registration as early as possible. Applicants should expect it to take approximately one year until receiving registration approval for the trademark. During this period, the application is reviewed by one of the USPTO's trademark attorneys and evaluated for its compliance with regulations and for potential conflict with existing registered marks. Having passed such tests, a trademark will subsequently be published in the USPTO's *Gazette* for review and possible challenge by competitive parties.

Once registration has been achieved, a trademark must remain in commercial use in order for the rights of registration associated with it to remain in force. For newly registered trademarks, a renewal application will need to be filed in order to extend the term of registration (those registered prior to November 16, 1989, need be registered only every 20 years). The only exception to this rule is that between the fifth and sixth year of initial registration a supplemental affidavit must be filed with the USPTO. Provided that the relevant conditions are met, registered ownership of a trademark can continue indefinitely.

Benefits of Registering a Trademark

Federal registration of a trademark grants the owner a competitive advantage in the use of the mark. In addition to nationwide public notice of the legal claim being made, the owner has the benefit of legal appeal in federal court concerning matters of dispute and infringement. National evidence of ownership can provide a basis for achieving international registration of the trademark and for preventing importation of international goods, which infringe on the registrant's rights in the United States.

Enforcing a Trademark

Once a trademark is registered with the USPTO, the owner of the mark may use the federal registration symbol ® in association with its mark. This will inform others of the exclusive rights afforded by the mark. Until such time as official registration occurs, it is a good idea to use the TM symbol as a way of notifying others that rights are claimed in association with use of your mark. The SM symbol may be used in the case of service marks.

Even when properly registered, and kept in constant use, there is no guarantee that others will not infringe on the trademark. Where infringement is deemed to have taken place, the USPTO should be notified. A decision to pursue legal recourse for damages should hinge upon the existence of actual or potential financial loss as a result of the infringement, although owners of marks are entitled to file suit even where no such losses are readily apparent. In cases where injury is minimal, it may make more sense to simply notify the infringing party of infringement, providing records of your rights and a request to terminate usage of the mark. Document this action so that you can use it in future prosecution should the infringing party fail to comply. Where compliance is not observed, or where significant financial interests are at stake, a qualified attorney should be contracted do perform prosecution.

It should be noted that in order for infringement to exist, a mark need not be identical to that used by the infringed party, only similar enough to cause confusion. Similar marks are more likely to infringe upon one another when used in the same or similar spheres of commerce. Furthermore, infringement need not be intentional in order for damages to be awarded. It is the obligation of any party employing a mark to be certain that its use is unrestricted. Determination of intent, nonetheless, can strengthen a case against an infringing party and result in the award of greater damages than in cases where intent does not exist.

COPYRIGHTS

What Are Copyrights?

Copyrights are instruments of legal protection given to authors of original works of writing, art, musical composition, photography, and architectural design, to name a few. In addition to the conditions of originality, protected works must be expressed and recorded in a fixed medium, such as in print, by brush stroke, recorded on vinyl disc, and so on. Computer programs are among the works that may be copyrighted. With rare exception, names may not be copyrighted. The same is true of titles, slogans, and short phrases, all of which are potentially securable by way of trademark. One exemption from this exception pertains to representations of names, titles, and so on, presented in a sufficiently original style or manner. Where the name for a brand might not be copyrighted (remember that trademark protection is available for such protection), and if that name is rendered in an original manner with sufficient artistic content, for example, it may be copyrighted in that particular form. As is the case with all copyrighted work, it is not idea content, per se, that is copyrighted, but the original expression of that content.

How Do Copyrights Help the Entrepreneur?

For entrepreneurs holding copyrights, the fundamental importance of such is in the potential to harvest profit from a marketable piece of copyrighted work. The owner of a copyright generally has the exclusive right to reproduce, distribute, sell, publicly display, and publicly perform (where applicable) their protected work, or newer derivative work based on the protected work. Persons other than the owner of a copyright wishing to use the work protected by it in any material way must receive permission from the copyright owner to do so. Unauthorized use may carry stiff penalties under U.S. law. Nonmaterial use of protected work might take the form of quoting small portions of a written text and providing proper citation in a new document. The law outlining the boundaries of copyright infringement is specific but complex and ought to be consulted carefully where copyright infringement may be of concern.

The means of capitalizing upon one's copyright are largely at the discretion of the copyright owner. By itself a copyright is a vehicle for revenue generation only if material infringement upon that copyright takes place and can be demonstrated in a court of law. To gain value of one's copyright, negotiation for sale, use, or other consumption of the work must be undertaken with some party interested in the work. As with other forms of intellectual property, ownership of a copyright itself may be transferred via sale or some other mode of conferment. Where real money is at stake, whether negotiating for revenue or suing for infringement, the use of a copyright attorney is highly advisable.

The U.S. Copyright Office (USCO) supplies a list of licensing organizations and publication rights clearinghouses on its web site at www.loc.gov/copyright/. Many of these organizations would be a good place to start for entrepreneurs interested in harvesting the value of copyrighted IP.

How Does One Obtain a Copyright?

In most cases, the author of a work owns the copyright at the moment of its creation. The only exception is in the case of a work made for hire. Work for hire is defined as not owned by the author or when the work is performed in some other salaried or compensated capacity. An example of such a work made for hire could be an article written by an individual author freelancing for a magazine or employed by the same. In the case of a work made for hire, copyright ownership is again present at the moment of a work's creation, but is the intellectual property of the party employing or otherwise compensating the actual author.

Because it is copyrighted by virtue of its existence and conformity with specific requirements, an original work need not be registered with the U.S. Copyright Office. Registration is, nonetheless, a very good idea where IP value is of potential concern, because registration is necessary before any legal action can be taken against infringement. The U.S. Copyright Office makes it very easy for authors of original works meeting the copyright criteria to register their works federally. A mere $30 must be sent along with a simple application form and nonreturnable copies of the work to be registered. Once the work is registered, an author will receive a certificate of registration for his or her work; his or her copyright will be part of the public record and may become part of the collections at the Library of Congress. Registration typically takes approximately eight months but may take as long as a year. Unlike trademarks, copyrights needn't universally be renewed for their power to remain in force, though a variety of specific legal conditions can require renewal steps to be taken. The USCO's *Circular 15* and *15a* should be consulted for detailed renewal conditions and benefits.

Contacting the U.S. Copyright Office

By mail:

Copyright Office
Library of Congress
101 Independence Avenue, SE
Washington, DC 20559-6000

By phone:

Public information   (202) 707-3000
Application forms   (202) 707-9100
TTY   (202) 707-6737

PATENTS

What Do Patents Do?

The U.S. government originally established patents as a way to encourage invention and technological progress by granting those who brought such progress to the nation rights from which they could gain personally. In the United States, patents are issued by the United States Patent and Trademark Office (USPTO) in Washington, D.C. In most cases, a patent grants the inventor (or his or her heirs or assignees) specific property rights for a term of 20 years from the date of patent application filing. In cases where a patent application refers to an earlier filing, the 20-year period extends from the date of the earliest referenced filing. Lastly, it should be noted that the rights granted the inventor apply only within the United States and its territories and possessions. Inventors concerned about securing their rights outside of the United States need to file additional foreign patent applications to do so.

In the United States, a patent grants its holder the right to exclude others from making, producing, selling, or otherwise engaging in some particular activity. For its value to be realized, the restrictive power of a patent must be exercised, yielding the patent holder competitive advantages from which to profit, or presenting the patent holder with financial compensation for allowing others to participate in the activities otherwise restricted by the patent.

What Are the Various Patent Classifications? How Do They Differ?

1. Design patents are issued to individuals who have invented novel elements of design and/or appearance only. A design patent does not include the elements of structure and function.

2. Plant patents are issued to individuals who have invented or discovered a novel type of plant and who have been able to reproduce that plant asexually. Plant patents are not issued for either tuber-propagated or uncultivated plant varieties.

3. Utility patents are issued to individuals who have invented novel processes, machines, and compositions of matter. The majority of information contained herein applies most specifically to utility patents—the most complex and common of all patents issued.

What Qualifications Must Be Met for a Patent to Be Granted?

The U.S. government has very specific rules for qualifications in a particular invention in order to be granted patent status. Broadly speaking, there are five major categories of requirements that all inventions must meet if they are to be considered patentable. These categories pertain to the scope of an idea, its utility, its novelty, the extent to which it might be nonobvious, and the possibility that it may be reduced to practice.

- ✔ *Scope.* Patents can be issued to cover only a limited range of ideas. Among the things that may not be patented are naturally occurring objects, entities, laws, and phenomena, as well as abstract ideas. Some manners of plants may be patented, but only in the cases where scientists have genetically manipulated DNA in a unique way that may yield some novel and useful benefit to humankind, however great or little said benefit might be.

- ✔ *Utility.* Nonuseful inventions may not be patented. Any useful machine, process, composition of matter, or improvement upon the same may be patented provided that said machine, process, and so on is not disclosed in the prior art (see "Prior Art" section later in this chapter).

- ✔ *Novelty.* A number of very specific conditions must be met in order for an invention to qualify as novel. Novelty requires that the original invention predate knowledge and include the use or sale of the invention by others within the United States or any foreign country. Also to be included is the description of the invention in a U.S. publication or foreign country. The application must also be submitted within one year of the applicant's public use or the sale of the invention.

- ✔ *Nonobviousness.* If an invention is judged to have been obvious to any person of average skill in the field relating to the invention, it may be barred from receiving patent approval.

- ✔ *Reduction to Practice.* At one time, it was necessary for inventors to present the USPTO with an actual working model in order to receive a patent. Today, a *constructive* reduction to practice requirement stipulates that only the method of manufacture or effectuation of an invention needs to be made clear (not to the layperson, but to one skilled in the realm of art pertaining to the invention). The method requirement ensures that only inventors who can actually deliver on the technological promise of their inventions be granted a patent.

STARTING SECURELY

Many inventors find it useful to begin protecting their IP before applying for a patent. Depending on the sophistication required to both comprehend and harvest the idea, unprotected conversations with other people may or may not constitute a serious threat security. If there is truly some potential value to your ideas, it is especially important to begin protecting early and to err on the side of conservancy. Have a simple nondisclosure agreement (NDA) or confidentiality agreement (CA) drawn up to be signed by any person you discuss your ideas with before any substantive conversation takes place. Where the costs of having such an agreement prepared professionally are of concern, the inventor may wish to review some of the popular prepackaged legal software available in bookstores and libraries or books on the subject for examples on which to base simple CAs (see sample in Chapter 1).

Another step you should consider is the protection of your working notes. Even simple measures such as using a safe or encrypting your computer records could potentially go a long way toward preserving the idea.

Finally, be careful about how much involvement you allow from others in helping to develop your idea. If you need their assistance, prepare an outlined agreement specifying the precise nature of any compensation due and include ownership and control.

Professional Assistance

In order to be certain that adequate background and preparatory work is done in producing an application for submittal, it is advisable that inventors seek the services of a registered patent agent or attorney. These individuals are skilled in carefully addressing the details that might stand in the way of a successful patent application.

Registered Patent Agents

Patent agents are not attorneys-at-law, but are registered to practice patent law by and before the U.S. Patent and Trademark Office. While the range of duties these individuals are legally authorized to perform is not as extensive as that of patent attorneys, patent agents are generally equally qualified to perform all of the basic work that many inventors will require in obtaining patents for their inventions. Patent agents generally have an advanced degree or work experience suiting them to their legal function. In addition, all agents not having served for at least four years as an examiner within the USPTO must pass a special exam given by the USPTO to guarantee competence in the field of work. These individuals do not work for the government, but may be found in private organizations that serve the needs of inventors.

Registered Patent Attorneys

Registered patent attorneys must successfully complete the same exam issued to individuals wishing to become patent agents, but hold higher credentials which allow them to perform legal services above and beyond those executed by patent agents. Most importantly, patent attorneys are authorized by virtue of their Juris Doctorates to litigate in matters of patent law in whichever states they are licensed to practice law. It should also be noted that, having been admitted to the bar, attorneys are bound by a code of ethics. Even if attorneys fail to adhere to the ethics they pledge to uphold, their qualifications also permit them to be sued, should such be necessary.

Choosing Your Representative

Generally speaking, one should expect to pay more for the services of a patent attorney, who is licensed to litigate over matters of intellectual property, than for the services of a patent agent, who is not licensed to litigate over such matters. Fees for professional services vary substantially between agents and attorneys and among the members of the groups themselves. However, considering what many inventors have at stake, the cost of even highly priced professional services may be indispensable. It is advised that total fees be determined before entering into a binding contract with any agent or attorney, as many of the flat rates quoted by attorneys and agents do not actually cover work required after submission of an application. For convenience, the following table provides a starting point, with some average figures obtained from a selection of queried professionals. These rates apply to small entities. Large corporations will pay much more for comparable services.

Service Description	Agent	Attorney
Initial consultation	Free	Free
Hourly rate	$100	$250
Preparation and submission	$3,000	$4,500
Expected total costs	$4,500–$7,500	$6,000–$10,000

These figures apply most specifically to utility patent applications. Design applications can cost far less, sometimes half the amount of a utility application, and plant patent applications usually come in somewhere between design and utility patents in terms of cost. Office actions taken by the USPTO require responses from inventors, and rejected applications will require additional capital outlays in order to be disputed. Agents and attorneys may charge by the hour for such work, or these costs may be included in a fixed rate. Many agents and attorneys give inventors the option of paying flat fees, hourly rates, or some combination of the two. Again, the figures given here are rough averages only. Inventors can expect to find that costs may vary considerably given such factors as the complexity of their inventions.

The most important criterion for selecting a representative will be the relative amount and quality of experience in practicing patent law. You will also want to learn what sorts of activity the representative has regularly engaged in and his or her success. Where there any complaints registered? Each of these questions must be answered and their answers weighed carefully in your decision.

Whenever possible, use an agent or attorney who specializes or has knowledge in the scientific or technical field pertaining to your invention. The added insight that comes with such an understanding can be especially helpful in guiding development in the most appropriate manner.

As a final note, it is worth addressing the fact that nonregistered agents, attorneys, organizations, and the like do not practice within the jurisdiction of the USPTO, and so fall outside of the realm of regulation that the USPTO has over registered professionals. This will be of key concern to inventors who may have grievances with their attorney, agent, or other representative.

DOCUMENTING YOUR IDEAS

The U.S. government gives rights to the first in conceiving an idea, provided that it can be proven. Therefore, it is very important to keep a well-documented account of the invention's development wherever possible. This may very well be the most important step an inventor can take in the process of protecting the IP rights. It is common knowledge that mailing a disclosure of one's work to oneself via registered mail is a useful way to establish a verified date of idea origination for legal purposes. What is not commonly known is that there are more effective methods of establishing the origination of such dates. It would be a good idea to employ these methods in one's own work to best safeguard intellectual property.

The Disclosure Document Program

Send a document disclosing the invention, which must contain a comprehensive explanation of the invention and the manner that it is produced and used. Where applicable, drawings should be included as well. Further, a disclosure should be made as to the purpose of the invention and how it is "novel" compared to any existing inventions. For the sake of efficiency, the USPTO mandates a specific format for disclosure documents. Contact the USPTO for details on the latest requirements and fees.

The Patent and Trademark Office will keep the disclosure document for a period of two years. During that time, the documents will be considered evidence of the earliest date of conception for the invention. If no official patent application is filed before the end of this initial two-year period, the disclosure documents will be destroyed. It is incumbent upon the inventor to proceed with the patent process in as expeditious a manner as possible to fulfill the intended purpose of safeguarding the date of origination of property rights.

Upon receipt of the successfully completed disclosure document, the USPTO will return a receipt form identifying the date of receipt and an identification code for the document. Remember that specific reference must be made to the original disclosure document date of receipt and identification number at any such time as further documents, such as an official patent application, are submitted to the USPTO.

Other Options

Another effective way of safeguarding property rights is to maintain a witnessed, permanently bound, and page-numbered notebook that records the ideas in an orderly and clearly understandable fashion. This notebook should record as much of the invention's features as possible, including notes as to the novel and useful distinctions and advancements over any existing similar art. Every time new material is added to this record, have an objective witness sign and date beside said additions as soon as possible. Forms of notarized records other than the bound book may be kept also.

PRIOR ART

Before beginning the often lengthy and expensive campaign to get one's idea or invention patented, it is highly advisable that one conducts a search for prior art. The term *prior art* refers to all subjects that do not meet the condition of novelty, as explained earlier in the section on patent qualifications.

The first thing that the USPTO examiner will do in evaluating a patent application is to review the prior art. Discovery of the existence of prior art will immediately nullify any possibility of the application's approval. Consequently, it ought to be clear that beginning the patent process without having conducted a prior art search may very well be an exercise in futility.

Search Options

Since professionals usually charge somewhere between $500 and $1,000 for a simple prior art search, it makes sense for most inventors to explore prior art initially on their own. While there's no way one can be sure how long the search may take, one could easily discover that the invention is already disclosed in the prior art within just the first few minutes of searching. There are a variety of tools that can assist the inventor in homing in on a discovery of the prior art status. Some are listed below.

Internet Searching The most easily accessible tool is the World Wide Web. By performing even simple searches on Internet search engines, the inventor will find hundreds of sites devoted to intellectual property, from university programs to home pages for law firms. For best results, try using search terms related to your topic such as "intellectual property" and "patent." The USPTO's own home page, located at www.uspto.gov, is perhaps the most indispensable Internet site, replete with all of the information needed to successfully patent a qualifying invention. See the additional sources at the end of this chapter for URLs of numerous other sites worth visiting.

Agencies and Organizations There are several public and private agencies to assist the inventor in discovering prior art. Costs of employing them can vary considerably, but so does the effectiveness of each organization's searching capabilities. Inventors choosing to use professional assistance should research the firms, agents, and attorneys that they're dealing with before entering into any binding agreements. Look for a track record of success, among other things.

Government Resources The USPTO provides physical facilities for the general public to use in pursuing intellectual property research.

> United States Patent and Trademark Office
> Crystal Plaza 3
> 2021 Jefferson Davis Highway
> Arlington, VA 20231

Independent Resources Independent search firms often employ the same computer databases available through the USPTO and PTDL sites. Whether paying an hourly rate or a fixed sum, inventors are likely to spend several hundred dollars for search services. Although some firms possess technical expertise in prior art search, there is no guarantee that the patent examiner will not question the technical application. Another factor is that some firms average four to six weeks to return the results of the prior art searches, though services may usually be expedited if a fee is paid for express service. The high cost of employing expert services this early in the patent process may be unwarranted given the complexity of many inventions. This matter calls for consideration on the part of the individual inventor.

In addition to the independent search firms, patent agents, and attorneys offering search services, a variety of other organizations exist that offer various forms of service. The services offered by many of these companies and organizations may also be available through some of the aforementioned firms, agents, and attorneys.

Typically, an inventor will be able to find both local and national inventors' organizations offering a broad range of services which can be equally helpful to both the novice working on the first invention and the veteran with one or more patents. Some of these organizations are nonprofit, and many require no fees or only moderate fees to join. In addition to being a valuable resource, organizations are often good launch pads for inventors looking for other resources such as journals, magazines, and other organizations. The World Wide Web and the local Yellow Pages are good places to start when seeking such organizations. Consult the additional sources at the end of this chapter for some additional information.

Some Words of Caution

Before using the services of any organizations, it would be a good idea to check with the local Better Business Bureau to see if any complaints have been lodged. Be particularly wary of services that ask for up-front fees to promote your invention. The USPTO issues a warning on its web site about "inventor services." It states that "there are many firms who prey on small inventors" essentially starting with a small fee and grossly escalating charges while providing little in the way of substantive assistance. The Federal Trade Commission (FTC) is currently conducting an operation investigating such companies. Any inventor considering using an unfamiliar firm should contact the FTC for more information. Should an inventor already be mired in a troublesome relationship, it is wise to seek assistance from the FTC. Poor quality of work done for the inventor by firms can actually do more harm than good to the inventor's long-term intellectual property rights. This is not to say that all such firms are untrustworthy, but forewarned is forearmed.

APPLYING FOR A PATENT

Generally, only the inventor may apply for a patent. In cases where more than one inventor is responsible for generating the idea, inventors must file jointly. Only in cases of insanity or death may another person legally apply instead of an inventor. Exceptions are when an inventor declines to apply or is unable to apply, in which case some person with an exclusive interest in the intellectual property may apply on an inventor's behalf.

The USPTO offers a choice of two patent applications depending on what state of development an inventor's subject is in at the time application is made. Essentially, the inventor with a complete concept who is fully prepared to submit a comprehensive case for patentability will submit a *nonprovisional* application. Inventors who want to establish a filing date, but are not prepared, can file a *provisional* application giving them one full year from the date of filing to complete development of the invention. Concerns regarding marketability, licensing, capital requirements, and the like should also be included. Only inventors seeking design patents are limited to use of the nonprovisional application form. Inventors seeking utility or plant patents may use either form.

Provisional Application Provisional applications serve to establish an official date of filing with the USPTO. The applications are not as complete as the nonprovisional application form and must be succeeded within 12 months of initial filing in order for the formal patentability review process to follow.

The provisional patent application must include the following:

1. A cover sheet consisting of:

   Statement that identifies the application as provisional.

   Inventor name(s).

   Inventor residence(s).

   Title given to the invention.

   Correspondence address.

   Identification of any U.S. government agency with a property interest in the IP.

   Name and registration number of any attorney(s) or agent(s) involved.

   Docket number (if applicable).

2. A partial specification. This sort of specification may simply be an adequate description of the invention. No specific claims are necessary.

3. A drawing, in cases where such is necessary.

4. A fee (consult the USPTO for fees, as they change annually).

Nonprovisional Application The nonprovisional application is the more complete of the two application forms offered by the USPTO. Submission of a nonprovisional application will initiate the process of examination leading to a USPTO judgment on patentability.

The nonprovisional patent application must include the following:

1. A specification: a written description of the invention that makes at least one specific claim.
2. An oath or declaration.
3. A drawing, in cases where such is necessary.
4. A fee (consult the USPTO or updated fee schedule for current fees).

The claims must be as comprehensive as possible. They will form the basis for an invention's patentability and serve to settle legal considerations concerning infringement after such time as a patent might be issued.

Drawing Up Claims

Claims are the most important element of the patent application. They officially designate the property rights of the inventor. In a very real sense, the claim *is* the intellectual property. When making claims, the inventor should detail all intellectual property rights.

Patent Review Process

Once the completed nonprovisional application has been filed with the USPTO, it will be assigned to a specific examination group knowledgeable in the realm of technology where the invention falls. From within this group, a particular examiner will take up the review. Reviews are conducted in the order in which patents are filed, or as otherwise prescribed by the Commissioner of Patent and Trademarks. Inventors who wish to make a case for special consideration, including early review, must have appeals approved directly by the Commissioner.

Twelve Steps: From Idea, to Patent, to Enterprise

1. Conceive an idea and perform a preliminary analysis of the market and patent potential. Take preparatory steps to protect your idea, limiting exposure and documenting carefully.

2. Document a brief, descriptive record of the idea. Define what is being protected. There are numerous forms of protection and each may vary to a single attribute or range of services. This can include product features or an entire line of products.

3. Select an intellectual property law firm. Consider the success of the firm in handling applications and its experience in the realm of technology related to the patent. Visit the firm for an initial consultation, usually provided free of charge. It might be helpful to compare the services and costs of using registered agents and attorneys.

4. Conduct a preliminary research. Depending on your financial position, you or your attorney should perform the initial prior art search. This search may be done using the online resources of the USPTO or with on-site computers dedicated for this purpose. Attorneys and agents will have their own resources with which to perform this search. If no prior art is discovered, you may proceed to the next step.

5. Conduct a detailed search and in-depth review of identifying and reviewing related patents. This research must be disclosed to the patent office. If there are no conflicting patents, you can proceed further.

6. Prepare the patent application using diagrams and flow charts. File the patent with a law firm and receive filing data from the patent office.

7. It takes approximately 9 to 12 months to get a response from the patent office in the form of an Office Action letter. More than one such letter may require a response.

8. Respond to the Office Action letter. This is your opportunity to address any objections or issues raised by the USPTO with regard to the application.

9. For the next four to six months, wait to hear if the patent is accepted or rejected. It may come to pass that only part of the patent or claims are accepted. If you and your representatives have done a good job, the entire application will hopefully be approved.

10. The patent is accepted and a patent number is issued.

11. Embark on your new enterprise. Options may include licensing the patent for use by others. Ultimately, an exit strategy involving the sale of the patent should also be considered.

12. Maintain vigilance and safeguard your rights by searching for patent infringement and prosecuting appropriately.

TRADE SECRETS

In the realm of intellectual property, there are times when information is best left undisclosed, even if disclosure and registration with the federal government would afford a measure of legal protection. Vital information not shared with the general public, but valuable to the success of an entrepreneurial entity, may fall within the realm of trade secrets.

What Are Trade Secrets?

Modern trade secret law dates back to the industrial revolution in England, but its precedent may be found in ancient Roman law, which imposed punishment upon persons found to be guilty of impelling others to disclose secrets of trade. In the United States, the Uniform Trade Secrets Act (UTSA) was drafted by the National Conference of Commissioners on Uniform State Laws. The protection of trade secrets differs from state to state, so it is important that entrepreneurs familiarize themselves fully to best safeguard trade secrets.

Broadly speaking, trade secrets may constitute any manner or form of information that, by way of its secrecy, yields its user potential or actual economic value and economic and/or competitive advantage over others. It is generally stipulated that in order for a trade secret to be legally defended as such, its owner must take reasonable steps to ensure its secrecy. Information subject to common knowledge may not be protected as a trade secret, but trade secrets needn't be complex or novel in order to qualify as such. Among the many forms a trade secret may take are those of formula, pattern, device, and process. Even a customer list may serve as a trade secret when meeting the requirements. In some cases, such trade secrets are more appropriately referred to as business secrets.

Advantages and Disadvantages of Trade Secrets

The trade secret's greatest advantage over other forms of IP may be in the potentially limitless duration of its value and service to its owner. Coca-Cola is a good example of a company that has maintained a trade secret for over 100 years and continues to enjoy the economic benefit of such. Coke has been successful in keeping the formula for its popular soft drink secure from outside discovery, but not all business entities can rely on similar success. This is an important consideration to keep in mind, because any formulation, process, or other form of IP maintained as a trade secret by one party can be lawfully employed by an outside party if development is done independently and without any infringement. Even Coke's valuable trade secret might one day be reproduced and used competitively by an outside party.

Because the value of a trade secret may be compromised even under the best cases of internal protection, the decision to maintain some IP as a trade secret rather than filing and registering for a patent, for instance, must be weighed carefully. To help make such a decision, first determine whether the value of some IP might be reasonably expected to endure beyond the period of protection afforded by a patent. If only 5 to 10 years of real value are expected, a patent may be the way to go, as patents provide a more guaranteed form of protection. On the other hand, filing for, registering, and defending patents can often be far more costly than maintaining trade secrecy. Here a cost/benefit analysis must be employed.

Trade Secret Licensing

As with other forms of IP, licensing can be a viable business option for owners of trade secrets. Trade secret licensing is remarkable, however, as it may present the most interesting example of IP longevity yet. While the value of a trade secret may be compromised in the event that independent discovery occurs, once a trade secret has been licensed under specific terms, that license remains inviolate regardless of what kind of information falls into the hands of the general public. Only the licensing party has the authority to amend the terms of a licensing agreement, should such be requested on the part of the licensee. Even if the licensed IP becomes less valuable to the licensee, or to the licenser for its own use, the licensing fees and other financial provisions of a licensed trade secret may be enforced for as long as a trade secret license remains in force.

Protecting Trade Secrets

The first step in protecting a trade secret lies in its identification. It is important that the entrepreneur or business entity engage in a competitive analysis to determine whether the trade secrets exist. Once identified, the trade secret must be actively protected. Failure to take clear and decisive precautions in this regard can lead to the loss of a valuable trade secret.

One of the most effective ways of maintaining a trade secret is to limit disclosure. The smaller the number of persons exposed to a trade secret, the lower the likelihood that it will fall into the hands of competition. Where possible, it is a good idea to only expose part of a trade secret to any given individual in whom some trust must be place (such as a worker required for completing only part of a process). An even more important consideration than the number of persons exposed is the nature of persons exposed. Better to place faith in a large number of individuals who can be relied upon to maintain the secrecy of some information than in just one who cannot. Members of a venture who have a vested interest in maintaining trade secrecy are naturally more likely to be reliable regarding key knowledge. Keep the trade secret disclosure on a need-to-know basis, and in all cases make sure that some form of CA, NDA, or other employment agreement is filled out and kept safe as early as possible.

Special attention is called for in cases where an employee, partner, or other individual may be leaving a venture. In such cases, filing of a *noncompete agreement* would also be advisable. Agreements should also be made with entities working outside of the venture itself, such as venture capitalists, attorneys, engineers, suppliers, vendors, and other business partners.

Any *proprietary* information fundamental to the ongoing success of a venture should be considered worthy of protection. Whether it take the form of a supplier list or a supplier's price list, sensitive financial information, computer programming code, a manufacturing process, recipe, or marketing strategy, information that yields competitive and economic advantage must be safeguarded.

noncompete agreement

legal agreement preventing the signer from joining or starting a similar venture.

proprietary
that which is owned, such as a patent, formula, brand name, or trademark associated with the product/service.

SUMMARY

The United States government provides provisions for the protection of various forms of intellectual property. Among these are copyright, trademark, patent, and trade secret. The government's purpose in granting protection for IP is to encourage the advancement of "science and the useful arts" by offering those who make such advancement rewards for doing so. The importance of intellectual property to the entrepreneur is in its ability to provide profit or some other form of competitive advantage. Intellectual property has many of the same characteristics as other forms of property. It may be used, bought and sold, licensed, or otherwise transferred.

The development and protection of intellectual property can be a painstaking and costly process. Many tools exist to assist entrepreneurs in pursuing IP rights, some of which can add significantly to the costs involved, but which can prove invaluable to doing the job right. The government agencies responsible for the oversight and administration of IP matters are among the most accessible, inexpensive, and useful resources available to entrepreneurs. In addition, there are a variety of public and private organizations available for hire in pursuing IP rights. Registered patent agents and attorneys may be the most qualified to help entrepreneurs. In spite of the higher fees charged by agents and attorneys, their qualifications and expertise can add value in overcoming the complex hurdles encountered in the pursuit of IP rights.

Each form of IP offers different levels of legal protection by the federal government. Protection for IP differs widely, internationally, and may even vary from state to state within the United States, in the case of trade secrets. Promoting and protecting IP is an active process and steps should be taken to protect this asset. It is equally important to defend one's IP, as it is to avoid infringing on another's.

If you are involved in IP infringement, a cost-benefit analysis should be employed in determining what legal remedies, if any, to employ. The costs of prosecution can be daunting and may not prove worthwhile unless real financial gain is at stake. Where significant value may be in jeopardy, it is recommended that entrepreneurs engage legal counsel.

The field of law pertaining to intellectual property is complex and in constant flux. Recent developments in technology have only added to the complexity of IP law. It is recommended that the entrepreneur stay abreast of current developments and consult early with professionals in the field. The way in which entrepreneurs handle the development, protection, enforcement, and prosecution of intellectual property can make or break any enterprise. It also can be of particular consequence to start-up companies with less experience and fewer resources. Conscientious attention to detail and a commitment to one's project are vital to ensuring the success of an IP-based enterprise.

ADDITIONAL INTELLECTUAL PROPERTY RESOURCES

Internet IP Source Sites

✔ About.com Inventors' Page: www.investors.tqn.com

✔ American Intellectual Property Law Association: www.aipla.org

✔ Derwent-Thomson Scientific: www.derwent.com

✔ Everything You Want to Know about SEC Filings: www.10Kwizard.com

✔ Franklin Pierce Law Center: www.fplc.edu

✔ Hoover's Corporate Information: www.hoovers.com

✔ IBM Intellectual Property Network: www.patents.ibm.com

✔ Inventors' Alliance: www.inventorsalliance.org

✔ Inventors' Digest: www.inventorsdigest.com

✔ Inventors Resource Homepage: www.gibbsgroup.com

✔ IPWorldwide: www.ipworldwide.com

✔ Licensing Executives Society: www.les.org

✔ Patent Café: www.patentcafe.com

✔ Thomas Register of American Manufacturers: www.thomasregister.com

✔ U.S. Copyright Office: www.loc.gov/copyright

✔ U.S. Patent and Trademark Office: www.uspto.gov

Additional Sources

Avoiding Patent, Trademark, and Copyright Problems
U.S. Small Business Administration
SBA Publications
P.O. Box 30
Denver, CO 80201-0030

The Complete Copyright Protection Kit
Intellain, Inc.
P.O. Box 6492
Denver, CO 80206

Inventors Clubs of America
Alexander T. Marinaccio
P.O. Box 450621
Atlanta, GA 31145-0261
(800) 336-0169

The Inventor's Notebook, 2d Edition
Fred Grissom and David Pressman
Nolo Press
950 Parker Street
Berkeley, CA 94710
(800) 955-4775
(510) 549-1976

Licensing Industry Merchandisers' Association
350 Fifth Avenue, Suite 2309
New York, NY 10118
(212) 244-1944

Building the Resources and Setting Up the Company

Objectives

1. Assess the factors in deciding which form of ownership is best suited for a potential business.

2. Outline the advantages and disadvantages of a sole proprietorship and partnership.

3. Explain the corporate form of ownership and describe how a business is incorporated.

4. Understand the S corporation and the limited liability company (LLC).

5. Know how to set up stock options and employment agreements.

INTRODUCTION

Some of us start businesses and determine the structure of the company with lots of thought and planning. Others find themselves establishing a company without much regard to how the business should be structured. However, one of the most important decisions you will make is how to legally structure your business.

Before you decide how to organize a company, you need to identify the legal structure that will best meet the requirements of the business. This is due to the tax laws, liability situation, and ways to attract capital.

Profile: Roy Wetterstrom, President of Micro Modeling Associates—Remaking the Company from Top to Bottom

Micro Modeling Associates (MMA) grew out of the need for automated tools in the Merchant Banking Division of First Bank System (now U.S. Bancorp) in Minneapolis, where Wetterstrom worked as an analyst. Soon, his Lotus 1-2-3 models became the department's standard. Eventually, Wetterstrom was placed in charge of building a state-of-the-art Windows-based corporate finance model in Microsoft Excel. With the bank's permission, Wetterstrom and a partner marketed the model to Wall Street. Merrill Lynch was impressed and promised to keep Wetterstrom and his partner busy for three months. With this promise and $40,000 that Wetterstrom and his partner scraped together from various sources, Micro Modeling Associates was born. MMA also secured a $20 million equity investment from TA Associates, a Boston-based investment firm, and a $15 million line of credit from Fleet Bank, Boston. Initially, the company was organized as a subchapter S corporation. The purpose was to limit ownership in the company, pass through losses to the owners, and maintain control for future growth. However, as the business grew, his $54 million client/server consulting business required changes in structure and strategy.

The plan was to transform Micro Modeling Associates into a top-tier Internet service, strategy, and developmental company. To meet this mission, the company changed its name to "Plural" and became a Delaware C corporation. This name and structure change positioned the company to become a top-tier Internet player and gave "Plural" the power of a potential public offering. The new strategy also included discounted rates to dot-com companies for services and making up the difference by taking an equity stake in the company. Roy's goal was to build a mutual fund of pre-IPO dot-com companies and use the equity to retain employees and attract new talent. Additionally, a search firm was hired to recruit a president and chief marketing officer to meet and complete the transformed company image.

When Wetterstrom and his partner first started the firm, it was virtually the only company doing Excel-based applications for the financial industry. Since that time, by organizing the company structure and strategy, the firm has expanded its client base to other industries while consistently keeping ahead of the technology curve. The firm is now on the cutting edge of Internet and e-solutions consulting development.

Many companies provide added incentives for keeping key employees, by providing an equity interest in the company. This is usually in the form of common stock or options to acquire common stock. We will discuss in this section how companies should establish a qualified stock option plan and how selected employees receive options to purchase stock in the company.

The legal form of the business proprietorship, C corporation, S corporation, partnership, and LLC, should be determined in light of the business's short- and long-term needs. In this chapter, we will examine the pros and cons of each of them and how to prepare a checklist to start the business. Your specific situation, circumstances, and issues will determine the choice.

WHICH FORM OF OWNERSHIP IS BEST?

In choosing a form of ownership, entrepreneurs must remember that there is no single "best" form; what is best depends on the individual's circumstances. The following questions will help determine which form of ownership is best for you:

1. How big can this business potentially become?

2. How much control do you need in the decision-making process of the company? Are you willing to share ideas and the business's potential profits with others who can help build a more successful business?

3. How much capital is needed to start the business?

4. What tax considerations are important? What sources of income are there, and how are they to be sheltered?

5. In case of failure, to what extent are you willing to be personally responsible for debts created by the business?

6. Is it important that the business continue in case of owner incapacity or death?

7. Who will be the sole or major beneficiary of the business success? Is the owner the type of person

who doesn't mind taking all the risks but expects to reap all the benefits if successful?

8. Can you put up with the time-consuming bureaucratic red tape associated with more complicated forms of ownership? What is the emotional reaction to government regulations and their accompanying paperwork requirements?

FORMS OF DOING BUSINESS

The legal form of the business (sole proprietorship, C corporation, S corporation, partnership, or LLC) should be determined in light of the business's short- and long-term needs. Because there are significant tax and nontax differences among the forms, the results and requirements of each form should be carefully considered to ensure that the business form chosen best meets the requirements. A brief analysis of each of the forms of doing business is presented to stimulate the process and meet the business requirements.

SOLE PROPRIETORSHIP

A *sole proprietorship* is a form of business that has a single owner and requires only local business licenses to open. If the plan is to start a business under a name other than that of the owner, the owner must file a name in order to operate "doing business as" (for example, Jack's SmartCard Consulting). The business can be dissolved or closed at any time and always ends upon death of the owner. The sole owner has the right to make all the decisions for the business.

However, the biggest disadvantage is that the owner is personally liable for all debts and contracts of the business. There is no distinction between personal and business debts; so if the business cannot pay its bills, the creditors can sue to collect from personal assets. In matters dealing with taxes, income from the business flows directly through and is taxed at the individual rate. If the owner does not plan to take a salary, the income is the profits from the business. There is no carryback or carryforward of losses.

 sole proprietorship a business firm owned by only one person and operated for his or her profit.

Advantages of a Sole Proprietorship

Sole proprietorships are popular because they have a number of attractive features:

✔ *Simple to Create.* One of the most attractive features of proprietorships is how fast and simple it is to begin operations. If the proprietor wishes to operate the business under his or her own name the individual simply obtains the necessary local licenses and begins operations. In a proprietorship, the proprietor is the business. It is not difficult to start up a proprietorship in a single day if the business is simple.

✔ *Low Start-up Fees.* In addition to being easy to begin, the proprietorship is generally the least expensive form of ownership to establish. Legal papers do not need to be filed. Rather, the proprietor goes to the local government and states the nature of the new business. The government assesses the appropriate fees and license costs. Once these fees are paid, the owner may conduct business in that jurisdiction.

If the business has a trade name, a "Certificate of Doing Business under an Assumed Name" can be obtained from the state in which the business will operate. The fee for the certificate is usually nominal. Acquiring this certificate involves conducting a name search to determine that the name is not already registered with the secretary of state as a trademark or service mark. Filing this certificate also notifies the state of who the owner of the business is.

✔ *Profit Incentive.* One major advantage to the proprietorship is that after all the debts are paid, the owner receives all the profits (less taxes, of course). Profits represent an excellent scorecard of success.

✔ *Total Decision-Making Authority.* Because the sole proprietor is in total control of operations and can respond quickly to changes, this becomes an asset in rapidly shifting markets. The freedom to set the company's course of action is another major motivation for selecting this ownership form. For the individual who thrives on the enjoyment of seeking new opportunities and then modifies the business as needed, the free, unimpeded decision making of the proprietorship is vital.

✔ *No Special Legal Restrictions.* The proprietorship is the least regulated form of business ownership. In a time when government requests for information seem never-ending, this feature has much merit.

✔ *Easy to Discontinue.* When the owner cannot continue operations, he or she can terminate the business quickly, even though the owner will still be liable for all outstanding debts and obligations.

Disadvantages of a Proprietorship

As advantageous as the proprietorship form of ownership is, it does have its disadvantages:

✔ *Unlimited Personal Liability.* The greatest disadvantage of a sole proprietorship is unlimited personal liability; that is, the sole proprietor is personally liable for all business debts. The proprietor owns all the business's assets. If the business fails, these assets can be sold to cover debts. If there are still unpaid debts, creditors can sell the owner's personal assets to cover the remaining debt. Failure of the business can ruin the owner financially. Because the law views the proprietor and the business as one and the same, the business's debts are the owner's debts. Laws protecting an individual's assets to some degree may vary from one state to another. Most states require creditors to leave the failed business owner a minimum amount of equity in a home, car, and some personal items.

✔ *Limited Skills and Capabilities of the Sole Owner.* The owner may not have the needed skills to run a successful business. Each individual has skills and talents reflective of education, training, and work experience. However, the lack of skills and knowledge in other areas is what often causes failure. The sole owner who fails might have been successful if he or she had had previous knowledge of possible problems and had obtained good, timely advice. Sole owners need to recognize their shortcomings and then find help in becoming proficient in those areas. Also, successful entrepreneurs are always seeking to keep abreast of the changes in their area of interest.

✔ *Limited Access to Capital.* For a business to grow and expand, a sole proprietor generally needs financial resources. Many proprietors put all they have into their businesses and often use their personal resources as collateral on existing loans. In short, proprietors, unless they have great personal wealth, find it difficult to raise additional money while maintaining sole ownership. The business may be sound in the long run, but short-term cash flow difficulties can cause financial headaches. Most banks and lending institutions have well-defined formulas for borrower's eligibility. The proprietor in most cases cannot obtain the credit needed to weather the financial storm.

✔ *Lack of Continuity for the Business.* Lack of continuity is inherent in a sole proprietorship. If the proprietor dies or becomes incapacitated, the business automatically terminates. Unless a family member or employee can effectively take over, the business could be in jeopardy. If no one is trained to run the business, creditors can petition the courts to liquidate the assets of the dissolved business to pay outstanding debt.

C CORPORATION

The C corporation is the most common of the forms of business ownership. It is a separate entity apart from its owners and may engage in business, issue contracts, sue and be sued, and pay taxes.

When a corporation is founded, it accepts the regulations and restrictions of the state in which it is incorporated. A corporation doing business in the state in which it is incorporated is a domestic corporation. When it conducts business in another state, that state considers the corporation to be a foreign corporation. Corporations that are formed in other countries but do business in the United States are alien corporations.

Generally, the corporation must report annually its financial operations to its home state's attorney general. These financial reports become public record. If the stock of the corporation is sold in more than one state, the corporation must comply with federal and state regulations governing the sale of corporate securities.

How to Incorporate

Once the owners decide to form a corporation, they must choose the state in which to incorporate. If the business will operate within a single state, it is probably most logical to incorporate in that state. There are differences in the requirements each state places on the corporations.

Every state requires a Certificate of Incorporation or charter that is filed with the secretary of state.

Information Required in the Certificate of Incorporation

✔ *Name of the Corporation.* The corporation must choose a name that is not similar to another firm in that state as it causes confusion or deception.

✔ *Purpose of the Corporation.* State in general terms the nature of the business. The purpose must, of course, be lawful. An illustration might be "to engage in the sale of office furniture and fixtures." The purpose should be broad enough to allow for some expansion in the activities of the business. It can be as broad as "to engage in any activity permitted by the state."

✔ *Time Frame of the Corporation.* In most cases, corporations are with no specific termination date; they are formed in perpetuity. However, it is possible to incorporate for a specific duration.

✔ *Name and Address of the Incorporators.* The incorporators must be identified and are liable under the law to attest that all information is correct. In some states, one or more of the incorporators must reside in the state in which the corporation is being incorporated.

✔ *Place of Business.* The post office address of the principal office of the corporation must be listed. This is the address to which all official correspondence will be sent.

✔ *Capital Required at the Time of Incorporation.* It should be determined whether the state of incorporation requires a specific percentage of the par value of the capital stock be paid in cash and deposited in the bank prior to incorporation.

✔ *Provision for Preemptive Rights.* Give preference to some stockholders to buy a specified proportion of new stock issues that are granted to stockholders.

✔ *Restrictions on Transferring Shares.* Many closely held corporations, often family members, might require shareholders to offer their stock to the corporation first. This is called a right of first refusal and allows the corporation better control of its ownership.

✔ *Names and Addresses of Initial Officers and Directors of the Corporation.*

✔ *Rules under Which the Corporation Will Operate.* Bylaws are the rules and regulations established by the corporation for its internal management and operations. Once the attorney general has approved your request for incorporation and fees are paid, the approved articles of the incorporation become its charter. With the charter in hand, the next order of business is to hold an organizational meeting for the stockholders to formally elect directors, who in turn will appoint the corporate officers.

✔ *Capital Stock Authorization.* Include the amount and class (or type) of capital stock the corporation wishes to issue. This section also must define the different classifications of stock and any special rights, preferences, or limits each class might have.

Advantages of a Corporation

✔ *Limited Liability of the Stockholders.* The corporation allows investors to limit their liability to the total amount of their investment. This legal protection of personal assets beyond the business is of critical concern to many potential investors. Because start-up companies are so risky, lenders and other creditors often require the owners to personally guarantee loans made to the corporation. By making these guarantees, owners are putting their personal assets at risk (just as in a proprietorship) despite choosing the corporate form of ownership.

✔ *Ability to Attract Capital.* Based on the protection of limited liability, corporations have proved to be the most effective form of ownership to accumulate large amounts of capital. Limited only by the number of shares authorized in its charter (which can be amended), the corporation can raise money to begin business and expand as opportunity dictates.

✔ *Ability of the Corporation to Continue Indefinitely.* Unless limited by its charter, the corporation as a separate legal entity theoretically can continue indefinitely. The existence of the corporation does not depend on any single individual.

✔ *Transferable Ownership.* If stockholders in a corporation are displeased with the progress of the business, they can sell their shares to another individual. Stocks can be transferred through inheritance to a new generation of owners. If any person wishes to own some shares in a firm and there is someone who would like to sell his or her interest in that firm, an exchange is possible. During all this change of ownership, the business continues.

✔ *Skills, Expertise, and Knowledge.* Unlike the proprietor who is often the only active member of management, the corporation can draw on the skills, expertise, and knowledge of its officers and board of directors, and people whose knowledge and experience can be used to shape the direction of the firm. In many cases, the board members act as advisers, giving the stockholders the advantage of their years of experience.

Disadvantages of a Corporation

✔ *Cost and Time Involved in the Incorporation Process.* Corporations can be costly and time-consuming to establish. The owners are giving birth to an artificial legal entity and the gestation period can be prolonged for the novice. In some states an attorney must handle the incorporation, but in most cases entrepreneurs can complete all of the requirements.

✔ *Liability of Closely Held Corporate Owners.* Corporations offer limited liability to the owners, which means the owners cannot be sued for the debts of the business unless they have personally guaranteed those debts. Therefore, the potential loss for you, the owner, is limited to the capital that you invested. (Capital does not have to be money; it can be property, machinery, skill, or labor.) Debtors can sue only the corporation and can claim only the assets of the business. For this reason, banks usually require closely held corporate owners to sign or guarantee any loans.

✔ *Double Taxation.* The corporation is a separate legal entity, and the income is taxed by the federal, state, and local government. Before the shareholders receive income as dividends, the corporation must pay taxes. Then, corporate shareholders must pay taxes on the dividend share they receive from these same profits. This double taxation is a distinct disadvantage of the corporate form of ownership.

 S corporation (Subchapter S corporation) a firm that has elected to be taxed as a partnership under the Subchapter S provision of the Internal Revenue Code.

SUBCHAPTER S CORPORATION

The *S corporation* (*Subchapter S corporation*) is a corporation that is treated like a partnership in that profits and losses are typically taxed directly to the individual shareholders. It is your responsibility to report the gains or losses on individual income tax returns. To become a Subchapter S corporation, the following must occur:

- ✔ The company must be a domestic company.
- ✔ Only one class of stock is allowed.
- ✔ Only individuals and certain trusts may own stock.
- ✔ There cannot be any nonresident aliens as shareholders.
- ✔ There can be a maximum of only 35 shareholders.
- ✔ The shareholders must elect to become an S corporation.

Advantages of an S Corporation

The S corporation retains all of the advantages of a regular corporation such as continuity of existence, transferability of ownership, and limited personal liability. The most notable provision of the S corporation is that it avoids the corporate income tax (and the resulting double taxation) and enables the business to pass through operating profits or losses to shareholders. In effect, the tax status of an S corporation is similar to that of a proprietorship or partnership.

Entrepreneur Fanny Chin, who launched Creative Calendars in 1998 as an S corporation, maintains that form of ownership today. "Since there were no shareholders except me, I didn't see any advantage to C corporation status since my earnings would have been taxed twice."

Another advantage the S corporation offers is avoiding the tax that C corporations pay on assets that have appreciated in value and are sold. Also, owners of S corporations enjoy the ability to make year-end payoffs to themselves if profits are high. In a C corporation, owners have no such luxury because the IRS watches for excessive compensation to owners and managers.

Disadvantages of an S Corporation

When the Tax Reform Act (TRA) of 1986 restructured individual and corporate tax rates, many business owners switched to S corporations in an attempt to lower their tax bills. For the first time since Congress enacted the federal income tax in 1913, the maximum individual rate was lower than the maximum corporate rate. However, Congress has realigned that structure by raising the top personal tax rate from 31 percent to 39.6 percent. The new rate is 4.6 percent higher than the current corporate tax rate of 35 percent. As a result, owners of many S corporations are considering making the switch back to C corporations. However, entrepreneurs must weigh the difference between the two rates against the double taxation disadvantage of the C corporation.

When Is the S Corporation a Wise Choice?

Choosing the S corporation status is usually beneficial to start-up companies anticipating net losses and to highly profitable firms with substantial dividends to pay out to shareholders. In these cases, the owner can use the loss to offset other income or is in a lower tax bracket than the corporation, thus saving money in the long run.

Similarly, small companies with these characteristics are not likely to benefit from S corporation status:

- ✔ Highly profitable personal service companies with large numbers of shareholders, in which most of the profits are passed on to shareholders as compensation or retirement benefits.
- ✔ Corporations in which the loss of fringe benefits to shareholders exceeds tax savings.
- ✔ Corporations with sizable net operating losses that cannot be used against S corporation earnings.

partnership
business association of two or more people. There are two types of partnerships: general and limited.

PARTNERSHIP

A *partnership* is usually defined as an association of two or more people carrying on as co-owners of a business for profit. There are typically two types of partnerships. The first type, a general partnership, declares that each partner participates in all profits and losses equally or to some previously agreed-upon ratio. Normally, a general partner has unlimited liability, which includes personally owned assets outside the business association. A general partnership can be created by a formal agreement or an oral understanding. Additionally, it has banded together for profit-producing motive and is generally not considered a legal entity separate from the partners. A general partnership may not sue or be sued in the firm's name. Each partner shares potential joint and several liabilities. The second type of partnership, a *limited partnership*, limits the liability of the *limited partners* to the extent of their capital contributions. A limited partnership must have at least one general partner.

limited partnership
a financial arrangement in which partners' liability toward their business's creditors is limited.

Advantages of a Partnership

✔ *Ease of Establishment.* Like the proprietorship, the general partnership is easy and inexpensive to establish. The partners must obtain the necessary business license and submit a minimal number of forms. In most states, partners must file a Certificate for Conducting Business as Partners if the business is run under a trade name.

limited partner
an individual who has limited liability in a partnership. He or she cannot participate in management.

✔ *Complementary Skills of Partners.* In sole proprietorship, the owner must wear many different hats and not all of them will fit well. In successful partnerships, the parties' skills usually complement one another. For example, one partner in a software firm says, "My co-owner provides the vision, energy, and enthusiasm needed in a deal situation. I am more negative and careful. Together we're a solid team."

✔ *Division of Profits.* There are no restrictions on how profits must be distributed as long as they are consistent with the partnership agreement and do not violate the rights of any partner.

✔ *Larger Pool of Capital.* The partnership form of ownership can significantly broaden the pool of capital available to the business. Each partner's asset base improves the ability of the business to borrow needed funds. Therefore, each individual has more to contribute in equity capital and together their personal assets will support a larger borrowing capacity.

✔ *Ability to Attract Limited Partners.* There can be any number of limited partners as long as there is at least one general partner. A partnership can attract investors who, with limited liability, still can realize a substantial return on their investment if the business is successful. There are a great many individuals who find it very profitable to invest as limited partners in high-potential small businesses.

✔ *Little Government Regulation.* Like proprietorship, the general partnership form of operation is not burdened with red tape.

✔ *Flexibility.* Although not as flexible as sole ownership, the partnership can generally react quickly to changing market conditions, because no giant organization stifles its quick and creative responses to new opportunities.

✔ *Taxation.* The partnership itself is not subject to federal taxation. Its net income is distributed directly to the partners as personal income, and the partners pay income tax on their distributive shares. The partnership, like the proprietorship, avoids the double taxation applicable to the corporate form of ownership.

Disadvantages of a Partnership

✔ *Unlimited Liability of at Least One Partner.* At least one member of every partnership must be a general partner. The general partner has unlimited personal liability.

✔ *Capital Accumulation.* Although the partnership form of ownership is superior to the proprietorship in its ability to attract capital, it is generally not as effective as the corporate form of ownership. This is due to the fact that the partnership usually has limitations and restrictions to raising capital as well as shares.

✔ *Restrictions of Elimination for the General Partnership.* Most partnership agreements restrict how partners can dispose of their share of the business. It is common to find that partners are required to sell their interests to the remaining partners. But even if the original agreement contains such a requirement and clearly delineates how the value of each partner's ownership will be determined, there is no guarantee that the other partner(s) will have the financial resources to buy the seller's interest. When the money is not available to purchase a partner's interest, the other partner(s) may be forced either to accept a new partner who purchases the partner's interest or to dissolve the partnership, distribute the remaining assets, and begin again. When a general partner dies, becomes incompetent, or withdraws from the business, the partnership automatically dissolves, although it may not terminate. Even when there are numerous partners, if one wishes to disassociate his or her name from the business, the remaining partners will probably form a new partnership.

✔ *Lack of Continuity for the General Partnership.* If one partner dies, complications arise. Partnership interest is often nontransferable through inheritance, because the remaining partner(s) may not wish to be in partnership with the person who inherits the deceased partner's interest. Partners can make provisions in the partnership agreement to avoid dissolution due to death if all parties agree.

✔ *Potential for Personality and Authority Conflicts.* Friction among partners is inevitable and difficult to control. Disagreements over what should be done or what was done have dissolved many a partnership. For example, when the cofounders of a successful communications company got into a dispute over its future direction, the firm lost its edge and momentum in the market. While the partners fought over buyout terms, the business floundered. Ultimately, the business was sold at a very low price.

LIMITED LIABILITY COMPANY (LLC)

An LLC is a blend of some of the best characteristics of corporations, partnerships, and sole proprietorships. It is a separate legal entity like a corporation, but it is entitled to be treated as a partnership for tax purposes and therefore carries with it the flow-through or transparent tax benefits that corporations do not have. It is very flexible and simple to run, and, like a sole proprietorship, there is no statutory necessary to keep meeting minutes, hold meetings, or make resolutions, which can trip up many corporate owners. The owners are called members, who can be individuals (residents or foreigners), corporations, other LLCs, trusts, pension plans, or other entities.

Filing an Articles of Organization form with the secretary of state and signing an LLC agreement forms an LLC. The corporation division of most secretary of state offices handles LLCs. Most states require an annual report be filed to keep them apprised of current status, but other than that there are no other ongoing reports or forms. The LLC is not a taxpaying entity. Profits, losses, and so on flow directly through and are reported on the individual members' tax returns. The LLC files a partnership return under Subchapter K of the Internal Revenue Code.

Advantages of an LLC

- ✔ Owners do not assume liabilities for debt.
- ✔ LLCs offer different classes of stocks.
- ✔ There are no restrictions on the number and types of owners.

Disadvantages of an LLC

- ✔ There is difficulty in business expansion out of state.
- ✔ Transferring ownership is restricted.
- ✔ Requirements are different for each state.
- ✔ LLCs cannot be used for professional services such as accounting or attorneys.

Other Aspects

An LLC is taxed as a partnership. The pass-through is similar to the S corporation's tax.

An S corporation limits the number of shareholders to 75. Unlike an S corporation, an LLC has no limit on the number of members and owners.

BUSINESS START-UP CHECKLIST

Now that you have a good beginning to understand the legal forms of the organization, a business start-up checklist is presented. This checklist will be your guide for the first 30 days, 60 days, and year-end activities.

First 30 Days

✔ Obtain an employer identification number from the IRS by completing federal form SS4.

✔ Select a lawyer.

✔ Select an accountant.

✔ Prepare a business plan.

✔ Select a banker or banking institution.

✔ Select an insurance agent.

✔ Obtain business insurance.

✔ Order business cards and letterhead.

✔ Obtain a business license or permit from the city hall or county office.

✔ Establish bank accounts.

✔ Establish merchant credit card service allowing your business to accept major credit cards (if applicable).

✔ Pick a year-end date.

✔ Corporations hold an organizational meeting where:

Bylaws are adopted.

A board of directors is elected.

Share certificates should be distributed to shareholders once purchased, and these transactions should be recorded on the corporation's stock ledger.

Company members and/or managers and officers are elected.

Any corporate business that needs immediate attention is addressed.

✔ An LLC should have an organizational meeting where:

An operating agreement is adopted.

Membership certificates are distributed.

Company members and/or managers are elected.

In some states, publishing is required of your operation of an LLC.

First 60 Days

✔ Establish presence on Internet with domain name registration.

✔ Contact suppliers.

✔ If selecting S corporation status, file Form 2553 within 75 days.

✔ Obtain business insurance (liability, health and dental, workers' compensation, etc.).

✔ Join a professional organization.

✔ Some states such as Nevada require a list of officers and directors to be filed with the state.

By First Year-End

✔ Obtain federal tax forms.

✔ Obtain state tax forms.

✔ Pay corporate franchise tax or annual state fees.

✔ Order mail-forwarding service.

✔ Obtain financing.

✔ Establish a line of credit.

Contacting Your Attorney

Laws and legal requirements for setting up a company can vary greatly from state to state. An attorney should be consulted to meet many of the legal requirements facing the business. This can include:

✔ Forming the business.

✔ Preparing the contracts to get started.

✔ Establishing relations among equity holders.

✔ Hiring employees and agreements (confidentiality, work for hire, noncompetition, nonsolicitation, etc.).

✔ Addressing product liability and environmental concerns.

✔ Raising equity capital.

Contacting Your Accountant

The accountant should be a practical business adviser who can set up a total financial control system for the business and render sound business advice. At the outset, the accountant should work to establish accounting and reporting systems, cash projections, financing strategies, and tax planning. In addition, as the company matures, the following services can be provided:

✔ Vendor services and payment options.

✔ Cash management or fiscal accounting.

✔ Cost-reduction planning using invoices.

✔ Compensation plan for employees.

✔ Merger, acquisition, and appraisal assistance.

✔ Management information systems to determine the accounting software requirements.

Name Registration

A business adopting an assumed business name must register the name with the state of incorporation and each state in which the business is doing business. This should be done before taking any other steps to do business in the state. The registration will protect the name from infringement. The amount of registration fee varies by state.

In most states, a corporation's name must include "corporation," "company," "incorporated," "limited," or an abbreviation of one of these words. A competent attorney can assist with this phase of establishing a new business.

Federal Identification Number

Any business must obtain an identification number from the Internal Revenue Service, except for a sole proprietorship that has no employees other than the owner. An identification number can be obtained by filing Form SS-4, "Application for Employer Identification Number."

Insurance Issues

Most businesses require insurance of one form or another. State law may require some forms, such as workers' compensation. The entrepreneur should shop around to find the insurer that offers the best combination of coverage, service, and price. Trade associations often offer special rates and policies to their members.

The entrepreneur should consider the following forms of insurance, even though not required by law.

- ✔ Fire.
- ✔ Automobile.
- ✔ Employee, health, and life.
- ✔ Fidelity bonds that insure the employer from employee theft.
- ✔ Crime coverage that reimburses the employer for robbery, burglary, and vandalism losses.
- ✔ Business interruption that compensates the business for revenue lost during temporary halt in business caused by fire, theft, or illness.
- ✔ Key person that compensates the business for the death or disability of a key partner or manager.
- ✔ Liability that protects the business from claims of bodily injury, property damage, and malpractice.
- ✔ Product liability.

SETTING UP EMPLOYER–EMPLOYEE AGREEMENTS

It is important to establish employment agreements for your management team and key employees in the company. The agreement describes the obligations of the employer and employee and varies widely among companies and even among employees within the same company. Usual provisions included in the agreement should emphasize the following employee issues:

✔ Employees cannot disclose any confidential information about the company either during or subsequent to employment.

✔ They must return all materials that belong to the company at the time of termination of employment.

✔ They cannot engage in a new business during the period of employment without the consent of the employer.

✔ They will not compete with the company for a period of time subsequent to employment.

✔ They will disclose and assign to the company all inventions during their employment.

Employment agreements can present an element of coercion. The employee may assume that because the employer is given the agreement for signature, the employee has little choice but to sign it or seek employment elsewhere. If the employer tries to enforce an agreement, the sympathies of the court usually lie with the employee. Seldom will a court enforce an employment agreement if it deprives the ex-employee of a means of making a living. For these reasons, employment agreements should be drafted, read, and agreed to prior to actual employment.

The best employment agreement serves as an incentive for the employee and provides protection against the employee damaging the company subsequent to employment. The incentives may include stock options, payments for inventions, or bonuses.

SETTING UP STOCK OPTIONS AGREEMENTS

Many companies provide added incentives for keeping key employees, by providing an equity interest in the company. This is usually in the form of common stock or options to acquire common stock. Companies should establish a qualified stock option plan under which selected employees receive options to purchase stock in the company. Qualified stock options are restricted to employees and are not available to others. The word "qualified" indicates the plan is qualified for certain tax benefits under Section 422A of the Internal Revenue Code of 1986. Under such an arrangement, the employee pays no tax at the time the option is granted. Another feature of the option plan is that the ownership of the options can vest over a period of years, so that if the employee is terminated prior to the terms of the option, only a portion of the options are received.

A qualified employee stock option plan must meet certain requirements. Some of the most important features to consider are:

- ✔ A plan must be adopted by the board of directors and approved by the stockholders of the company. The board can adopt the plan and put it into effect, subject to approval by the stockholders, at the next annual or other meeting within 12 months.

- ✔ The plan must state the aggregate number of shares being set aside for the options and the employees or class of employees (for example, "key employees") for which options will be made available.

- ✔ No options may be granted more than 10 years after the plan is put into effect without board approval.

- ✔ The option must not be transferable and is exercisable during the lifetime of the employee.

Stock Option Plan

A stock option plan can be a powerful incentive, particularly in a start-up situation. There is a minimum of red tape in establishing such a plan, and you can prepare your own documents. It is advisable to have your tax accountant review the proposed plan before its adoption to make sure it meets the statutory requirements to qualify for the tax benefits.

Shares Issued for Compensation and Tax Implications

Attracting and maintaining talented employees is necessary for the success of a new organization. The carrot used to attract these employees might take many different forms. For example, competitive cash compensation, retirement plans, transferring property (automobiles, real estate, equipment, etc.), equity, along with many other forms could be used to attract employees. Sometimes this compensation might take the form of golden handcuffs, which would place vesting period restrictions on the receipt by an employee on a form of property received by the employee for a period of time. No matter what form the compensation comes in, it will have a particular set of tax-related problems.

The Internal Revenue Code (IRC) Section 83 governs the tax treatment accorded to transfers of almost all kinds of property to an employee in the course of employment. The key point of Section 83 is that when property is transferred by an employer to an employee, in connection with the performance of services, the difference between the price paid and its fair market value is treated as compensation. This is included in the employee's gross income in the year ownership is vested. Additionally, under this section, the employee stockholder would be required to pay taxes on the amount seen as income (the spread) upon it fully vesting at the tax rate of 39.6 percent, or whatever their individual income tax rate is at the time.

As an alternative to the tax structure, the employee stockholder can elect the use of IRC Section 83(b) to pay the income tax in the year the stock was received. When the stock is later sold, the employee will pay a capital gains tax on future appreciation of the gain.

Example of Tax Implications In year one, a start-up company sells stock to a key employee, Allison, at $8 per share. The fair market value of the stock is $10 per share. In year five, when the restriction lapses, the fair market value of the stock is $110 per share. The restriction is that Allison must still be working for the company in five years. If she quits, she must sell the stock back to the company at the cost of $10 per share.

Tax Implications for Allison	83(a) Default	83(b) Election
Year one	None	The difference between fair market value and the price sold to Allison is taxed at ordinary income. Tax rate = 39.6 percent Tax due = $.79 per share
Year five (when restriction is removed)	$110 – $10 = $100 = taxable compensation Tax rate for ordinary income = 39.6 percent Tax due = $39.60 per share	Taxed only if stock is sold. Taxed at long-term capital gains rate of 28 percent on the amount stock has appreciated above original value. If sold, tax due = $28 per share.
Upon selling the stock	Taxed on further appreciation of stock above is $110 at 28 percent.	Taxed on appreciation of stock at 28 percent. Benefit of additional tax deferral. If the stock were not sold prior to Allison's death, the gain would never be taxed.

Setting Up the Nonqualified Stock Options (NQSOs)

This type of option allows the employee to purchase shares of employer stock at a stated price over a given period of time. This option plan is not subject to strict regulations and allows for flexibility in setting the exercise price and term of conditions. The terms of the plan usually include the following provisions:

- ✔ *Exercise Price.* This is usually equal to the fair market value of employer shares at the time of the grant. Any difference between the option exercise price and the fair market value of the option at the date of grant is a compensation expense and would reduce earnings for accounting purposes.

- ✔ *Vesting Restrictions.* Vesting in its daily equal installments over a three-to-five-year period is most common.

- ✔ *Term.* Ten years is a typical term. Option values increase with the length of the exercise period; a shorter term may be appropriate if the recipient is close to retirement or the employer anticipates quick and extreme appreciation of the shares and is concerned about the potential dilutive effects of outstanding options.

- ✔ *Posttermination Exercise Restrictions.* Most limit the posttermination exercise period to 90 days or one year following death or disability.

- ✔ *Form of Payment.* Payment may be in cash where a value price has been established. Shares used for payment should be owned for at least six months to avoid potential Section 16(b) issues under the securities laws.

Advantages to the Employee

- ✔ The possibility of a large gain is not limited by any accounting considerations.

- ✔ The employee can choose the timing of exercising the option to maximize gains.

✔ There are no statutory limitations on exercise after retirement.

Advantages to the Employer

✔ The company can take a tax deduction.

✔ There is no charge on the income statement, although there may be a negative impact on earnings per share.

✔ It provides increase in capital to the company.

✔ The plan is simple to design and administer.

✔ Setting up is by board resolution or may require shareholder approval in the same states.

✔ There is no need to establish specific performance standards; value is determined by the price of stock.

Disadvantages

✔ The employee may need to borrow the cash to exercise the option. A program can be arranged through a broker to pay the purchase price.

✔ The profit or gain may not meet the benefits for employment.

✔ The compensation may not provide the cash rewards based on the particular performance of the employee.

Setting Up the Incentive Stock Options (ISOs)

These options provide the right to purchase shares of stock at a stated price over a given period of time. However, ISOs must satisfy certain statutory requirements:

✔ The option price is not less than the fair market value (FMV) of the stock at the time of the grant.

✔ The option by its terms is not exercisable after the expiration of 10 years from the grant date.

✔ The option is nontransferable other than by will and exercisable during the life of the agreement.

✔ Individuals owning more than 10 percent of the outstanding shares are subject to a minimum exercise price of 110 percent of fair market value at the date of grant and a maximum exercise period of five years.

✔ The plan must be approved by shareholders, must state the number of shares to be granted and who is eligible, and must be granted within 10 years of the shareholder approval.

✔ The value of all options vesting in a given year per individual may not exceed $100,000. This provides limitations to senior executives.

Disadvantages for the plan include:

✔ There is a mandatory waiting period of two years from date of grant and one year from date of exercise to qualify for long-term capital gain treatment.

✔ There is a three-month exercise limitation after termination of employment, including retirement. One-year limitation on exercise after death or disability.

✔ There are limitations on the maximum amount of $100,000 that may vest in any year.

✔ There is no grant to an executive owning more than 10 percent of the voting power of all classes of stock before the option is granted, unless the option expires within five years of the grant and the exercise price is 110 percent of FMV on the date of the grant.

✔ There is a possibility that the individual may need to borrow cash to finance the option.

✔ The plan requires action by the board of directors and shareholder approval.

✔ There is no tax benefit to the company.

SUMMARY

The material in this chapter is a good beginning to understand the legal forms of the organization. It can provide you with guidelines on the legal form most appropriate for your situation.

The most common forms of business ownership are the sole proprietorship, the partnership, and the C corporation. Other forms of ownership include the limited liability company (LLC) and the S corporation.

A sole proprietorship is a form of business owned and managed by one individual and is the most popular form of business ownership. Approximately 65 percent of all businesses are proprietorships.

A partnership is usually defined as an association of two or more people carrying on as co-owners of a business for profit. There are typically two types of partnerships. The first type, a general partnership, provides that each partner participates in all profits and losses equally or to some previously agreed-upon ratio. Normally, a general partner has unlimited liability, which includes personally owned assets outside the business association. A general partnership can be created by a formal agreement or by an oral understanding.

The C corporation is the most complex form of business ownership. It is a separate entity that can participate in any business and pay taxes to the federal and state agencies. The owners are called shareholders. Stockholders are not liable for the debts of the company and can lose only the money invested in the business.

A limited liability company, similar to an S corporation, has the benefits of pass-through tax benefits and the limited liability of a C corporation. It is very flexible and simple to run, and, like a sole proprietorship, you do not need to keep meeting minutes and hold regular meetings. The owners are called members, and two or more are required to file the articles of organization. The members can be the management and are not personally liable for the company's debts or liabilities.

An S corporation passes the profits and losses of the corporation to the stockholders. It is treated like the LLC and partnership in the sense that if the business earns a profit, that profit becomes the income of the stockholders, and the owners pay the tax on that profit at their individual tax rates.

✔ It can have no more than 75 stockholders.

✔ Shareholders must be U.S. citizens or residents (partnerships and corporations cannot be shareholders).

✔ It can have only one class of stocks issued and outstanding; that is either preferred or common.

✔ No more than 25 percent of the corporate income can be derived from passive investments, such as dividends, rent, and capital gains.

The S corporation cannot be a financial institution, a foreign corporation, or a subsidiary of a parent corporation.

The chapter summarizes the major forms of the legal organization—proprietorship, partnership, and corporation. The advantages and disadvantages of each were discussed, and a list of questions was highlighted to help you decide which form of ownership is best for you. In addition, a checklist was prepared to assist you in the first 30-day, 60-day, and year-end periods to maximize the best performance for the business.

You should also find legal advice to assist in the preparation of articles, name registration, and other documents to ensure the proper registration of the form of business.

References

Chapter 1 Developing Ideas and Business Opportunities

Interview with Fanny Chin of Creative Calendars, June 1998.

Interview with Larry Meistrich of Shooting Gallery, January 1999.

Jack M. Kaplan, *Smart Cards, the Global Information Passport*, International Thomson Computer Press, 1996, pp. 15–17.

Karl H. Vesper, *New Venture Experience*, Prentice Hall, 1996, pp. 130–135.

David Bangs Jr., *The Real World Entrepreneur*, Upstart, 1999, p. 65.

Chapter 2 Analyzing the Market, Customers, and Competition

Leonard Fuld, *Competitive Intelligence*, New York: John Wiley & Sons, 1993, pp. 9–10.

John B. Vinturella, *The Entrepreneur's Field Book,* Prentice Hall, 1999, pp. 62–64.

Robert Hisrich, *Entrepreneurship*, Irwin McGraw Hill, 1998, p. 170.

Courtney Price, Ph.D., and R. Mac Davis, *The Entrepreneur's Fast Trac II Handbook*, Entrepreneurial Education Foundation, 1997, pp. 109–112.

Interview with Stephen Hanson of B. R. Guest, March 1999.

Chapter 3 Starting Home-Based Businesses, Opening Franchises, and Buying Existing Businesses

John B. Vinturella, *Entrepreneurship Field Book*, Prentice Hall, 1999, p. 116.

Donald Kuratko, *Entrepreneurship*, Dryden Press, 1998, p. 396.

"Entrepreneur of the Year, Richard Schulze of Best Buy," Ernst & Young, LLP, Fall 1999, p. 12.

"Entrepreneur of the Year, Mark Logan of VISX," Ernst & Young, LLP, Fall 1999, p. 24.

Chapter 4 Preparing a Winning Business Plan

Jack M. Kaplan, *Smart Cards, the Global Information Passport*, International Thomson Computer Press, 1996, pp. 187–190.

Eric Siegal, *The Ernst & Young Business Plan Guide*, John Wiley & Sons, 1987, pp. 59–60.

"Entrepreneur of the Year, Christy Jones of pcOrder," Ernst & Young, LLP, Fall 1999, p. 44.

Interview with Margaret Green of Creative Enterprises, February 1998.

Chapter 5   Getting the Funding

"Where Has All the Money Gone?, Inc.", April 2000, pp. 100–102.

Amar Bhide, "Bootstrap Finance," Harvard Business Review, November 1992, p. 112.

"Entrepreneur of the Year, The High Tech Bubble," Ernst & Young, LLP, Fall 1999, pp. 28–30.

Robert Hisrich, *Entrepreneurship*, Irwin McGraw Hill, 1998, pp. 365–367.

Virginia O'Brien, *Fast Forward MBA in Business*, John Wiley & Sons, 1996, p. 86.

Interview with Mati Weiderpass of Watch World International, January 2000.

Chapter 6   Bank Loans and Debt Financing

John Tracy, *Fast Forward MBA in Finance*, John Wiley & Sons, 1996, pp. 59–62.

Donald E. Vaughn, *Financial Planning for the Entrepreneur*, Prentice Hall, 1997, p. 55.

Chapter 7   The IPO Process (Going Public)

"Entrepreneur of the Year, Capital Improvements," Ernst & Young, LLP, Fall 1999, pp. 18–19.

Ira A. Greenstein, *Going Public Source Book*, RR Donnelley Financial, 1999, pp. 5–7.

Stephen C. Blowers, *The Ernst & Young Guide to the IPO Value Journey*, John Wiley & Sons, 1999, pp. 97–99.

Interview with Laurence Charney of Ernst & Young, May 2000.

John B. Vinturella, *Entrepreneurship Field Book*, Prentice Hall, 1999, pp. 298–299.

Chapter 8   Launching an Internet Business

Michael Clark, *Cultural Treasures of the Internet*, Prentice Hall, 1995, p. 68.

Interview with Don Rappaport of Impower, November 2000.

"ABCs of ASPs," Forbes, July 17, 2000, pp. 86–87.

Chapter 9   Discovering Value in Intellectual Property: The Competitive Edge

Robert Goldscheider, *The New Companion to Licensing Negotiations*, Clark Boardman Callaghan, 1997, pp. 37, 47.

Interview with Eric Hirsch, May 2000.

Douglas K. Smith and Robert C. Alexander, *Fumbling the Future: How Xerox Invented, Then Ignored, the First Personal Computer*, William Morrow and Company, 1988, pp. 14–15, 18–19.

Margaret Cheney and Robert Uth, *Tesla—Master of Lightning*, Barnes & Noble, 1999, pp. 67–70.

Chapter 10 Building the Resources and Setting Up the Company

Gordon B. Baty, *Entrepreneurship for the Nineties*, Prentice Hall, 1990, p. 219.

James H. Donnelly Jr., *Fundamentals of Management*, Richard B. Irwin, 1990, pp. 656–658.

Kathleen R. Allen, *Launching New Ventures*, Houghton Mifflin Co., 1999, pp.155–159.

Interview with Roy Wetterstrom of Micro Modeling/Plural Company, March 1999.

Interview and consultation with Ann Chamberlain of Richards & O'Neil, LLP, May 2000.

Norman Scarborough, *Entrepreneurship and New Venture Formation*, Prentice Hall, 1996, pp. 172, 183, 191.

Glossary

accredited investors   individual or institutional investors who meet the qualifying SEC criteria with respect to financial sophistication or financial assets.

acid-test ratio   method of judging firm's ability to meet current debt quickly. The formula: Total cash + receivables / current liabilities. One common standard ratio is one to one (1:1).

angel   a private investor who often has nonmonetary motives for investing as well as the usual financial ones.

asset-based financing   financing an enterprise by using its hard assets for collateral to acquire a loan of sufficient size with which to finance operations. Widely used in leveraged buyouts (LBOs).

board of directors   the people elected by stockholders of a corporation who are responsible to that group for overseeing the overall direction and policy of the firm.

buy-sell agreement   contracts between associates that set the terms and conditions by which one or more of the associates can buy out one or more of the other associates.

comment letter   a letter from the staff of the SEC describing deficiencies noted in its review of a registration statement. Comment letters request additional information or changes that must be made before the offering can become effective and the shares offered to investors.

common stock   shares that represent the ownership interest in a corporation. Both common and preferred stock have ownership rights, but the preferred normally has prior claim on dividends and, in the event of liquidation, assets. Both common and preferred stockholders' claims are junior to claims of bondholders or other creditors. Common stockholders assume greater risk, but have voting power and generally exercise greater control. They may gain greater rewards in the form of dividends and capital appreciation. Common stock and capital stock are terms often used interchangeably when the company has no preferred stock.

copyright   an exclusive right granted by the federal government to the processor to publish and sell literary, musical, and other artistic materials. Honored for 50 years after the death of the author.

debt capital   funds or assets acquired by borrowing.

dilution   the reduction of a stockholder's percentage of ownership in an enterprise, usually done by selling more common stock to other parties. Sometimes called watering the stock.

due diligence   the responsibility of those preparing and signing the registration statement to conduct an investigation in order to provide a reasonable basis for their belief that statements made in the registration statement are true and do not omit any material facts. Proper due diligence can help protect these parties from liability in the event they are sued for a faulty offering. The company, on the other hand, has strict liability for errors or omissions in the registration statement.

EDGAR online   Electronic data gathering for SEC filings.

entrepreneur   derived from the French *entreprendre*, "to undertake." Someone who is willing and eager to create a new venture in order to present a concept to the marketplace.

equity   total assets minus total liabilities equals equity or net worth.

Form 10-K   the annual report required to be filed with the SEC.

Form 10-Q   the quarterly report required to be filed with the SEC.

going public   the process by which a corporation offers its securities to the public.

goodwill   the difference between the market value of a firm and the market value of its net tangible assets.

IPO   the initial public offering process.

joint venture   usually refers to a short-lived partnership with each partner sharing in costs and rewards of the project; common in research, investment banking, and the health-care industry.

lien   an interest of a creditor in any real assets or property as security for repayment of credit. A legal claim against property.

limited partner   an individual who has limited liability in a partnership. He or she cannot participate in management.

limited partnership   a financial arrangement in which partners' liability toward their business's creditors is limited.

line of credit   short-term financing usually granted by a bank up to a predetermined limit; debtor borrows as needed up to the limit of credit without need to renegotiate the loan.

marketing plan   a written plan for achieving the marketing goals and strategies of the venture, usually on an annual basis. Business plans always contain a marketing plan section.

multiple   a firm's price-earnings ratio. Used for quick valuations of a firm; for example, a firm that earns $5 million a year in an industry that generally values stock at 10 times earnings (multiple of 10) would be valued at $50 million.

new venture   a new business providing products/services to a particular market.

noncompete agreement   legal agreement preventing the signer from joining or starting a similar venture.

nondisclosure agreement   legal agreement stipulating that the signer not disclose confidential information about the company and/or product.

partnership   business association of two or more people. There are two types of partnerships: general and limited.

patent   federal governmental grant to an inventor giving exclusive rights to an invention or process for 20 years from date of patent application filing. A U.S. patent does not always grant rights in foreign countries.

proprietary   that which is owned, such as a patent, formula, brand name, or trademark associated with the product/service.

private placement   the sale of stocks or bonds to wealthy individuals, pension funds, insurance companies, or other investors, done without a public offering or any oversight from the Securities and Exchange Commission.

public offering   the sale of a company's shares of stock to the public by the company or its major stockholders.

registered stock   stock that has been registered with the SEC, and thus can be sold publicly.

SBA loan   loan providing SBA guarantee for 90 percent of a loan obtained from banking sources.

S corporation (Subchapter S corporation)   a firm that has elected to be taxed as a partnership under the Subchapter S provision of the Internal Revenue Code.

sole proprietorship   a business firm owned by only one person and operated for his or her profit.

start-up capital   money needed to launch a new venture during the pre-start-up and initial period of operation.

stock certificate   a document issued to a stockholder by a corporation indicating the number of shares of stock owned by the stockholder.

stockholders' equity   the portion of a business owned by the stockholders.

venture capitalist   an investor who provides early financing to new ventures— often technology-based—with an innovative product and the prospect of rapid and profitable growth.

warrant   an option to buy a certain amount of stock for a stipulated price that is transferable—it can be traded.

working capital   the amount of funds available to pay short-term expenses. Seen as a cushion to meet unexpected or out-of-the-ordinary expenses. It is determined by subtracting current liabilities from current assets.

Index